Table of contents

UNIVERSITY COLLEGE BIRMINGHAM
COLLEGE LIBRARY, SUMMER ROW
BIRMINGHAM. B3 1JB
Tel: (0121) 243 0055

DATE OF RETURN

Please remember to return on time or pay the fine

JUTA

Introduction to Integrated Marketing Communications

First published 2011 by Juta & Co.
1st Floor, Sunclare Building
21 Dreyer Street
Claremont
7708

ISBN 978-0-70217-793-4

Project Manager: Corina Pelser
Editor: Ulla Schüler
Typesetter: WaterBerry Designs cc, Somerset West
Cover designer: Nic Jooste, Comet Design
Typeset in 9/12 ITC Stone Informal Medium

Printed in South Africa by Academic Press, Parow Industria, Cape Town

Preface

....

Promotion, the 4th P, is all about the brand. Marketers and their advertising agencies are pursuing brand success by using a variety of marketing communication tools. The challenge is to successfully integrate these tools. To get advertising, promotions and media to work together in an effective way.

This text is an Introduction to Integrated Marketing Communications. It focuses on the IMC mix, principles of communication, planning the advertising campaign, advertising media and media planning, principles of Advertising, Personal Selling, Sales Promotion, Direct Marketing, Public Relations, Sponsorship and principles of Digital Marketing. I would like to give credit to the 2004 team who prepared the original chapters on which this text is based:

- Rory Duckles (Direct Marketing)
- Norman Blem (Personal Selling)
- Brian Connett (Intro to IMC and Sales Promotion)
- Chris Skinner (Public Relations)

Also, Japie Swanepoel for the information from which the Digital Marketing chapter was prepared.

We are living in a new world today. Above-the-line advertising like television and print went from being the primary communication channels to simply being two channels among many. Marketers are, in the current economic crisis, seriously looking at communications tools that can provide and prove results (such as direct marketing, sales promotions and sponsorship). New technology are providing Internet, Web, mobile media and social media opportunities. These are new opportunities to explore but the Big Idea still needs to be integrated, regardless of which tool(s) will be used. Where possible, reference to the new media opportunities are made in the text.

To help students each chapter provides Learning Outcomes, but Key Learning Points and Self Assessment items or questions will be available separately.

I would like to thank Mike Cant, Consulting Editor for his input, Juta Academic for publishing the book, Ulla Schüller for proofreading the text and Corina

Pelser for managing the project. Also everyone not mentioned here who directly or indirectly contributed to the success of this text. Above all, Soli Deo Gloria.

I trust that students, and perhaps practitioners, will greatly benefit from this Introduction edition and that it will instill in them a keen interest in the exciting world of marketing communications.

Ludi Koekemoer (PhD)
Editor
2011

1 The Integrated Marketing Communication Mix

AIM OF THIS CHAPTER

The focus of this chapter is on marketing communication and its place in the organisation. As an introductory book on marketing communications the focus will be to explain what the marketing communication mix is, to focus on the evolution of the Integrated Marketing Communication (IMC) concept, to explain the six marketing communication mix elements, the three modes of marketing, the use of the marketing communication mix by marketers, marketing communication planning and strategy, organising for marketing communication and to give an overview of the trends in marketing.

LEARNING OUTCOMES

After studying this chapter you should be competent in:
- identifying and discussing the six marketing communication elements
- discussing the evolution of the IMC concept
- discussing marketing communication strategy and the marketing mix and indicate how product, price and place 'communicate' with customers
- discussing the three modes of marketing
- explaining the relative importance and usage of the six marketing communication mix elements
- describing the marketing communication planning and strategy process
- illustrating how a small, medium and large corporation can organise for marketing communication
- briefly outlining the future of marketing communication

1.1 INTRODUCTION

For any business to be successful it is important that the business communicates with its customers or market. No communication or incorrect ways of communicating will result in the market not being aware of the company and its products and services, which in turn may mean that the company may not survive. In today's difficult economic times it is becoming more and more important that businesses communicate with their market, because if they do not, their competitors might. In fact, everything a company does is some form of communication with the market. This process of communicating with consumers and customers is called marketing communication. In order to understand how marketing communication 'works', consider the following example. A company decides to offer a product or service to a group of customers (target market), who share some similar characteristics and needs and who may or may not be located in the same geographical area. In order to be able to sell this product or service to this group or target market a strategy is developed by the company.

In reaching and influencing the selected target market, the marketer uses what is known as the marketing mix. The basic elements of the marketing mix, commonly referred to as 'the four P's' are Product, Price, Place (distribution) and Promotion. The aim of the business is to put these elements into a combination where it will lead to the target market buying the product and in so doing, meet the profit objectives of the company. This is put in writing in a format that is referred to as the marketing plan.

Product as indicated above refers to the need satisfying offering the company presents to the target market in order to meet their needs. This can be a service as well or a combination of a product and service based on the customer needs. For example, the City Lodge group offers accommodation to customers, which includes peace of mind, a welcome drink, newspaper, breakfast, wake-up call and so forth. These add-ons are based on customer needs and wants as identified by means of market research that has been done. *Price* as the second element is the amount that the customer is prepared to pay for the product or service. The price is determined based on the cost to render the service as well as the price charged by competitors for similar products. In the case of City Lodge the fee per night may be R850 per night, excluding breakfast which means additional fees will be charged for breakfast if the customer wants it. *Place or distribution* refers to the place where the product or service is made available as well as the activities involved to get it there. Having a City Lodge in all major cities and in areas which is frequented by tourists means that the needs of the market is taken into account when deciding where to locate it. It must be located where it will most benefit customers. *Promotion* (or marketing communication), the fourth element of the marketing mix deals with the way the company informs its customers about the product or service, what it includes, the price they will pay and where it can be obtained. This element, promotion, itself consists of six elements namely advertising, personal selling, sales promotion, direct marketing, public relations and sponsorship. These six elements are also the focus of this book, as well as new trends in this field. The objective of this book is to illustrate what these elements are, how they work, their advantages and disadvantages, and how they should be combined to work synergistically in an optimum blend known as the marketing communication mix. Marketing communication involves a combination of marketer-initiated techniques directed to target audiences in an attempt to influence attitudes and behaviours. The ultimate goal of marketing of marketing communications is to reach some audience to affect its behavior. In order to inform, persuade and remind targeted customers effectively, marketers rely on one or more of the major elements of the communication mix. (Du Plessis, 2005:3)

While this definition refers to the fact that it is a combination of techniques, it nevertheless implies that marketers may use the elements selectively rather than synergistically. Nowadays, marketers cannot afford to take the risk of failing to communicate effectively with their target markets – competition will ensure that ineffective communicators fail. Marketers can improve their communications effectiveness by taking an *integrated marketing communication* approach and by managing the marketing communication strategy.

1.2 EVOLUTION OF THE INTEGRATED MARKETING COMMUNICATION CONCEPT

In the sixties, seventies and even eighties (and sometimes even today), the various elements of the marketing communication mix were regarded as separate functions and were handled by experts in the relevant areas. It was not uncommon that different messages were communicated to the target market as these departments (sales, advertising, sponsorships, etc) each had their own objectives and no coordination took place. It happened often that an advertising agency would be responsible for designing and managing the advertising campaign, the sales manager the sales force, sales incentives, specials and other activities and outside technological experts manage the Web site and other technological activities – and they do not even talk to each other. The net result of such a system can lead to total and utter chaos as the activities will be uncoordinated and frequently inconsistent. The results achieved were, therefore, less than optimum. There simply had to be a better way to do things – which there was namely integrated marketing communications (IMC).

To some extent, some of the factors that led to this new era of marketing communication were the empowerment of consumers, significant political and social changes, and rapid technological development, including the social networks such as Facebook, Twitter, and products such as the iPhone and iPad, which has brought a whole new dimension to marketing communication. These powerful forces have all contributed to creating a business climate in which marketers can no longer afford to 'dictate' to their target audience. Consumers were becoming more informed and empowered to choose what they wished to read or listen to and, more importantly, to 'talk back' and make themselves heard. Facebook is one such medium where consumers have made themselves heard on a wide range of topics including politics and social issues.

The most profound changes that has taken place over the past years, and which has and still are shaping communication methods, is in information technology. The dramatic reduction in the *real* price of computers, the ease of access to the Internet, and the birth of social networking (Facebook, Twitter, blogs), have been both the catalyst for individual consumer 'freedom' and the solution for marketers dealing with this new environment. It is significantly cheaper to employ online social networking strategies than to pay for advertising – many companies have claimed social networking successes, but the effectiveness has as yet not been proven. When you use social networks, you can for example pre-screen potential customers. You learn what your prospects like and what they don't. The personal relationship an advertiser gains when they connect with their potential customer is more valuable than what they would get had they advertised. Advertising is regarded as impersonal as one message for all does not seem to work anymore. Connecting with potential customers on a personal level builds trust and credibility. A general rule of thumb is to offer your services, expertise or help before you ask for it (Yeshin:2004).

Through the growth and development in the field of technology, the ability to gather, store, manipulate and retrieve vast amounts of data has given marketers unprecedented capability to communicate with consumers one-on-one. Indeed, even a new word in marketing segmentation has been added to the vocabulary of marketers, namely narrowcasting. The 'wealth' of marketers is no longer simply products and brand equity – it is now information. Much has changed in the marketing landscape over the last decade and marketers have learned to adapt to this new environment. It is an environment in which consumers are much better able to evaluate the offers being made to them and to decide more independently how to satisfy their requirements. Consumers are far more selective than they ever were and competition, both local and global, will ensure that they are provided with precisely what they want, when they want it. Needless to say, this has led to significant changes in the way marketers promote their product offerings to consumers.

According to the American Association of Advertising Agencies,

> *IMC is a concept of marketing-communications planning that recognizes the added value of a comprehensive plan that evaluates the strategic roles of a variety of communication disciplines – for example, general advertising, direct response, sales promotion, and public relations – and combines these disciplines to provide clarity, consistency, and maximum communications impact.*

The IMC concept centers around the integration of the various marketing-communication elements to provide added value to the customer and increase positive relationships (Yeshin:2004).

Strategically the focus of integrated marketing communications is on the consumer or customer. Figure 1.1 shows the importance of the consumer in planning the integrated marketing communication strategy.

INTEGRATED MARKETING COMMUNICATION STRATEGY

1. **The consumer**
   - Target buying incentive:
     - What is the perception of the consumers of this product?
     - What do they buy? How do they buy and use the product/s? When do they buy? Why do they buy? Where do they buy?
     - What is the profile of the customers in terms of lifestyles, psychographics, attitude, etc towards the product?
     - What else would the consumers want from the product category that they are not getting now?
     - Target buying incentive: I will buy a product that gives me better value for money than any other product in the category.
   - Recommend target buying incentive for group. Why?

➔

2. **Does the product fit the group?**
   - The reality of the product:
     - What's in it?
     - Why is it different?
   - How does the consumer perceive the product?
     - How does it look, feel, taste, etc?
   - How does the consumer perceive the company behind the product?
   - The 'naked truth'.
   - Does the product fit the group? Recommendation.

3. **How will the competition affect our objectives?**
   - What is the network, the competitive frame? Why?
   - What do competitors now communicate to the consumer?
   - How are competitors perceived by the consumer?
   - How will competition retaliate against our programme?
   - How vulnerable is competition? From whom will we take business?

4. **What is the competitive consumer benefit?**
   - Must be a benefit – solve a consumer problem, improve the consumer's way of life, etc.
   - Must be one benefit.
   - Must be competitive – 'better than' the competitive frame.
   - Must not be a slogan or ad phrase.
   - Must be one sentence.

5. **How will marketing communications make the benefit believable to the consumer?**
   - Product reason why.
   - Perceptual support.
   - Communication support.

6. **What should the personality of the brand be?**
   - What unique personality will help define the product and differentiate it from the competitive frame?

7. **Objectives**
   - What main point do you want the consumer to take away from the communication?
   - What action do you want the consumer to take as a result of the communication?
     - Try product?
     - Send for more information?
     - Use product more often?
     - Other?

→

8. **Perceptual effect**

   ■ If communication is successful ... months or years from now the consumer will perceive the product as ... compared to the competition.

9. **Consumer contact points**

   ■ To most effectively reach the consumer with a believable, persuasive message, the following consumer contact points should be considered. Why?

10. **Future research**

   ■ List types of research needed in the future to further develop the communications strategy. Why?

Figure 1.1: Koekemoer (2004:4–6).

Schultz et al (1995:85) expressed doubt that a marketer can establish effective communication with its target market if it only uses mass communication tools such as advertising, publicity, etc. It is the rapport, the empathy, the dialogue, the relationship and the communication the marketer establishes with the prospect that makes the difference, that separates him or her from other companies. Therefore, the marketer should recognise that, to be successful, the integrated marketing communication concept must start at the corporate level. Thus, the overall corporate strategy sets the tone for the organisation's marketing strategy. This, in turn, consciously combines the elements of the integrated marketing communications plan. It is imperative, therefore, to understand just how the four elements of the marketing mix 'communicate' with the organisation's target market. See Figure 1.2 on page 7.

1.2.1 Product

Etzel et al (2004:209, 210) define a product as

> ... a set of tangible and intangible attributes, which may include packaging, color, price, quality, and brand, plus the seller's services and reputation. A product may be a good, service, place, person, or idea.

Many other definitions do exist but for the purposes of this book this definition is regarded as appropriate, since it presents the broadest possible scope of an organisation's product offering, whether it is a commercial venture or a non-profit entity.

Any marketer, it can be assumed, will at least have a good idea what they want to offer to the market and which they believe will meet specific needs in the market. This 'product offering' or 'good idea' as it is referred to, forms the very basis of the intended business venture. Notwithstanding the dramatic changes that have taken place in the field of marketing the past years, many marketers still make the mistake of developing a product and then looking for someone to buy it. This is referred to as a *product orientation*, as opposed to the desirable approach, which is marketing or *consumer orientation*. In the latter approach, the marketer established what the target market's needs and wants are and then attempts to offer a product

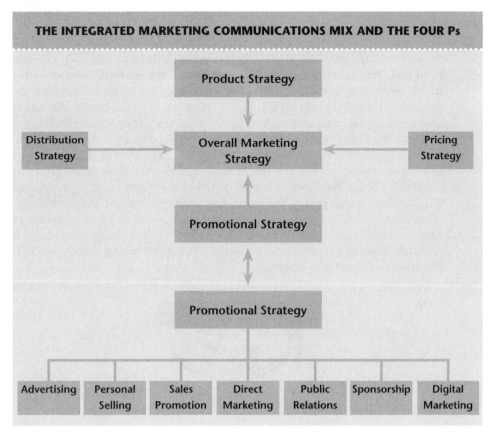

Figure 1.2

which can meet these wants and needs. However, the fact remains that a key element of the marketing mix is the product offering – and the marketer's product offering is always a principal 'communicator' with the target market.

How the product offering communicate with the consumer is through both tangible and intangible attributes. Both these attributes are highly visible to consumers and therefore communicate by virtue of their appearance. In the case of tangible products the product has to look good on the shelf and is as simple as for example an attractive package or as complex as the benefits and features of a product like a cell phone.

Intangible products such as an airline flight pose different challenges to marketers in terms of communication but are nevertheless highly 'visible' to consumers. A passenger on an airline sees a host of physical evidence of the service he or she is experiencing, not the least of which is the cabin crew and the aircraft itself. If the aircraft looks 'good', if it is clean and in good repair, the passenger (customer) is suitably impressed and feels confident in travelling on that airline. Reports in newspapers of safety concerns, technical problems and so forth will have the opposite effect. A decision to visit a day spa, for example, will be influenced by the qualifications of the therapists and the ambiance of the spa. The customers will have a sense that they 'know what they are doing' if they see the certificates and if the spa looks neat and classy.

It is not only the physical product that communicates with the user, but also the name, for example Edgars, Pep and so on. All products have a name, usually referred to as the *brand name*, by which they can be identified. Even the 'no-name brands' actually have a brand name – that of the retailer for whom they are manufactured and packed. Very often, one of the key attributes of a product is the brand name. A *brand* could be described as a name, term, design, symbol or any other feature that identifies one seller's product offering as distinct from those of other sellers. The brand name is that part of the brand that can be spoken (letters, numbers or words), whereas the *brand mark*, often referred to as the logo, is that part of the brand that cannot be spoken. Brand marks or logos, are commonly symbols, pictures, designs, distinctive lettering, colour or some combination of these. The well-known Mercedes Benz three-pointed star is a good example of a symbol logo, while the distinctive lettering of Sony products identifies that brand very clearly.

An example of a logo

It is unthinkable today that a marketer or company will not register its brand as a trademark as much money is invested in building up the brand and creating loyalty for the brand. The trademark is a legal term meaning the same as a brand. If this is done, the product label or package will carry the letter 'R' circled (®) following the brand mark or brand name to signify that it has been registered and is, therefore, legally protected. This in itself is a strong marketing tool as it says to the customer that: *this product is guaranteed to be the genuine article*. To competitors it says: Do not attempt to steal our good name! In the case of a service, a registered service mark (SM) is the same thing as a registered trademark (TM).

Traditionally packaging was designed to protect a product and nothing else. Over time this has changed and packaging has become a major marketing tool – in fact, it has become so important that in many instances the package sells the product and not the product. Think of ladies perfume and how the packaging/bottle is in many cases the reason why it is bought. Further to this, packaging has become a source of information. Today most food products have full nutritional values on the packaging, the ingredients, warnings and so forth. This information is based on legal requirements, consumer demand and dietary requirements. Attractive and innovative packaging will often give the product 'eye appeal' which will get the attention of consumers who might otherwise not even have noticed the product.

1.2.2 Price

The second component of the marketing mix is price and may be described as *the amount of money a willing buyer is prepared to pay a willing seller for a product offering at a point in time.* Simply viewed, price is the only component that generates money and the most important task of price is to cover costs.

It is not easy to establish the 'right' price as many factors can and will impact on it. Whether or not the product offering will compete against an existing product or products, it is important for the marketer to send the appropriate 'message' to the chosen target market about what sort of product is being offered. Evidence suggests that in the absence of any specific knowledge about a particular product, consumers will equate a high price with high quality. In fact, many marketers of 'upscale' products will deliberately try to 'distance' their product offering from those of competitors by pricing it somewhat higher than other, lesser-quality products. Therefore, it can be said that price will give some indication of a product offering's quality. However, we must never forget that quality is a *relative* construct. What consumers do in practice is to make judgments on quality based on what they can afford and thus speak of *value* (for money).

Irrespective of the price charged and the strategy followed, the truth is that consumers today simply will not accept products that fail to deliver the basic level of satisfaction or performance that is expected of a particular type of product. A good example is the motor industry. Motorists who purchase the most inexpensive car on the market still expect that car to have adequate safety features, such as good brakes and steering and other benefits.

Price is used to *differentiate* products from one another and provides consumers with very valuable information. Indeed, one of the most basic roles of pricing is the informational role. Even within a particular product line, various versions of the same product may be offered at different prices to inform consumers that the marketer is catering to a number of target markets depending, for example, on their income level. Thus we see that price, in a very direct and important way, 'communicates' with consumers. Professional marketers know the importance of this element of the marketing mix and how to effectively incorporate it into their marketing communication strategy.

1.2.3 Distribution

The third component of the marketing mix, distribution can be described as *the process of ensuring that the marketer's product offering is made available to the targeted consumers in the right place/s, at the right time, in the right quantities, in the 'right' (ie, good) condition and at the 'right' (ie, competitive) cost.* In practice, a variety of intermediaries is used to ensure that this takes place. Collectively, these intermediaries are referred to as the distribution channel.

A marketer will very soon discover that having decided on what to offer the chosen target market and how much to charge for it, a vital step is how to get the product offering to the consumers being targeted. This means that the marketer will have to decide on a suitable distribution strategy. Naturally, much will depend on the type of product and the type of consumers being targeted. Essentially, there are three basic distribution channel structures available to the marketer: intensive, selective and exclusive. If a marketer decides that the product offering warrants *intensive distribution* and attempts to make it available in every possible retail outlet, the 'message' given is that this product is for everybody. Typical products offered in this way include bread, milk, newspapers, etc. It is also linked to the classification of products and the products that consumers are not keen to spend a lot of time on getting (consumer products) are usually intensively distributed, ie at as many outlets as possible.

Selective distribution is linked to shopping goods or goods that customers usually buy by first comparing prices, quality and so forth. The customer is therefore prepared to go to some extra trouble to buy the product. The marketer decides to make the product available only in selected outlets. It therefore becomes important to decide which outlets to select since this will automatically 'communicate' to consumers which of them are being targeted. This not only relates to the geographical location of the outlet but also to the type of retail outlet. The marketer may decide, for example, to make the product available only in retail establishments that offer a certain level of customer service. Some health supplements, for example, are only offered through Dischem, Clicks and pharmacies to create a bit of an exclusive image as well as to create the perception of it being a 'prescription' type product. Customers tend to form such associations based on the distribution channel used. Think of the number of advertisements where it states that 'only available at leading pharmacies'.

Exclusive distribution means just what it says. However, in this case, the type of product offering is such that it is only required to be available in an extremely small number of retail outlets. Customers do not buy such products frequently and when they do, they are prepared to search out the exclusive outlets that carry the particular product. The customer, who for example wants to buy an Armani suit, will expect to purchase the product at exclusive retail shops selling the brand. Similarly, the number of jewelry stores selling Rolex watches are few and dispersed in line with the buying habits of customers who are prepared to go to some trouble to buy this product.

1.2.4 Promotion (marketing communication)

The fourth component of the marketing mix is promotion and also the main focus of this book. Promotion is the combination of a number of activities and actions that are bound together in a specific way in order to inform the market of a new product, idea or service, to remind the market of a product, idea or service and to persuade them to buy the product or even just to test the product.

Promotion or marketing communication is not something marketers 'do' *to* consumers. It is what occurs when marketers are sensitive to consumers' needs and wants and communicate *with* them in a responsible, respectful and relevant way. Remember that effective communication is a two-way process. Merely telling someone about your product is a one-way process and is hardly likely to elicit much positive response. In order to communicate effectively, marketers must use all the promotion mix elements appropriately and integrate them successfully.

1.3 THE MARKETING COMMUNICATION MIX

The marketing communication mix consists of a number of elements and consists of a blend of the following seven elements:

- advertising
- personal selling
- sales promotion
- direct response marketing
- public relations
- sponsorship
- new or digital media

The following is a brief discussion of each of these elements:

1.3.1 Advertising

Many people see marketing and advertising to be synonymous or the same – which is far from the truth. Advertising can be defined as

> *all forms of paid non-personal communication through the mass media of ideas, goods and services by an identified sponsor.*

Advertising is one of the most visible manifestations of a marketer's communication efforts and few would claim that it is possible to be immune to the constant barrage of advertisements aimed at consumers. Advertising messages are delivered in a wide variety of formats using many different media including print, television, radio, outdoor and, most recently, the Internet and social media. The distinguishing feature of advertising is that it is a one-way form of communication with targeted consumers, referred to collectively as the target audience.

Advertising has four main purposes, namely to attract attention, to inform, to persuade and to remind. When a product is new to the market, advertising's main objectives are to grasp the *attention* of the prospective customers and to *inform* the target audience about the new product. Advertising messages will be mainly informational, even educational – 'educating' the target audience about new technology, for example – and persuasive.

The role or task of advertising changes over the product life cycle. The role of advertising in the introduction phase of the life cycle, for example, will be to create primary demand for the product and to make people aware of the product. As the product moves into the growth phase of the life cycle, the emphasis will shift to persuading customers to buy the product. This may be done by means of highlighting differences with competitors. During the maturity phase the focus will fall more on reminder advertising and in the decline phase advertising may be stopped altogether as the company do not want to spend money on a product that may soon be discontinued.

1.3.2 Personal selling

Personal selling is *a person-to-person process by which the seller learns about the prospective buyer's wants and seeks to satisfy them by offering suitable goods or services and making a sale.* As established by empirical research, this element dominates the marketing communication mix (in terms of money spent) in almost all situations for reasons that are not hard to find. It would probably be true to say that virtually all organisations start off by selling to a relatively small number of customers and this is best accomplished by personal selling. In many cases the nature of the product offering is such that it is absolutely essential to present it in a personal way. Personal selling certainly has several advantages, not the least of which is that each customer can be approached in a unique way. But personal selling is expensive. It is therefore necessary to establish whether or not it can be justified before simplistically assuming that it will be a part of the organisation's marketing communication mix.

1.3.3 Sales promotion

Sales promotion is *any activity that offers incentives for a limited time period to induce a desired response, such as trial or purchase, from those who are targeted.* Sales promotion is frequently misinterpreted and thought to mean literally anything that is done to 'promote' sales. This is not the case in professional marketing terms. In particular, it is essential to understand that sales promotion should be directed at three groups to be effective. The first group to be targeted is internal, ie within the marketing organisation. In most instances this would mean the sales force. The next group would be the members of the channels of distribution, such as wholesalers and retailers and finally consumers would be targeted. Specific objectives should be set for sales promotion to be effective.

1.3.4 Direct response marketing

Direct marketing is an *interactive system of marketing that uses one or more advertising media to effect a measurable response or transaction at any location.* However, the real key to the understanding of this rapidly growing element is the word *measurable.* Indeed, more than with any of the other elements of the marketing communication mix, the marketer is able to measure the effectiveness of a particular campaign with surprising accuracy. And therein lies its appeal, since marketers are under increasing pressure to account for the money they spend on any form of marketing communication. But there are also some concerns with direct marketing. One of the main criticisms is that it frequently makes use of *direct mail*, which is often inferior in quality and is consequently labeled 'junk mail'.

1.3.5 Public relations

The Public Relations Institute of South Africa (PRISA) defines public relations as

> ... *the management, through communication, of perceptions and strategic relationships between an organisation and its internal and external stakeholders.*

Many people erroneously believe that public relations 'personnel' are paid to 'waste' the organisation's money on needlessly and lavishly entertaining customers and shamelessly 'buying' their favours (whatever they may be). This is patently a very cynical and inaccurate view of public relations. Used appropriately it can significantly enhance an organisation's marketing efforts. Fortunately there are sufficient examples of sound and effective public relations efforts that have won national and even international acclaim for their quality. The most 'visible' result of an organisation's public relations activities is *publicity*. This is frequently (and mistakenly) referred to as 'free' publicity. Whilst it is true that if an organisation succeeds in obtaining favourable publicity in a newspaper or trade journal or, perhaps even more desirable, 'air time' on television, that space or air time is not paid for. If BMW were to donate for example 12 BMW 320is to the police to combat crime and it is reported in the newspaper, it is publicity – and positive as well.

1.3.6 Sponsorship

Sponsorship is *the marketing communications activity whereby a sponsor contractually provides financial and/or other support to an organisation or individual in return for rights to use the sponsor's name (company, product, brand) and logo in connection with the sponsored event or activity*. Sponsorship is an important part of IMC, but very often large amounts of money are expended without the sponsor receiving much benefit from the sponsorship. The donated BMWs stated above is a sponsorship, as is the sponsorship of Currie Cup rugby by Vodacom or the Nedbank Confederation Cup in the case of soccer. Corporate sponsorship of events have become a major promotional activity for many companies. A good example in this case is the 2010 FIFA Soccer World Cup and its range of sponsors which included Telkom, Coca-Cola, MTN and many others.

1.3.7 Electronic media

In the past 10 years electronic media has become very prominent and important in marketing actions. The use of the Internet, World Wide Web, email and mobile technology such as MXit has become everyday mediums. Imagine a world without Internet or emails or even a cellphone. Most consumers in their teens have grown up with mobile technology as the norm and not as something new. Some marketers talk about screenagers and the mobile youth. These are consumers who communicate with their mobile mediums (primarily cell phones) on Facebook, Twitter, MXit, and who are connected wherever they are via BlackBerry, GPRS or 3G.

The potential of these media is still in its infancy but it is certain that more and more emphasis will be placed on these media in the future.

1.4   THE THREE MODES OF MARKETING

The above discussion focused on a broad introduction of the nature of marketing communications and promotion management and it is appropriate to tie the concepts discussed previously into a more thorough framework called the three modes of *marketing*.

According to this perspective, the overall marketing function consists of three overlapping sets of activities, whereby marketers seek to manage the demand for their offerings. The three modes are mode 1: *the basic offer*, mode 2: *persuasive communication* and mode 3: *promotional inducements* (Shimp, 1990:13–21).

Figure 1.3 illustrates the relation of the three modes and the connection between the traditional 'marketing concept' and the 'promotion concept'. The *marketing*

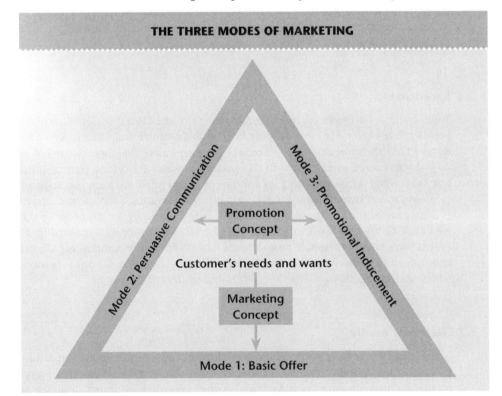

Figure 1.3

concept embodies the notion that the marketer adapts the company's offering to the customer's needs and wants. The basic offer is the mode that is primarily responsible for fulfilling the marketing concept. By comparison, the *promotion concept* attempts to adapt the customer to the marketer's needs and wants. This is accomplished by the other two modes, persuasive communication and promotional inducements.

There must be a meaningful coordination of efforts to satisfy both the marketing and promotion concepts. Excessive emphasis on customer fulfillment (the marketing concept) may lead to unnecessary expenditure and lost profit. Similarly, excessive emphasis on marketer fulfilment (the promotion concept) can lead to disgruntled customers and lost business.

1.4.1 Mode 1: The basic offer

The basic offer consists of the regular, usual and even additional benefits that the marketer offers to his or her targets as a possible solution to some problem. The basic offer has two components: the *product itself* and associated *terms of sale*, such as price, credit terms, warranties, availability and delivery promises. The role of the basic offer is to satisfy customers' needs and move them to action by offering superior value in comparison with substitute offerings. In general, superior value results from providing customers with more benefits and/or lower cost.

1.4.2 Mode 2: Persuasive communication

Persuasive communication consists of various forms of marketing communications messages designed to enhance customers' impressions of the basic offer. These consist of non-personal verbal messages (advertising, sponsorship, publicity, new media), personal verbal messages (personal selling and word-of-mouth support) and non-verbal messages (such as packaging cues and retailer imagery).

Whereas the basic offer is designed to meet customer needs, persuasive communication is intended to stimulate wants by encouraging customers to imagine the benefits of the basic offer. Marketers attempt to stimulate wants by supplying facts or by appealing to the customer's imagination.

1.4.3 Mode 3: Promotional inducements

Promotional inducements are substantive or extra benefits, beyond the benefits of the basic offer, intended to motivate particular customer actions. 'Promotional inducements' is a descriptive way of referring to what is more commonly called sales promotion. Marketers can use three forms of promotional inducements: those representing the *character of the basic offer* (for example, free samples, trial usage, extra goods at the same price), *price-related* inducements (discounts, money-off coupons, trade allowances for dealers) and inducements that are *external to the basic offer* (premiums, contests and trading stamps).

The role of promotional inducements is to motivate retailers and consumers to adopt the marketer's plan of action. In the case of retailers, this means stocking more of the marketer's product, providing better display space and promoting the marketer's product more aggressively. In the case of consumers, this means buying more of the marketer's product, buying it sooner than originally planned and buying it more frequently. Marketers induce these actions by providing retailers and consumers with some form of reward (for example, price savings or free merchandise).

EXAMPLES OF THE THREE MODES OF MARKETING

Basic offer

- Product itself
- Terms of sale:
  - availability and delivery;
  - price;
  - credit terms; and
  - guarantees or warranties.

Persuasive communication

- Non-personal verbal messages:
  - publicity;
  - measured advertising: radio, TV, newspaper, magazine; and
  - unmeasured advertising: direct mail, catalogue, trade shows, point-of purchase, Internet, World Wide Web, SMS, mobile media.
- Personal verbal messages:
  - personal selling messages; and
  - word-of-mouth support.
- Non-verbal messages:
  - packaging of product; and
  - symbolism derived from resellers, pricing, etc.

Promotional inducements

- Character of basic offer:
  - free sample;
  - free trial;
  - extra goods at same price; and
  - special terms of sale (other than price).
- Price related:
  - introductory discounts;
  - money-off coupons;
  - price specials;

→

- buy-back allowances to dealers; and
- manufacturer's rebates.
- External to basic offer:
  - premium promotions: trading stamps, contests, sweepstakes, games, free gift in pack, continuity coupons;
  - 'free' offers to customers;
  - 'right to buy' other products: 'self-liquidator', 'commodity continuities'; and
  - cash awards: sales contests, 'spiffs' to dealers.

Figure 1.4: Koekemoer (2004:18).

1.5   THE USE OF THE MARKETING COMMUNICATION MIX

The marketing communication mix is not something that is set and used in the same way over and over. The combination of elements for the same product may differ from campaign to campaign and even from month to month as the marketer adapts or adjusts the use of different elements. The combination in which these elements will be used depend on perceived conditions in the market and the market to be addressed, economic factors, competitors actions and launch of new products and marketing campaigns. In some instances the company may rely heavily on publicity in newspapers to carry the message across (such as in the case of a unique concept or invention) while in others the uses of sales personnel to demonstrate the product may be more important. The 'secret' of an effective marketing communication mix is therefore not a set way of combining the elements. A marketer may spend the majority of the promotion budget on, say, advertising, but may also spend a little money on public relations, which results in some favourable publicity.

This, in turn, may lend just the right amount of credibility to the marketer's advertising claims. The real 'secret' is to be able to judge just how to allocate the marketing communication budget to the various elements of the mix. The objective is to integrate them in a way that produces the best possible synergy. This is frequently referred to as 'getting the most value for your money spent'.

To do this is however not so easy. It might even be argued that there is no way to determine the optimum blend of the marketing communication mix elements as there are a magnitude of factors that can and will impact on the effectiveness of the mix. But with experience and a constant evaluation of results it is possible to improve the mix and to move closer to securing a more optimal response for the market. This is not only done by playing around with different combinations but also by seeing what competitors are doing, the types of combinations they are using and the response to their efforts.

Each element of the marketing communication mix is designed to do a specific job and it would be counterproductive to think in terms of any one being 'better' than any other one. The effective marketing organisation will establish which elements of the marketing communication mix will work best for its product offering and target market and then will enhance the performance of the appropriate elements by intelligently integrating them into a cohesive marketing communication strategy.

1.6 MARKETING COMMUNICATION PLANNING AND STRATEGY

A very important part of marketing communications is the planning and managing thereof. The planning and managing of marketing communication involves six basic steps (see Figure 1.5).

Step 1: Performing a situation analysis.

Step 2: Setting marketing objectives.

Step 3: Determining the marketing communication budget.

Step 4: Management of the marketing communication programme.

Step 5: Coordinating and integrating efforts.

Step 6: Evaluating, controlling and following-up.

Let's briefly review these steps:

■ *Step 1: Situation analysis*

A thorough situation analysis includes an examination of each of the following issues:

◆ *Internal organisational strengths and weaknesses* – for example, monetary resources, established policies and procedures, personnel skills, management track record, history of brands, reputation, etc.

◆ *Target markets* – for example, market segmentation, targeting of selected segments, positioning, etc.

◆ *Competitive analysis* of the direct and indirect competitors.

◆ *External or uncontrollable factors* – for example, political, economic, legal, sociocultural, technological, environmental and international factors.

■ *Step 2: Setting marketing objectives*

The marketing objectives could include sales objectives, market share and growth objectives, service and relationship objectives, etc.

■ *Step 3: Determining the marketing communication budget*

This step involves the determination of the money appropriation in total and to each of the various elements in the marketing communication mix.

■ *Step 4: Management of the marketing communication mix*

Within the limitations of the promotion budget and the monies allocated to each of the marketing communication mix elements, the following issues will receive attention regarding each element:

◆ objectives (how much or how many, and by when?);

◆ strategy (what 'blend' to use?);

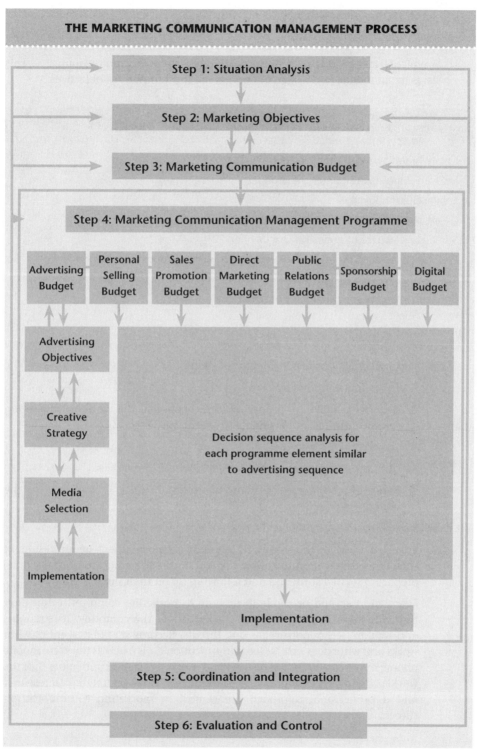

Figure 1.5: Adapted from Koekemoer (2004:22).

◆ method (how will it be used?); and

◆ implementation (when, where, by whom?).

A typical list of marketing communication objectives is given in Figure 1.6. This list is by no means exhaustive but covers the most important objectives.

TYPICAL MARKETING COMMUNICATION OBJECTIVES

- Create brand awareness for your company
- Increase the consumption of the product
- Enhance brand loyalty
- Create awareness of a new product offering
- Stimulate purchase of goods on special offer
- Change consumers' perceptions or attitude towards a product or organisation
- Convey positive information about the marketer
- Build the image of the product or organisation

Figure 1.6

■ *Step 5: Coordination and integration of efforts*

There are four main issues involved here:

◆ How to achieve a proper balance between the various marketing communication mix elements to get the best effect.

◆ Scheduling the activities.

◆ Utilisation of personnel and outside agencies or services.

◆ Budget appropriation revision to optimally allocate resources to the various mix elements.

■ *Step 6: Evaluation, control and follow-up*

This step involves the setting of standards, measurement of the results of each marketing communication element and of the programme as a whole, preparing revised strategies and following up on their implementation.

Every effort should be made to prepare a marketing communication plan that will work, bearing in mind the culture of the company, its strengths and weaknesses, opportunities and threats. Records should be kept of what works and what does not. New communication tools (such as the Web, mobile phone, Internet, etc) should be tried and marketers should remember that the world around us is changing and so should we. However, relying on research and a professional approach are central to marketing communication success.

1.7 ORGANISING FOR MARKETING COMMUNICATION

As is clear from the discussion above the management of the marketing communication process is not easy and it is imperative that the 'right' organisation is in place. This may range from a number of very sophisticated and interrelated internal departments to a straightforward understanding of 'who does what'. The defining factors, of course, will be the size and resources of the organisation. A large, financially strong organisation may be able to justify the establishment of a number of specialised departments, each handling a specific area of marketing communication. However, an important point is that the activities of departments (or whatever else they are called) must be coordinated in order to achieve optimum results. This is very much in line with the concept of IMC. Let's now look at various ways of organising for marketing communication.

Assuming the organisation is large enough to justify a full marketing communication operation, marketing communication should fall under a marketing manager or director. Depending on a number of factors, principally the type of product offering and the target market/s, the most likely 'departments' in such an organisation will be a sales department, an advertising department and possibly a public relations department. Historically, one of the things that seems to present the most difficulty in a marketing organisation is the conflict that arises between sales and the 'other' departments, collectively referred to as 'marketing'. This is unfortunate and reflects a lack of understanding of the true meaning of marketing.

Sales is an integral part of marketing and not a separate discipline or function. Unfortunately, however, in many organisations the sales department is indeed separated from the other marketing communication functions. While it is essential to maintain strict control of the sales function, sight should never be lost of the support that can be given to the sales force by the other marketing communication elements. In order to do this the sales manager or director should report to the marketing manager or director. In some 'older' organisations this may not sit too well with certain individuals, usually the sales manager or director, who previously would most probably have reported directly to the general manager or managing director. Whatever personal feelings may be involved, it is essential to put these aside for the good of the organisation.

The areas of sales promotion and direct response marketing are a little more complex because of the specialised nature of these activities. Whether they are handled by separate departments within the organisation or by outside specialists, the most important point is to ensure that they are still ultimately under the control of the marketing manager or director – there simply *must* be overall control and integration.

The key issues to note in organising for effective marketing communication are that overall responsibility rests with the marketing manager or director and that each of the various departments is seen to be 'equal' in status. No inference is made here to the actual status of the individuals involved since it should be clear that the scope of the positions may be significantly different. Neither is it the intention to imply that each functional area is precisely as 'important' as the others. The key concept to grasp is the fact that they are all *equally important contributors* to the ultimate success of the organisation. It makes no difference if one functional area 'only' does a certain amount of work or has a significantly lower budget than any of the others. What that particular functional area does, may have a vital and synergistic influence on another area, again illustrating the importance of the concept of integrated marketing communication.

1.8 THE FUTURE OF MARKETING COMMUNICATION

A number of trends in the field of marketing communication are taking place in the market and the marketer must be aware of these as well as integrate new trends as far as possible which are appropriate to his specific market. Some trends identified are as follows:

- *Traditional marketing methods* are losing their grip on customers at an alarming rate. Trade shows, trade publications and direct mail deliver a fraction of the ROI they did only two years ago.

- *Consumers themselves have changed beyond recognition*

  Their behaviour is more complex, their media habits are different, and they are more outspoken. They have a different relationship with brands these days, and are less tolerant, less obedient, less loyal and more demanding.

  Previously, marketers could define their brands for consumers. They could make one TV commercial and run it in some top rating TV show where millions of consumers would see it, and the job was done!

  Today, consumers are defining brands, even redefining them. And because consumers experience brands multi-dimensionally these days, it's no longer good enough to produce a wonderful TV commercial or anything else for that matter — extolling the virtues of a brand if the brands claims do not match up to the actual brand experience because especially in this age of fast networked communications, consumers themselves will share good and bad experiences with their friends without fear.

- *Consumers today have far more control*

  They must be shown enormous respect as people if marketers are to have any hope of them respecting their brands.

- *Communication channels are exploding and fragmenting*

  The term mass media threatens to become an oxymoron. Audiences are diminishing as they are given more choices and more distractions than ever before. Against this scenario, we find conventional advertising agencies and marketing service companies in denial.

  It is not that interruptive advertising does not work, it's more that with an over proliferation of interruptive communications combined with a fragmenting media environment, only the very best interruptive marketing can work when combined with huge spending on media.

For several years now, the Internet, mobile media and the Web have been dramatically altering the traditional view of advertising and communication media as we used to know them. The Web provides an efficient channel for advertising, marketing, and even direct distribution of certain goods and information services and the mobile phone is emerging as the other key player in this fast changing marketing landscape.

REFERENCES

American Productivity and Quality Center. 1998. *Integrated Marketing Communications: A Consortium Benchmarking Study*. Working Paper published by APQC International Benchmarking Clearinghouse: Houston, TX.

Beem, E.R. and Shaffer, H.J. 1981. *Triggers to Customer Action – Some Elements in a Theory of Promotional Inducement*. Marketing Science Institute: Cambridge, Massachusetts.

Bennett, P.D. (ed) 1988. *Dictionary of Marketing Terms*. American Marketing Association: Chicago.

Cornwall, B. and Maignan, I. 1998. 'An International Review of Sponsorship Research'. *Journal of Advertising*, March.

Duncan, T. 2002. *IMC: Using Advertising and Promotion to Build Brands*. McGraw- Hill/ Irwin: Burr Ridge, IL.

Engel, J.F., Warshaw, M.R. and Kinnear, T.C. 1994. *Promotional Strategy*, 8ed Irwin: Homewood, Illinois.

Etzel, M.J., Walker, B.J. and Stanton, W.J. 2004, *Marketing*, 13ed Irwin/McGraw-Hill: Burr Ridge, IL.

Govoni, N., Eng, R. and Galper, M. 1986. *Promotional Management*. Prentice Hall: Englewood Cliffs, New Jersey.

Koekemoer, L. (ed) 2004, *Marketing Communications*, 3ed, JUTA Academic, Cape Town.

Schultz, D.E., Tannenbaum, S.I. and Lauterborn, R.F. 1995. *The New Marketing Paradigm. Integrated Marketing Communication*. NTC Business Books: Chicago, Illinois.

Shimp, T.A. 1990. *Promotion Management and Marketing Communicaton*, 2ed The Dryden Press: Orlando, Florida.

Van der Westhuizen, B. 1996. 'Promotion Mix Practices in South Africa: Implications for Marketing Strategy'. In Kaynak, E., Lascu, D-N. and Becker, K. (eds) *Proceedings of the Fifth Annual World Business Congress*. Hamilton: Bermuda.

Yeshin, T. 2004. *Integrated Marketing Communications*, 2ed Jordan Hill, Oxford.

http://www.books.google.co.za/books?id=JrAscbNarWIC&pg=PA68&lpg=PA68&dq= American+Association+of+Advertising+Agencies:Definition+of+IMC&source

2 Principles of Communication

AIM OF THIS CHAPTER

This chapter will focus on the nature of communication, communication objectives, the communication process, the 'meaning of meaning', the essence of persuasive communication and barriers to effective communication.

LEARNING OUTCOMES

After studying this chapter you should be competent in:
- explaining the communication concept and discussing the elements involved
- outlining communication objectives and marketing communication objectives
- discussing the communication effects pyramid
- indicating what constitutes a good communication objective
- describing the communications process by outlining some communication models
- discussing semiotics (or the 'meaning of meaning')
- discussing the variables influencing persuasive communication
- discussing the barriers to effective communication

2.1 THE NATURE OF COMMUNICATION

As mentioned in Chapter 1 the marketer needs to communicate with his or her market. For this the product, price and place can be used to some extent, but they also need to inform and persuade customers to buy the product.

Communication suggests that there must be some common thinking between two parties and information must be passed from one person to another. Establishing commonality in thinking is not always as easy as it might seem; many attempts to communicate are unsuccessful (Belch & Belch, 2006:139). Communication is, therefore, very important in the marketing process. The interaction of customer and salesperson, the exchange of information between the buyer and the seller and between marketer and consumer are indispensable to the distribution of goods and services in competitive environments. Mass communication is a necessity in today's business environment owing to the dynamics and the growth in the number and size of the markets and to the wide variety of products offered for sale.

In today's global economy, the marketing communication process is fairly complex and diverse. Not only is a company communicating with their customers, but also with their suppliers, stakeholders, distributors and so forth. Consumers engage in word-of-mouth communication with other consumers and publics. Meanwhile, each group provides communication feedback to every other group. For most companies, the issue is not whether to communicate but rather how to say it, when to say it, who to address, and so on.

Having said this, what is communication then?

Communication is the exchange of information, news, ideas, etc or the action to convey one's ideas, feelings, etc clearly to others. Communication can be defined as 'a dynamic process in which people attempt to share their internal states with other people through the use of symbols' (Samovar, Porter & McDaniel, 2009:16).

Communication has four important elements, namely (Anon. 2007):

■ *Information:* It may be from advertising campaigns to job interviews or brochures to newspaper TV listing – as long as someone sends a message across to someone else.

■ *People:* This may include employees, customers, or whoever needs to be given a message.

■ *Time:* One must choose the right time to pass on a message.

■ *Format:* One must choose the best way to convey the message. It may be in a letter, via email, a short video, etc.

In some instances the *communications process* is simple, while in others it is more complex. The success of the communications process depends on a variety of factors such as the nature and complexity of the message, the audience's interpretation of it, the environment in which it is received, the level of interference, etc. To these factors we can add the message receiver's attitudes to and perceptions of the source and the medium used to transmit the message. Often words, sounds, pictures, colours, even jewellery and clothing, as symbols, may have different meanings to different audiences, and people's perceptions and interpretations of them will vary.

When communicating with others the marketer must make sure that the audience will understand what they are saying. Rix et al (in Figure 2.1) points out five 'know your voice' aspects that need to be taken into account when communicating with the target audience.

2.2 MARKETING COMMUNICATION OBJECTIVES

As with all business functions objectives are needed in order to give direction to the activities. Marketing communication objectives are for example dependent on what the business wants to achieve through its marketing efforts.

The communication objective of a new shampoo may be to communicate to new and potential customers that the product is harmless to the environment and that it does not damage the ecology.

KNOW YOUR VOICE

It is useful to have a clear understanding of how you sound to others. Here are several aspects to consider:

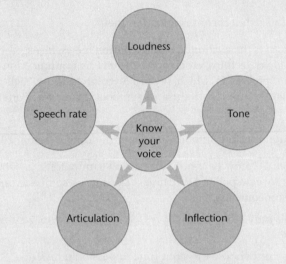

Loudness

The loudness of a person's voice can be either a deal maker or a deal breaker. The loudness of the salesperson's voice should be varied to suite the selling situation. The loudness of a voice is directly linked to the volume of the voice. Speaking with a loud voice can be intimidating and even chase people away. It is however important to use the loudness of a voice to emphasise certain issues or points. The loudness or softness of a voice can be used to emphasise a point.

Tone

To impress a potential customer's expectation, the salesperson's voice must constantly sound upbeat, warm, under control and clear. The tone of the voice can be improved through breathing exercises and to use gestures while speaking. A smile can go a long way to warm up the tone of the voice.

Inflection

Inflection refers to the change of tone at the end of a sentence. A drop in the tone generally indicates the completion of a thought. Salesmen should remember that when making a sales call, all body language disappear and the potential customer must rely on the words, tone and inflection.

Articulation

The salesperson must not mumble and it is important that each word is clearly spoken.

Speech rate

Speech rate refers to how fast a person speaks. There is a lot of evidence that the faster the speech rate the more negatively it impacts on sales. It is therefore important that salespeople focus on their rate of speech and make sure it is not too fast.

Figure 2.1: Rix et al (2001: 143–144).

The marketing objective could be to achieve eight per cent market share in the next year. This marketing objective can be achieved if the marketing communication objectives can be achieved, that is:

■ advertising objective: to increase awareness of the product to 80 per cent of the target market;

■ personal selling objective: to recruit 100 new accounts;

■ sales promotion objective: to persuade 40 per cent of the target market to try the product;

■ direct marketing objective: to persuade 80 per cent of the retailers to display the product at gondola ends (end-aisle displays);

■ public relations objective: to convince 85 per cent of the shareholders that the company is dynamic and profitable; and

■ sponsorship objective: to maintain brand awareness, enhance corporate image and build goodwill among key influencers.

In order to place marketing communication objectives in perspective compared to other company objectives Figure 2.1 shows an example of a car manufacturing company and the relationship of the marketing communication objectives to other company objectives.

Figure 2.2

2.2.1 Specific objectives

Generally speaking, all marketing communications efforts are directed at achieving one or more of the following objectives:

- to build primary demand;
- to create brand awareness;
- to provide relevant information (knowledge);
- to influence attitudes and feelings;
- to create desires;
- to create preferences;
- to facilitate purchase and trial; and
- to create loyal customers.

Figure 2.3 shows the various steps in customer movement towards purchase and loyalty. Many such hierarchy models exist, and although they may vary somewhat in terms of the intermediate steps they use, they essentially view customers as having to pass through cognitive, affective and conative stages in order to become loyal customers.

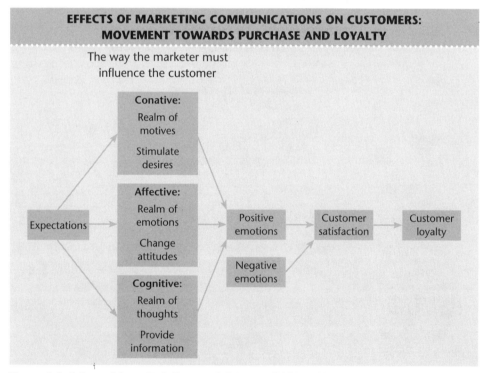

Figure 2.3: Adapted from Del, Bosque & Martin (2008:559).

Let's focus on eight important communications objectives:

■ *Objective 1: To build primary demand*

As most products have competitors the main aim of the marketer is to get the customer to choose their product over that of their competitors. It is often necessary to create or stimulate primary demand by building wants for a specific product category. For example, as more and more women work they have less time for cooking, sewing, their physical well-being, etc. Marketers can successfully create a demand for time-saving food recipes, for fun in sewing and knitting, for fibre-rich, fat-free, calcium-enriched food items, for easy ways to exercise, etc.

■ *Objective 2: To create brand awareness*

As soon as primary demand is created, marketers compete for market share by attempting to establish secondary demand for their specific brands. The first step in creating demand for a specific brand is to create awareness among the target audience. This can be done through repetitive advertising, a launch sales promotion, publicity and personal selling efforts.

■ *Objective 3: To provide relevant information (knowledge)*

Awareness involves familiarising customers with the marketer's brand via the marketing communication tools. Customers need information, rational or emotional, to form an opinion and to be able to choose between alter-native brands. Therefore, marketers use marketing communications to inform people about a product's special features, benefits, differences and why it is preferable to competitive brands. Often this information is 'nice to know' and will not motivate the target audience. Relevant information is not only essential to achieve the communication objectives but also motivational.

■ *Objective 4: To influence attitudes and feelings*

By successfully creating awareness and providing relevant information, communications can enhance, even change, attitudes and feelings. The objectives are to create a particular image, to position the brand and to establish favourable attitudes that will lead to a desire for the marketer's brand rather than for a competitive brand.

■ *Objective 5: To create desires*

Brand preference can only occur when the customers "like" the product. Liking is an attitude, a feeling that leads to 'I must have it' or 'I'd rather take that one' – in other words, a desire for this specific brand.

■ *Objective 6: To create preferences*

Marketers aim to achieve a position where there brand is preferred to those of competitors. It is therefore imperative that the marketer knows what makes a customer prefer one brand to another. In most cases it is the perception of value for money. Value for money is the relationship between the perception of quality and the perception of cost. To put it simply: 'What am I getting for what I'm paying?' Customers often do not form preferences because of the features of a brand (these could be nice to know), but because of what the brand can do for them (motivational benefits) which other brands cannot do. Successful communication not only creates awareness, provides relevant information, influences attitudes and feelings and creates desires but creates preferences by convincing the customer that the brand is better value for money than competitive brands.

■ *Objective 7: To facilitate purchase and trial*

Successful communication may lead to an intention to purchase, a conviction to try the brand. But if the brand is not available or priced too high relative to competitive brands, the likelihood of that brand being purchased is obviously reduced. Brand switching can then occur. Effective marketing communications serve to facilitate purchase and to overcome potential stumbling blocks (like a premium price) because the communication will convince the target audience that even at a premium price the brand is still excellent value for money. Infrequent purchase will hopefully lead to frequent purchase and regular use of the brand.

■ *Objective 8: To create loyal customers*

Repeat purchases of a company's products is the ultimate objective of a company. This implies that the needs of the customer must be totally satisfied or at least better satisfied by the company compared to the competitor's products. There is often a tremendous difference between the loyalty of merely satisfied and completely satisfied customers. In fact, any drop from total satisfaction results in a major drop in loyalty and can lead to brand switching. There are two types of loyalty: true long-term loyalty and false loyalty. Whenever these customers have choices they either remain rock-solid loyal or they defect. They defect or are lured away if they are not completely satisfied. Satisfied with what? Satisfied with the brand, the service quality, the price, the availability and a host of other factors. Marketing communications play an important role here in creating awareness, creating image, creating expectations (which may or may not be met), inducing trial and repurchase (by confirming that the customer made the right choice).

2.2.2 The communication effects pyramid

Belch and Belch (2004:203–5) state that communication objectives can be presented in the form of a communication effects pyramid. A way of understanding communications tasks to be performed by advertising and promotion is to view them as being analogous to building a pyramid by accomplishing lower-level objectives – such as awareness and knowledge or comprehension. Subsequent tasks involve moving consumers who are aware of or knowledgeable about the product or service to higher levels in the pyramid. The initial stages, at the base of the pyramid, will be easier to accomplish than those towards the top, such as trial and repurchase or regular use. Thus, the percentage of prospective customers moved to each level will decline as they move up the pyramid. We use the communication effects pyramid presented in Figure 2.4 to show how a company introducing a new sports drink targeted at 18 to 34 year-olds might set its advertising and promotion objectives.

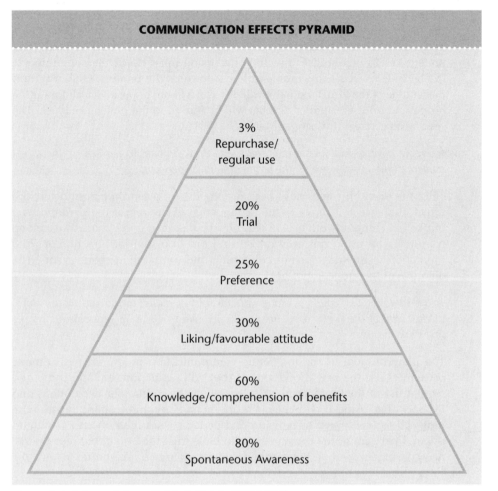

COMMUNICATION EFFECTS PYRAMID

3%
Repurchase/
regular use

20%
Trial

25%
Preference

30%
Liking/favourable attitude

60%
Knowledge/comprehension of benefits

80%
Spontaneous Awareness

Figure 2.4: Adapted from Belch & Belch (2004:204).

The first task of the marketing communication programme for a new product is to create a broad level of awareness among the target audience. This can be done through repetitive advertising in a variety of media, such as magazines, television and radio, that reach 18 to 34 year-olds. Thus, the specific objective would be:

To create an 80 per cent spontaneous awareness of the new sports drink among 18 to 34 year-old males and females during the first six weeks of the campaign.

The next step in the pyramid process is to communicate information so that a certain percentage of the target audience will not only be aware of the new product, but will also understand its features and benefits. Let's assume the new brand is being positioned as a sports drink that contains added vitamins and minerals. The specific objective for the second stage would be as follows:

To communicate the specific benefits of the sports drink – that it contains added vitamins and minerals – to 60 per cent of the target audience to make its members interested in the brand.

At the next level, the campaign is designed to create positive feelings towards the new brand. A certain percentage of the consumers who have been made aware of the new brand must be moved to the affective stages of liking and preference. To accomplish this, the advertising must effectively communicate the benefits to create favourable attitudes towards the product. Only a certain percentage of the target audience will develop a liking or positive feelings for the brand and an even smaller number will be moved to the preference block. The specific objective at this stage would be:

To create positive feelings towards the sports drink among 30 per cent of the target audience and a preference for the brand among 25 per cent.

Once the preceding steps have been accomplished, a certain percentage of the target audience will move to the action stage at the top of the pyramid. The marketing communication plan can now be designed to facilitate trial among consumers by using not only advertising but also sponsorships and/or sales promotion techniques, such as couponing and sampling at sports events. The objective at this stage might be:

To use sampling and coupons, along with advertising, digital media and sponsorships, to elicit trial of the sports drink among 20 per cent of 18 to 34 year-olds during the first three months.

The ultimate goal of the marketing communication programme is to make consumers use the new brand so that they will repurchase it. Repurchase and regular use of the sports drink will depend on the consumers' evaluations and feelings after using it. However, the marketing communications programme may call for continued advertising and periodic sales promotions not only to retain 3 per cent of the consumers, who have tried the brand, but also to take new consumers through the pyramid and get them to try the brand.

2.2.3 Characteristics of objectives

Good objectives have certain characteristics and it is important that communication objectives should be stated in terms of concrete and measurable communications tasks, a specific target audience, indicate a benchmark starting point and the degree of change sought and specify a time period for accomplishing the objective. Each of these requirements will now be examined more closely (Belch & Belch, 2004:206–8):

- ■ *Concrete and measurable.* The communications task specified in the objective should be a precise statement of what appeal or message the advertiser wants to communicate to the target audience. Advertisers generally use a copy platform to describe the basic message they hope to communicate. The objective should be specific and clear enough to provide guidance and direction to creative specialists who must develop the actual advertising message.

- ■ *Target audience.* It is not possible to set a good objective if the marketer does not know who his target audience is. The target market the communication is to be aimed at must be well-defined. Generally, the primary target audience for a company's product or service is identified and described in the situation analysis and may be based on descriptive variables such as geographics, demographics, psychographics and lifestyles, as well as on behavioural variables such as usage patterns, benefits sought and participation in digital media.

■ *Benchmark and degree of change sought.* An important part of setting objectives is knowing the target audience's present status concerning response hierarchy variables such as awareness, knowledge, image, attitudes and purchasing intentions, and then determining the degree to which consumers must be changed or moved by the marketing communications campaign. Determining the target market's present position regarding the various response stages requires that benchmark measures be taken. This often demands market research to determine prevailing levels of the response hierarchy.

Establishing benchmark measures is important as this gives the promotional planner a basis for detonating communications tasks that need to be accomplished, and for specifying particular objectives. For example, a pre-liminary study of a brand may reveal that awareness is high but knowledge of its specific benefits is low, as are consumer attitudes. Thus, the objective for the advertising campaign should not be to increase awareness but rather with improving the target audience's knowledge level of the brand and improving attitudes towards it.

■ *Specified time period.* All objectives should be set with a time line in mind. In order to be able to see if the communications used has had an impact, there should be time periods such as over three months, a year, etc. Appropriate time periods can range anywhere from a few days to a year or more. The length of the period depends on the situation facing the marketer and the type of response being sought.

2.3   THE COMMUNICATION PROCESS

In order to communicate with the target market a process need to be followed. Communication basically requires a sender (or source of the communication), a message and a receiver (or destination). A basic model is shown in Figure 2.5.

The sender's ability to successfully encode the message depends on his or her knowledge, past experiences, feelings, emotions and attitudes as well as his or her knowledge of the receiver's past experiences, feelings, emotions and attitudes and what will motivate the receiver to act. With this knowledge an effective appeal or message is encoded, the message is transmitted one-on-one or via mass media and the receiver will decode the message and respond to it, hopefully in the appropriate, intended way.

Successful communications are accomplished when the marketer selects an appropriate source, develops an effective appeal and then selects the media that will best reach the target audience and effectively deliver the message.

MODEL 1: A COMMUNICATION MODEL

The basis of this model is a message flow whereby the communication, starting with the source, is formulated into a message and is transmitted through a medium or channel to receivers constituting a target audience. The impact of the message is measured in terms of feedback in which the receiver's reaction to the message is communicated back to the source.

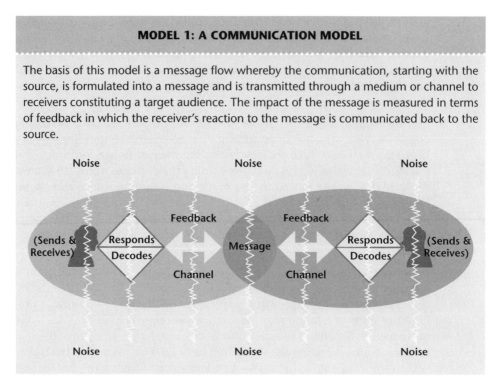

Figure 2.5: Adapted from Google Images.

Let's look at what is involved in the model:

- *Encoding.* The sender (source) encodes a message hoping that the message decoded by the receiver will be what is intended to be communicated.

  What are the requirements for good encoding? Knowledge, past experiences, feelings or emotions and attitudes all affect our ability to encode successfully. Knowledge of another's language, knowledge of the subject-matter of the communication, general education, background – all these play their part. Generally, excessive feelings, whether positive or negative or a total lack of feeling, tend to distort good communication through too much excitement or through apathy respectively. Empathy with the other person's cultural background is vital. Attitudes are the result of one's education, upbringing and culture and these can cause barriers to communication if the sender's attitudes are completely different from the receiver's.

- *The intended message/the encoded message.* The communicator's objective is to get the receiver to respond in a particular manner. And the intended message (the idea that the communicator wishes to convey to and have accepted by the receiver) should be the direct cause of the desired results. If the objective is to increase awareness, then the message should increase the receiver's familiarity with the brand. If the objective is to change beliefs, then the message should cause the receiver to reformulate his or her opinions.

The identification of the appropriate intended message comes from market analysis. If the communicator totally misunderstands the market and chooses an ineffective theme, no amount of creative expression will lead to successful communications.

The message, once encoded, can be presented in a variety of ways. We can classify messages according to their appeal and their 'tone of voice'. Appeals can be either emotional or rational. The tone of voice can be light-hearted, humourous, or serious. *Emotional appeals* are usually either negative or positive, for example, the consequences you will suffer for not doing something like insuring your car or the peace of mind for doing something like investing for your future.

Rational appeals can be simple or complex. A simple appeal could consist of a 25 per cent discount offer – a complex appeal could include a list of reasons for buying a certain product, such as technical specifications, quality, back-up service and a detailed comparison with the products of competitors.

■ *Message transmission happens through a medium or channel.* The medium of communication the sender chooses is the means of communication. This can take the form of either verbal or non-verbal communication. If verbal, then will it be spoken or written? If spoken, will it be a presentation, a meeting, a telephone message, a recording or a video? If a presentation, what kind of presentation? If a meeting, will it be formal or informal? If written, will it be a letter, a memorandum, a report, an advertisement, a poster with words, a graphic design with words? If non-verbal, will it be a picture, a poster without words, a chart, a film without words or a piece of music? All these questions concern the choice of medium.

The *channel of communication* can be formal or less formal and is the route or direction in which the message will travel. Some experts refer to the channel as the method of transmission and seem to treat medium and channel as a spoken message (the voice, the radio, television, computer or telephone). They refer to the channel for a written message as paper, an email, SMS or a fax. Some speak of the channel as vision or sound.

Very often noise can confuse the message or compete against communication. Noise could be any interference or disturbance, like literal noise (loud talking, a blaring radio, too many advertisements, continual coughing, the telephone ringing) or metaphorical noise (aspects competing for a receiver's attention like a lack of time, feelings of uncertainty, emotions, distrust, problems at home, etc).

■ *The receiver.* The receiver is the target of the communication efforts. It is important for the receiver to be able to decode the message, to want to attend to the message, to interpret the message, to retain the message and act on it. Let's consider these:

◆ *Ability to decode.* In many cases the receiver's ability to decode a particular message is influenced by his or her knowledge (of a language, a subject, etc), past experiences (favourable or unfavorable), feelings, emotions and attitudes.

◆ *Credibility of the source.* Source credibility is usually a function of two major characteristics, namely trustworthiness and expertise. Trustworthiness is the degree of confidence a receiver has in the intention of the sender.

◆ *Selective exposure, perception and retention.* A message cannot successfully communicate unless the receiver is aware of it, interprets the message in the intended way and remembers it. In planning the communication, the source must remember that perception by the receiver will always be selective and subjective. People do not pay an equal amount of attention to each of the thousands of commercial and non-commercial messages they are confronted with every day. Selectivity is practised: selectivity in exposure, in perception and in retention. Think of all the newspaper, magazine, radio, television, outdoor, Internet and direct response advertisements that you notice.We, as customers, avoid certain media or shops or sales pitches (selective exposure). Due to restrictions in income and lifestyle certain target groups will not be exposed to certain media. We may only pay attention to those communications that attract our attention and are relevant and meaningful to us.

■ *Response.* By capturing the receiver's attention, communicating relevant information and overcoming the dangers of selective perception and retention, the communicator has created a good opportunity to influence behaviour. The behaviour could be:

◆ Acceptance of a *particular* image. Most advertising messages are not intended to lead to immediate action but to create a particular brand-, user- or situation image.

◆ To have a clear *positioning* in mind. Most marketing communication messages are intended to position a product or service *vis-à-vis* the competitors' products or services.

◆ To experience a *sensation* (feeling, emotion, attitude) that stimulates the receiver to respond in a particular way. For example, a caring mother who loves her children feels the need to buy a course on study methods.

◆ To experience a *changed attitude.* For example, the brand is a natural product and must be preferable to artificial products.

◆ To have a *crystallised view.* Receivers may take action when they have been thinking about something but needed an extra push. For example, a person might have been thinking about redecorating a room and seeing the advertising for a furniture store's closing-down sale might crystallise the view sufficiently to trigger action. Why? Because the person can now afford it.

◆ To *buy* the product or to buy it *more often.* Successful communications can persuade the receiver to act now (buy the advertised brand) or can reinforce existing beliefs and attitudes (buy more of it more often).

In our model of communication, we identified the source, message, channel or medium, receiver and response. There are a number of variables influencing persuasive communication relating to the various elements in the model, as seen in Figure 2.6.

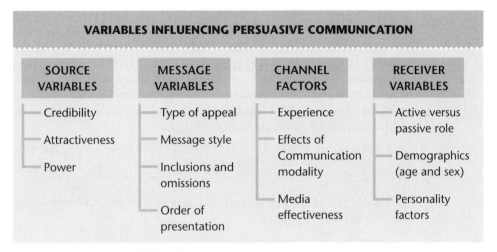

Figure 2.6: Koekemoer (2004:53).

- *Source variables*. The source element of the marketing communications process is multi-faceted, as a variety of sources can be involved. Examples are an article in a specialist publication, an announcer on radio, a salesperson, etc. The source can be judged by its credibility, its attractiveness and its power.

  - *Credibility* refers to the extent to which the source is perceived as having knowledge, skill or experience relevant to the communication topic and can be trusted to give a balanced opinion or present objective information on the issue. There are two important dimensions to credibility – expertise and trustworthiness. Expertise is a very important aspect of credibility, as a communicator who is perceived as being knowledgeable in a given area will be more persuasive than one who appears to have less expertise. Trustworthiness refers to the honesty, integrity and believability of the source and is also an important aspect of credibility. A source may be perceived as being very knowledgeable but his or her influence will be lessened if the audience members perceive the source as being biased or having no credibility. A source may be perceived as being very knowledgeable but his or her influence will be lessened if the audience members perceive the source as being biased or having underlying personal motives for advocating a particular position (such as being paid to endorse a product). It can be expected that expert and/or trustworthy sources would be more persuasive than sources who have less expertise or trustworthiness.

  - *Attractiveness* is probably the source characteristic used most by advertisers. When a receiver believes a source appealing, persuasion may occur through a process known as identification. The receiver can identify with a model, a situation, an emotion, etc. Marketers recognise that target audiences are more likely to identify with people who are similar to themselves. They would therefore select such people as models for their advertisements.

  - *Power* is the final source characteristic. A source may have power when he or she can actually administer rewards and punishments to the receiver.

When a source is perceived by the receiver to have power, influence occurs through a process known as compliance. Compliance results when the receiver accepts the persuasive influence of the source and hopes to obtain a favourable reaction or avoid punishment. In South Africa, distribution of fast-moving consumer goods is in the hands of a small number of buyers. These buyers can use their source power to demand that a certain amount of support for a brand (advertising, promotion, etc) be guaranteed before the brand is listed.

■ *Message variables.* We will focus on four message variables, namely the type of appeal, the message style, inclusions and omissions and the order of presentation.

◆ *The type of appeal.* In marketing communications, the most commonly used appeals are as follows:

- Card stacking: give as much information as possible.

- Fear: physical or social threats. Moderate fear appeals are more persuasive than low or high fear appeals.

- Humour: messages designed to amuse, entertain and provoke smiles or laughter.

- Repetition: increases the likelihood of a message being remembered. Message can be repeated evenly over a defined time period to remind consumers of a well-known brand or repeated in bursts to quickly increase awareness.

- Rational: emphasises logical or socially acceptable reasons for buying the product such as quality, durability, economy, effectiveness, functionality, etc. It has been proved, however, that pure rational appeals are not as effective as a mixture of rational and emotional appeals because customers are not strictly rational beings.

- Emotional: directed at consumers' ego and social motives such as friendship, love, security, prestige, status, self-esteem, etc.

◆ *Message style.* This has to do with the clearness of the message. Is the radio spot clear? Is there clutter in the print advertisement? Is there simplicity and a clear purpose? Message style also has to do with the skills used in presenting the message.

◆ *Inclusions and omissions.* This deals with what is included and what has been omitted, leaving it to the receiver to make his or her own conclusions. Persuasive messages are more effective if the source explicitly draws the conclusion rather than leaving it to the receiver to interpret the message in more than one way.

◆ *Order of presentation.* A basic consideration in the design of a persuasive message concerns the order of presentation of the message points. Should the most important message points be placed at the beginning of the message, in the middle or at the end? Research on learning and memory generally indicates that the points presented first and last are remembered better than those presented in the middle.

■ *Channel factors*. Channel factors include direct experience with an object versus communication about it, effects of communication modality and media effectiveness. Depending on the type of product involved, direct experience (for example, demonstration of a complex technical object) may be a lot more effective than communication about it. Certain products lend themselves to mood imagery which can be successfully created in advertising (for example, perfumes, bath salts, soap, etc). Communication modality deals with the choice between using a voice only, visual only or a combination of these. Again, it depends on the type of product and/or the circumstances. Radio is a good reminder advertising medium and largely depends on voice, music and sound effects. Print media and audio-visual media (television, cinema, video, etc) lend themselves to a combination of voice and visuals. Media effectiveness deals with a complex issue, namely: Is one medium superior to another? The superiority of one medium over another is difficult to ascertain and depends on the subject matter of the message. For example, if a demonstration is an important element in persuasion, personal selling or television can be effective. If it is necessary to supply a lot of technical arguments, a brochure or print advertisement may be preferable. The various advertising media are discussed in Chapter 4.

■ *Receiver variables*. Receiver variables include active versus passive roles (ie the involvement of the receiver), demographic factors (age and sex) and personality factors.

   ◆ The degree of *receiver involvement* influences the communications process. If a receiver is not highly involved, a persuasive message cannot lead to a cognitive change and therefore not lead towards a change in attitude and behaviour of a customer.

   ◆ *Age and sex* (demographic factors) are related to a receiver's persuadability. Generally, maximum suggestibility to persuasion increases up to the age of eight or nine. Thereafter it tends to decline. Some evidence indicates that women are more persuadable than men.

   ◆ *Personality factors* include self-esteem and intelligence. Generally speaking, the higher the self-esteem and intelligence, the more critical receivers are about believing messages.

2.4 SEMIOTICS

The process described in the preceding section focused on models of communication which could be one-on-one communication (as in personal selling) or mass communication (such as publicity, advertising, etc). Fundamental, however, to the communications process is the concept of meaning. Semiotics is the study of meaning and the analysis of meaning-producing events. Marketers attempt to convey meaning and customers receive and interpret meanings, which may or may not be similar to the meaning intended by the marketing communicator.

This section discusses the nature of meaning in marketing communications using a semiotics perspective.

2.4.1 The meaning of meaning

Meanings are internal responses to external stimuli. Many people have different meanings for the same words (Shimp, 2003:83). There is simple proof of this. Ask, for example, five business people to define what 'marketing' means to them. You will probably receive five decidedly different responses.

Semiotics (or semiology) examines how meaning is generated in communication messages via the use of signals, signs and symbols. Now let's define meaning.

> *Meaning can be thought of as the subjective perceptions (or thoughts) and affective reactions (or feelings) evoked when a person is presented with a sign or stimulus object* (Shimp, 2003:84–5).

We can see from this definition that:

- meaning is internal rather than external;
- meaning is subjective; and
- stimuli (signals, signs and symbols) do not have meaning – people attach meaning to them.

2.4.2 Signals, signs and symbols

Marketing communications make extensive use of signals, signs and symbols to communicate to specific target audiences.

- *Signals.* A product or specific brand is a signal if it is causally related to the meaning it generates. For example, consumers have learned in recent years that certain foods are high in fat content and cause obesity and coronary artery disease. Because red meats for many consumers have come to represent signals of poor eating habits and bad health, poultry consumption has increased while beef consumption has declined. It is for this reason that the beef industry has mounted campaigns to change people's beliefs and to alter the signalling relation.

  Because marketing communicators typically attempt to develop brand concepts that signal only positive relations, it is sometimes necessary for public policy officials to offset these efforts by stating warnings (e.g. on tobacco packs) or 'only sold to people over the age of 18' (e.g. liquor products), etc.

- *Signs.* Marketing communication in all of its various forms uses signs to create messages and convey meanings. A sign is something physical and perceivable by our senses that represents, or signifies, something (the referent) to somebody (the interpreter) in some context (Shimp, 2003:84).

  Consider, for example, the term 4x4. The primary and explicit meaning (denotative) of 4x4 is straightforward: it is a four-wheel-drive vehicle with either a double cab compartment for passengers in the front and loading space in the rear or a luxury imported vehicle. The secondary and implicit (or connotative) meaning of 4x4 could be totally different. A farmer could perceive it as a hardworking, multipurpose vehicle to transport animals, supplies and even farm equipment. The suburban professional or executive may use a 4x4 to travel to work every day and to the golf club on weekends. Thus, the 4x4 is a sign of success. When buying a sign we are buying the whole sign context: 'you are what you own'.

Most companies use signs as logos and these logos become synonymous with that company through frequent exposure on letterheads, in advertising, on packs, etc.

■ *Symbols.* Signals, signs and symbols are used to create meaning. In marketing communications they are also used to create and decode images. It is, however, symbols that create the greatest difficulty in transferring meaning from a sender to a receiver. This is due to misunderstandings of the role that symbols play in one-to-one communication, to using the wrong symbol and to a lack of efficiency in the way we develop, create, transfer and interpret symbols. How can we ensure that intended meaning is conveyed through symbols? We often use figurative or non-literal language in marketing communications. Shimp (2003:88) outlines three forms of figurative language, namely simile, metaphor and allegory.

◆ *Simile.* Simile uses a comparative term, such as *like* or *as* to join items from different classes of experience. For example, 'fresh as morning dew' (Timotei), 'love is like a rose', etc.

◆ *Metaphor.* Metaphor differs from simile in that the comparative term (*like* or *as*) is omitted. For example, 'SA's champion energy breakfast' (Jungle Oats), 'the prince of white wines' (Grünberger), etc.

◆ *Allegory.* Allegory is a word derived from a Greek term meaning 'other-speak'. Allegory conveys meaning in a story behind a story when something other than what is literally presented is occurring. For example, Mr Min personifies heavy-duty cleaning ability, and the (Ego) Axe man is always a cool, adventurous character. The story behind the story is that using Axe makes a man irresistible.

Allegory is often used in promoting taboo or sensitive products that are difficult to advertise without upsetting or offending audiences. Advertisers have found that using personifications (human-like animals or person-like product characters) makes advertising of these potentially offensive or risque products more palatable to audiences.

To summarise: signals, signs and symbols are used to share or convey meaning, but these tools and meanings are not synonymous. Meanings are individual internal responses to external stimuli like signs, etc. Meaning is found within an individual's perceptual field. No two people have exactly the same meaning for the same signal, sign or symbol – each one elicits a meaning specific to the individual's field of experience.

Meaning is developed through a process whereby stimuli (signals, signs and symbols) become associated with physical objects and evoke responses that are similar to those evoked by the actual physical objects. Marketing communicators use a variety of techniques to make their brands stand for something, to embellish their value, or, in short, to give them meaning. This is accomplished by firstly relating the brand to a referent in a cause-effect relation (signal), secondly relating the brand to a desirable referent in some context (sign) or thirdly relating the brand to a symbolic referent that has no prior intrinsic relation to the brand (symbol). Simile, metaphor and allegory are forms of figurative language that perform symbolic roles in marketing communications.

2.5 BARRIERS TO EFFECTIVE COMMUNICATION

There are a number of barriers to effective communication. No two people have the same biological, psychological and cultural makeup, therefore their field of experience, education levels, motivations, etc may differ extensively. Although there may be varying degrees of similarity, we can never presume that effective communication will result. It is more reasonable to assume that there are numerous obstacles that the marketer must try to overcome. The following barriers are involved in face-to-face communication (Ferreira, Erasmus & Groenewald, 2009:109–110):

■ *Managerial authority.* If there is no one in the organisation who can exercise authority, the organisation's goal will not be reached. The mere fact that there are supervisors in organisations causes barriers in the communication process.

■ *Specialisation.* Specialisation means that workers are separated from one another, even if they sit side by side. This prevents communication and can lead to the misinterpretation of messages. Jargon also makes communication difficult, as it consists of technical terms that belong to a specific field. This may cause misinterpretation.

■ *Network disruptions.* Negligence of managers to send information to a specific department is an example of a communication network disruption.

■ *Information overload.* When employees receive more information that they can handle, they are overloaded with information. Too much information can lead to certain important information being sidelined because management does not work selectively.

■ *Time pressure.* Many instructions must be dealt with within a certain timeframe. This might result in a message not being clearly formulated.

◆ *Failing to write to be understood.* Many people write to impress, not to express. They use long, haughty words in the mistaken belief that such words add dignity and strength to their messages. They don't.

◆ *Lacking knowledge of audiences.* Communicators must relate their messages to the specific characteristics, needs and interests of their audiences. They should know such things as educational levels and occupations, cultural differences, beliefs and attitudes, group loyalties and norms, and the disposition of the audience – friendly, hostile or indifferent.

◆ *Failing to realise that communication is a two-way process.* Many think communication is finished when information is imparted. They fail to consider that communication involves getting feedback and evaluating it.

◆ *Failing to observe common courtesies.* If communicators come across as impersonal or rude their ability to communicate with people will suffer. On the other hand, if they are respectful of others and treat them courteously their audiences will listen to what is said. More importantly, they are apt to understand and appreciate the message.

In their book *Getting it Right*, Adey and Andrew (1990) also outline, as communication barriers, noise (or interference) during the communication process, different perceptions, language problems, inconsistencies in communication, differences in status, distrust, emotional communication, apathy, resistance to change and cultural differences. Let's review these briefly (Adey and Andrew, 1990:26-48):

◆ *Noise*. Noise is any interference or disturbance that confuses the message or competes against communication. As stated earlier, it may be literal noise, for instance traffic noise, a faulty air-conditioning system, too much talking during a speech, an announcement on the intercom system, a blaring radio, a television set left on, dogs barking, a faulty line on the telephone, the crying of a child, continual coughing, rustling of papers or an interrupting telephone ring. These are easy enough to distinguish. Metaphorical noise, however, would include competing demands on a person's attention, such as domestic problems an employee is experiencing, too many demands on a person's time, feelings of insecurity, too much or too little emotion or distrust – in fact, any barrier can be considered noise in a figurative sense.

◆ *Differing perceptions*. As we know, each of us is unique: we see things differently from others. Speaking very literally, we can consider the differences in eyesight of short-sighted, far-sighted, partially blind and normal-sighted people. In the same way we can speak metaphorically of people seeing things differently. Look at the following drawings:

Figure A	Figure B	Figure C

Source: Koekemoer (2004:27).

What do you see in Figure A? A bird or a rabbit or both? Or something different? What do you see in Figure B? A vase or two people looking at each other or both? Look at Figure C. Which is the longer of the two parallel lines? Most of us will say the top one, but if you take a ruler you will see that they are both equal length.

◆ *Language usage*. Most differences in perception are caused by differences in visual or spoken interpretations. Language is the basis of most communication. The type of language used may be totally misunderstood by people of different cultural backgrounds. (Also see language under

'Cross-cultural barriers' at the end of this section.) Abbreviated sms text language may also cause a problem.

When language is used abstractly there is much room for inference, that is for an assumption or interpretation on the part of the listener. Abstraction in language means that there is some area of vagueness, some lack of precision, some room for interpretation or inference on the part of the receiver.

The use of jargon in communication often distorts a message. Users tend to assume that everyone understands it, whereas this is seldom true. Jargon tends to blur communication and to make people feel excluded if they don't understand – or superior if they do understand. This leads to dishonesty on the part of listeners because they do not want to admit to a lack of understanding and/or inferiority. Salespeople often use jargon, which can lead to confusion on the part of buyers and possible product dissatisfaction.

◆ *Inconsistencies in communication.* Inconsistency in communication can be involuntary. Often the spoken word conflicts with non-verbal behaviour or with the image that a communicator projects without even realising it.

In business, the image projected by a careless receptionist, telephonist or salesperson may distort the image the firm wishes to project. We need to see ourselves as others see us. This will make us more aware of our non-verbal behaviour and improve communication.

◆ *Differences in status.* There are two types of status, nominal status and real or deserved status. Often the difference between the two is blurred. The teacher expects his or her status to be accepted even though it may not be deserved – and the scholar may give token respect even though he or she resents it. There is, therefore, a third type of status: the perceived status of the person, how one person is perceived by another.

Perceived status influences communication: the sender of a message is judged by the receiver and the opinion formed affects the message itself. If the receiver respects the sender, he or she will be more inclined to accept the message. This is particularly true in social media. A lack of respect can distort the message and become a barrier to effective communication because it is no longer the actual message that is relevant but the perceived status of the sender.

◆ *Distrust.* Closely associated with status is distrust. Any signs of distrust or disbelief in the communication process are barriers to communication. If either the receiver or the sender doubts the credibility of the other, suspicion will dominate the communication and the effectiveness of the message will suffer. For example, there will be a barrier of distrust between two people who are constantly arguing. The same applies between a customer and a sales representative with a history of broken promises.

◆ *Emotional communication.* Inappropriate emotional appeals can distort messages. People tend to react to emotions (typical responses are aggressive or defensive) and the message is not communicated effectively.

Too much emotion threatens people. This is particularly true in dealings between superiors and subordinates and between sales representatives and customers. In mass communication, too little or too much emotion may have a negative effect.

◆ *Apathy.* Lack of any emotion is just as bad as too much emotion. Communication is enhanced by controlled emotions such as enthusiasm, friendliness, concern and sympathy. It is distorted by indifference, apathy and insensitivity. The customer gets the impression that the company doesn't care.

◆ *Resistance to change.* There was an enormous amount of change in the 20th century, and it is escalating year by year. The digital space became an unsettling factor to some and an exciting one to others, but many people fear change, particularly those who are older, insecure or uninformed. Computerisation has provided new ways of communicating and a host of advertising opportunities.

◆ *Cross-cultural barriers.* Whenever people of different cultures meet or communicate mutual understanding of habits, norms, attitudes, values, language, religion, etc is important for successful communication to take place. Often a barrier exists due to SRC (Self-Reference Criteria) or ethnocentricity (the tendency to evaluate other cultures according to one's own norms or values).

◆ *Language* is probably the most complex problem in cross-cultural interaction. Where cultures meet, different languages cause problems. Language is a precious part of our heritage, and a society is not easily persuaded to give it up. For example, the struggle for recognition of Black languages and Afrikaans in advertising media.

Generally, however, we tend to have an ethnocentric attitude towards our own language. We expect that what works for our culture or subculture should work for another culture or subculture. Ernest Mchunu, a prominent black marketing and management consultant who was involved in marketing Coca-Cola in South Africa, has pointed out that the popular advertising slogan 'Things go better with Coca-Cola' was a thoughtless slogan when applied to black people in South Africa during the years when things were definitely not going better for them! The history of multinational marketing is riddled with examples of mistakes caused by literal translations from the language of the marketers into the language of the consumers.

....

REFERENCES

Anon. 2007.5 Factors of communication. [Online] Available from: http://www.irradical.com/2007/05/5-factors-of-communication/ [Accessed: 2009/11-09].

Adey, A.D. and Andrew, M.G. 1990. *Getting it Right. The Manager's Guide to Business Communications.* Juta: Cape Town.

Belch, E.D. and Belch, M.A. 2004. *Advertising and Promotion*, 6ed Irwin: Homewood, Illinois.

Belch, E.D. and Belch, M.A. 2006. *Advertising and Promotion*, 7ed Irwin: Homewood, Illinois.

De Beer, A.S. (ed) 1998. *Mass Media Towards the Millenium*. J.H. van Schaik Publishers: Pretoria.

Del Bosque, I.R. and Martin, H.S. 2008. 'Tourist satisfaction a cognitive-affective model.' *Annuals of tourism research*, 35 (2):551–573.

Du Toit, M., Erdis, C., Klinkenberg, S. and Soke, B. 2006. *Study guide for Personal Selling*. Pretoria: Department of Marketing and Retail Management, University of South Africa.

Ferreira, E., Erasmus, A. and Groenewald, D. 2009. *Administrative Management*, 2ed Juta and Company Ltd: Cape Town.

Google Images. Retrieved from http://www.google.co.za/imgres?imgurl=http://plato.stanford.edu/entries/information-semantic/figure3.jpg8imgrefurl=http://plato.stanford.edu/entries/information-semantic

Govoni, N., Eng, R. and Galper, M. 1986. *Promotional Management*. Prentice Hall: Englewood Cliffs, New Jersey.

Jones T.O., and Sasser E. 1995. *Harvard Business Review*, November/December. Harvard: Boston, Massachusetts.

Koekemoer, L. and Bird, S. 2004. *Marketing communication*. Juta and Co. Ltd: South Africa.

Rix, P., Buss, J. and Herford, G. 2001. *Selling – A consultative approach*. 2ed New York: McGraw-Hill.

Samovar, L.A., Porter, R.E. and McDaniel, E.R. 2009. *Communication between cultures*, 7ed Wadsworth: Cengage Learning.

Seitel, F.P. 1992. *The Practice of Public Relations*, 5ed Maxwell Macmillan Publishing Company: New York.

Shimp, T.A. 2003. *Promotion Management and Marketing Communication*, 5ed The Dryden Press: Orlando, Florida.

3 Planning the Advertising Campaign

....

AIM OF THIS CHAPTER

To focus on the creators of the advertising campaign and the steps involved in planning and executing the advertising campaign.

LEARNING OUTCOMES

After studying this chapter you should be competent in:
- identifying the participants in the advertising process
- discussing the way the advertiser organises his- or herself to cope with the advertising challenges
- discussing why advertisers hire ad agencies
- discussing how an advertiser should select an ad agency
- outlining how an ad agency is structured
- discussing the types of ad agencies
- explaining how ad agencies are compensated
- outlining some future trends for ad agencies
- explaining how a good client-agency relationship can be developed
- discussing how advertising is developed using the total involvement method

....

3.1 INTRODUCTION

The planning process or the fact that a plan is prepared does not guarantee success because marketing and advertising successes are often due to factors like timing, place, price, effort, competitive actions, trade support, etc. However, success is more likely to be based on thoughtful marketing strategies and innovative, clever advertising plans.

Every company, to a greater or lesser extent, plans for its future. Corporate plans are concerned with questions of how the company can survive and grow from year to year. Such plans focus on the product range, the target market, the resources, the profit objectives and the company's goal to be a good corporate citizen. Corporate goals are translated into functional goals. For example, there will be an operations plan, sales plan, marketing plan, financial plan, development plan, information plan, etc. Plans for individual activities, projects, product groups or brands will flow from the functional plans. Within the overall marketing plans there will be a plan for the marketing of product groups, brands or services and each of these will cover a multitude of marketing activities. Advertising plans fall within the marketing plans and should help to accomplish the marketing and corporate goals.

Although this chapter deals with planning the advertising campaign more or less in isolation from the overall marketing plans, it must be remembered that all decisions regarding advertising (scale, scope, place, role, etc) depend on the marketing approach and policy of the company (the advertiser). Every company has its own approach and style and these are often evident in their advertising strategies. Some companies are aggressive, some are cautious. Some take risks, others test every element in their advertising programme. Some hardly ever change their advertising platform, others change it too often. Some build a relationship with their advertising agency over many years, others seem to have a new ad agency every year.

Planning the advertising campaign involves, therefore, a marketing strategy, setting advertising objectives, a budget, a message strategy and a media strategy. The planning is performed by a team consisting of the advertiser, the advertising agency and a number of service providers such as research companies, production houses, media advisers, etc. The final step in the planning process is an evaluation of the advertising effort. This chapter will deal with the creators of advertising (advertisers and advertising agencies) and the issues involved in planning the advertising.

3.2 CREATORS OF ADVERTISING

Most companies use some form of advertising and promotion. Large multinational corporations like Coca-Cola, Unilever, Procter & Gamble, etc spend millions on advertising every year, while smaller companies spend a lot less. Advertisers with large budgets either use advertising agencies or do their advertising in-house. A simple diagram can be used to illustrate who is involved (see Figure 3.1) and will now be looked at in more detail.

3.2.1 Advertiser (client)

There are many ways the advertiser could organise the company to cope with marketing and advertising challenges. The specific way in which the firm organises for these challenges depends on several factors, such as the size of the company, the number of products it markets, the role of advertising and promotion in the company's marketing mix, the size of the budget, etc.

While many people, both inside and outside the organisation are interested in or participate in the advertising and promotion process, the direct responsibility for administering the programme must be assumed by someone within the firm. In many companies, this is undertaken by an advertising department headed by an advertising or communications manager operating under a marketing director. This is known as a centralised marketing system. An alternative, used

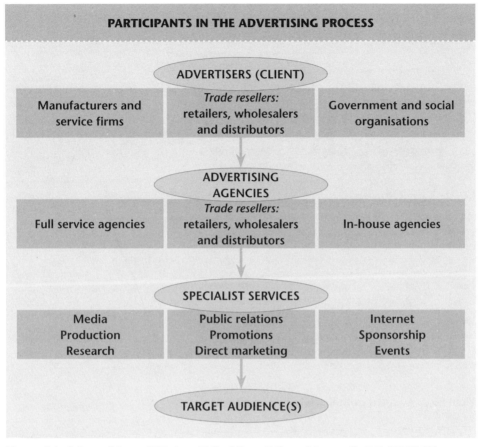

Figure 3.1: Adapted from O'Guinn, T.C., Allen, C.T. and Semenik, R.J. (2009:52).

by many large multiproduct firms, is to use a decentralised marketing or brand marketing system. Still a third option is to form a separate agency within the firm – or an in-house agency. Each of these alternatives is examined in more detail in the following sections (Belch & Belch, 2004:71–6):

■ *The centralised system.* In many organisations, marketing activities are divided along functional lines with advertising placed alongside other marketing functions such as sales, marketing research and product planning, as shown in Figure 3.2. Under this arrangement the advertising manager is responsible for all promotional activities except sales, with all advertising and promotion matters channeled through this department. The most common example of centralised system is the advertising department, where the advertising manager controls the entire operation: budgeting, coordinating creation and production of advertisements with ad agencies and specialist service providers, planning media schedules and monitoring and administering the sales promotion programmes for all the company's products or services.

■ *The decentralised system.* The centralised advertising department structure was the most commonly employed organisation system for many years.

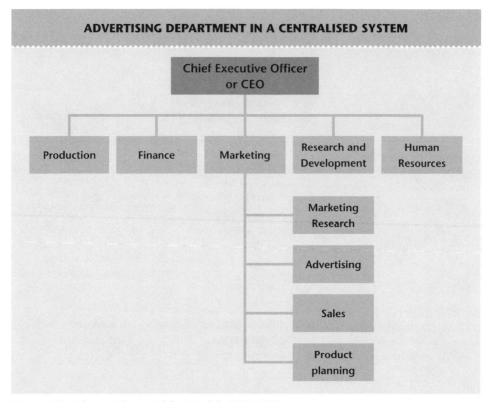

Figure 3.2: Adapted from Belch & Belch (2004:71).

However, many firms experienced problems with the traditional functional organisation. In this system a product group or category manager has the responsibility for the planning, implementation and control of the marketing programme for an individual brand or category of brands. The manager is also responsible for sales projections and profit performance of the brand or category and must develop and coordinate the budget. Companies utilising this form of organisation will generally support these managers with a structure of marketing services including sales, marketing research and advertising departments, as shown in Figure 3 .3. The product group manager will utilise the services in gathering information on customers, middlemen, competitors, product performance and specific marketing problems and opportunities.

In a product management system the responsibilities and functions associated with advertising and promotion are often transferred to the brand manager. The brand manager becomes the liaison between the outside service agencies and is involved with the ad agency in the development of the marketing communication programme.

Before we discuss the in-house agency it may be worthwhile to consider the advantages and disadvantages of the centralised and decentralised systems.

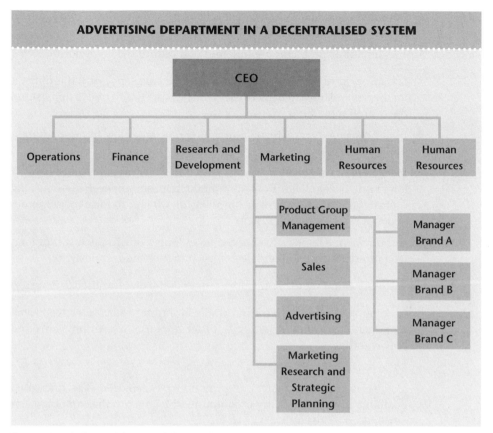

Figure 3.3: Adapted from Belch & Belch (2004:74).

The advantages of the centralised system are the following:

◆ *Facilitated communications.* Many companies prefer the advertising department organisation because it allows the advertising programmes to be developed and coordinated from one entral location. This facilitates communication regarding the promotions programme, making it easier for top management to participate in decision-making.

◆ *Fewer personnel required.* A centralised system can also result in a more efficient operation because fewer people are involved in the programme decisions, and as their experience in making such decisions increases, the process becomes easier.

◆ *Continuity in staff.* The staff appointed would normally be permanent staff and not as easily be affected by staff reductions if it should happen.

◆ *Allows for more top management involvement.* As the function is centralised it would normally be under the management of a senior member of staff and under closer scrutiny.

◆ *More control.* Centralisation by implication mean closer control over all the activities of the company and the coordination thereof.

◆ *Centralised planning.* All advertising need to be coordinated and planned from a central point.

At the same time, problems are inherent in a centralised operation:

◆ *Less involvement with and understanding of the marketing goals.* It is difficult for the advertising department to become involved with and to understand the overall marketing strategy for the brand.

◆ *Longer response times.* The department can also be slow in responding to the specific needs and problems of a brand.

◆ *Inability to handle multiple product lines.* Moreover, as companies become larger and develop or acquire new products, brands or even divisions, the centralised system can become impractical, which can force the company to adopt a decentralised system.

◆ *Less flexibility.* Adaption to changes takes longer due to the fact that long lead times are required and decisions cannot be made quickly.

On the other hand there are the advantages of the decentralised systems:

◆ *Concentrated managerial attention.* Each brand receives concentrated managerial attention resulting in faster response to both problems and opportunities.

◆ *Rapid response to problems and opportunities.*

◆ *More flexibility.* The product group manager system allows for increased flexibility in the advertising programme which means the campaign can be adjusted more easily.

There are also drawbacks or disadvantages to the decentralised approach:

◆ *Ineffective decision-making.* Brand managers often lack training and experience in advertising and promotion.

◆ *Internal conflicts.* They may be concerned with short-term planning and administrative tasks rather than with the development of long-term strategies.

◆ *Misallocation of funds.* Individual brand managers often end up competing for limited resources. That can lead to unproductive rivalries and potential misallocation of funds. The persuasiveness of the manager, rather than the long-term profit potential of the brands, may be the critical factor determining budgets.

◆ *Lack of authority.* The product group manager system has also been criticised for failing to provide the brand manager with the authority over the functions that are needed to implement and control the plans he or she develops. Some companies have dealt with this problem by expanding the role and responsibility of the advertising manager and his or her staff of specialists. The specialists counsel the individual brand managers and the advertising decision-making process involves the ad manager, the brand manager and the marketing director.

◆ *Lack of communication.* Communication with head office or group product management is sometimes not what it should be which can lead to problems and conflict.

■ *The in-house agency.* In-house agencies are advertising agencies owned and supervised by the companies who advertise. They are organised like independent agencies but can take a variety of forms. The advertising director for the company is usually the chief executive officer of the agency. The director supervises account managers responsible for brands or business groups. The in-house agency has writers and artists, traffic personnel and media specialists. If the company has a research department this specialty will probably not be duplicated in the in-house advertising unit. The in-house agency may do its own billing, paying and collecting, but it is more likely to use the company's accounting department. In-house agencies have the following advantages (O'Guinn, T.C. et al, 2009:58):

◆ *Coordination and control.* The coordination and control over the advertising and promotional message.

◆ *Savings.* The expense of staff duplication between the agency and the client can be eliminated. All profits that the firm would have had to pay commissions to any external agency are now kept within the firm.

◆ *Specialisation.* Companies in a highly technical or specialised field often find it difficult to get scientifically correct advertising messages from an agency. It may be better to have someone who knows the business on the staff in an in-house agency.

◆ *Priority service.* Clearly the in-house agency works only for the one company and is always available for high-priority projects.

◆ *Minimum staffing.* The in-house agency generally employs personnel for minimum continuous requirements and engages freelance staff to handle peak workloads. Freelance operators may not always be available and may not possess the required knowledge, although problems certainly can be controlled with good planning.

3.2.2 The advertising agency

In our discussion of the advertising agency, seven pertinent questions will be considered:

■ *Why do advertisers hire ad agencies?* An established agency has gained expertise through years of experience and can offer objective advice to its clients. Agencies are committed to solving problems for and delivering service to their clients. The following is a summary of the reasons advertisers hire ad agencies and endeavour to establish long-term relationships with them (Shimp, T.A. 2010:192):

◆ *Professional expertise.* An agency acquires experience by working with a variety of clients; agency professionals can apply lessons learned with one client to another. Applying a broad perspective gained from the varied backgrounds and skills of employees is the key to solving difficult advertising problems. This perspective is often lacking in smaller in-house agencies or limited departments. Just as a company may hire an outside law firm even though it has an attorney on staff, so too may a company hire an agency to work for its advertising department in order to benefit from the agency's professional expertise.

◆ *Objectivity.* Clients expect an agency to tell them when they are misreading the market or are out of step with consumers. Agency objectivity is a necessary part of the relationship. Someone from outside the client company is more likely to speak up and is better able to maintain an independent and detached view of the marketplace and the consumer. Advertising people are experts in their field, whereas few clients feel competent to approve as well as create advertisements. They depend on the agency for professional judgement.

◆ *Dedication and commitment.* Clients, especially those who nurture the relationship, receive dedication and commitment from their agencies. The agency becomes very much a part of the client team. This client agency relationship serves as an incentive for the agency to make an extra effort, take an interest in every aspect of the client's business and never be satisfied with 'good enough'. The commitment to a client's business and the need to remain objective can produce some of the most difficult decisions in the business. Agencies that hold fast to their point of view may lose a client but not their self-respect.

◆ *Specialist services.* An agency, especially a full-service advertising agency, can provide statisticians, strategic planners, media negotiators, special event coordinators, pack designers, market researchers, promotions experts, direct marketing experts, public relations experts, even people who can train brand managers in marketing and related topics.

■ *How should an advertiser go about selecting an advertising agency?* Selecting an ad agency is a very important task for the advertiser, as the advertiser and agency will form a team to prepare the advertising strategy. The most popular way to select an ad agency is the creative pitch. In the creative pitch the advertiser selects a limited number of agencies, gives them a briefing and requests them to prepare a presentation on which the advertiser will make his or her choice.

Each agency selected spends considerable time, effort and money to prepare an impressive presentation designed to sell the agency and the brand or service. Very often the client is given a distorted view of the pitching agency's abilities. The creative pitch is disruptive and expensive to the agencies and the advertiser may be better off looking for synergy in culture, personality and work ethics. It is often more sensible to select an agency by reviewing the quality of work produced for other clients, checking their track record, investigating the quality of services offered and meeting with the key people.

The following procedure is useful for selecting an ad agency (Koekemoer (2004:108).

Step 1: Analysis of company and requirements

Selecting an ad agency can be a complicated and risky task. Before the selection process begins, the advertiser should analyse the company (SWOT analysis, an enquiry into the company's Strengths, Weaknesses, Opportunities and Threats as well as its culture, requirements, budget size, growth potential, strategies, etc). Consideration should then be given to what type of agency is required – a large full-service agency or a specialised agency (such as a direct marketing agency or a prescription pharmaceuticals agency or a retail agency, etc).

Following the decision on large or small, specialised or full-service, domestic or global agency, it is necessary to determine and prioritise what types of service are required from an agency. For example:

◆ marketing expertise in strategy, planning and execution;

◆ creative performance in TV, print, radio, outdoor or direct response;

◆ media knowledge and clout; knowledge of the Internet;

◆ sales promotion and/or trade relations help;

◆ public relations and corporate or image-building ability;

◆ market and advertising research strength;

◆ knowledge in a specific area (such as fashion or beauty, etc);

◆ agency size and growth;

◆ location in relation to advertiser's office; and

◆ the culture and approach of the agency.

Specific requirements will dictate other factors, for example, previous experience in a particular product category, international links, awards won by the agency, etc.

Step 2: First selection procedure

This step involves the selection of a group of agencies (maximum of five) that seem to fit the advertiser's requirements. Before making this selection the advertiser can consult other advertisers and check published sources for information and ideas. Agencies responsible for successful advertising campaigns that have impressed the advertiser should also be identified.

A five-point scale such as the following can be used to rate the agencies selected:

◆ outstanding

◆ reasonably good

◆ average

◆ not so good

◆ unacceptable

It may also be necessary to give different values or weights to the agency attribute which relate to the advertiser's needs. These could include the following attributes as can be seen in Table 3.1 below:

Table 3.1 **IMPORTANT ATTRIBUTES OF ADVERTISING AGENCIES**

AGENCY ATTRIBUTES	
Creativity	Flexibility in meeting the client's changing requirements
Calibre of people	Personal attention given by top management
Strength and progressiveness of management team	Extent to which client will deal directly with people who work on the account
Ability to produce original creative ideas (creative reputation)	Previous experience in the client's type of market
Understanding of client's market and problems	Initiative (for example, in product development or new ideas)
Interest in client's products and markets	Growing and expanding versus losing accounts
Research orientation	Balanced account list and size
Integrity	Overall success

It is therefore very important to visit the agencies, ask for an agency presentation, do the assessment of the attributes and check whether there are any apparent conflicts with accounts already handled by the agency. Lately they also want to know about the agency's digital expertise. Advertisers must remember that when agencies consider a new account, the first question they ask is 'Which brands will be involved?' along with the amount of the potential billings.

Step 3: Final selection procedure

After the initial assessment it is necessary for the advertiser to reduce the original list of potential agencies to a manageable number of usually no more than three. These three are given a particular project and a budget to cover the cost of the pitch. The advertiser should again prepare an evaluation list for rating the remaining agencies on the same five-point scale. This list could be a lot more specific. It should also cover personnel who will supervise the account and how the account team will be staffed. Who are the creative people who will work on the account? Similarly, who will service the advertiser's needs in media, production (TV), strategic planning, research and sales promotion and how will they do it? What is the agency's track record in getting and holding on to business and in keeping key personnel teams together?

It is also very important to discuss financial arrangements. Will the account be a straight commission account, a fee account or a combination of both? Most marketers prefer a fee agreement. When is payment due?

■ *How is an ad agency structured?* Full-service ad agencies are usually organised around seven basic services as illustrated in Figure 3.5.

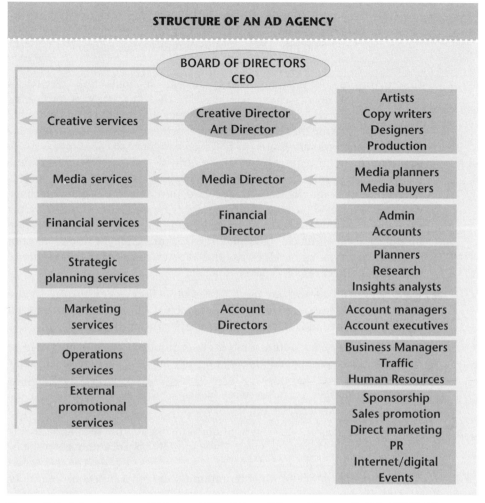

Figure 3.5: Adapted from O'Guinn, T.C., Allen, C.T. and Semenik, R.J. (2009:62).

The most important of these departments in terms of the allocated share of personnel and budget is the creative function. The people in this area develop the ideas and create the various advertising elements. They also arrange and supervise the production.

A second important area is media where strategies are planned and executed for placing advertising. The media department is responsible for the timing and geographic coverage of the advertising as well as for buying space in print media and time on broadcast media to ensure the most effective use of the marketing communication budget.

Closely allied with the media function is the financial function, which handles the internal administration of the agency and is responsible for billing clients and making payments to the various media. The operations function also handles the business aspects and looks after the human resources issues.

The strategic planning area is responsible for gathering and analysing data to enable the agency to answer a variety of questions, such as what are the latest consumer trends and insights, which is the most effective advertising theme, the best media mix, the most appropriate budget and so forth. It does strategic planning on specific brands.

Finally, the account management function in marketing services is responsible for agency-client relations. In the daily task of producing advertising the account executive on the agency side and the brand manager on the client side are the parties who work together closely. When an effective marketing and promotion strategy has been developed the account executive communicates the requirements of the strategy to the creative staff, the media planners and others in the various support groups of the agency as needed. Most large full-service agencies also have a senior executive responsible for new business. Sometimes this function is performed by the CEO, sometimes by a project team consisting of the CEO, creative director, media director, strategic planning director and one or more account directors. Separate subsidiaries usually exist to cater for public relations, promotions, direct response advertising, etc.

■ *What types of ad agencies are there?* In the preceding section the full service agency was discussed. In a full-service agency all of the seven internal functions outlined in Figure 3.5 are handled by the agency's staff.

Many advertisers, including some large companies, are not interested in paying for the services of a full-service agency but may be interested in some of the specific services agencies have to offer. Over the past few decades several alternatives to full-service agencies have evolved including the following (Koekemoer 2004:111–113):

◆ *Creative boutiques.* A creative boutique is an agency that specialises in and provides only creative services. These specialist agencies have developed in response to some advertisers' desires to utilise only the creative aspect of an outside provider while maintaining the other functions internally. The advertiser may seek outside creative talent because an extra creative effort is required or because personnel within the organisation do not have sufficient skills in this regard.

Creative boutiques are usually formed by members of the creative department of a full-service agency who leave the firm and take with them clients primarily interested in their creative expertise. These boutiques usually perform the creative function on a fee basis.

◆ *Specialist media agencies.* Modern media agencies specialise in media coordination for large advertisers. Both agencies and clients utilise their services, usually developing their own media strategies and using the buying service to execute them. Because media agencies purchase such large amounts of time and space they receive substantial discounts and can save money on media purchases for the ad agency or client. Media buying services are paid a fee or commission for their work.

◆ *À la carte agencies.* Many agencies offer for a fee just that part of their total services that the advertiser wants. The à la carte arrangement is used mostly for creative services, for media planning and placement and for research services.

◆ *Rolodex agencies.* These agencies are run by several advertising specialists, usually account and/or creative people and have no basic staff. They hire specialists – in marketing, media planning, creative strategy, writing, whatever – to work on a project basis. The concept is similar to using freelance creative people to execute ads except that the experts are hired as needed. Rolodex agencies claim to be able to give advertisers expertise that the small full-service agencies can't match.

◆ *Direct marketing agencies.* Direct marketing, using such strategies as online (Web), telemarketing, interactive video, television, radio and direct mail, etc is not commission bearing. Hence, it found its way into the full-service agencies only recently, largely by way of mergers. Nevertheless, numerous direct marketing shops have developed creative skills. Because direct marketing is growing dramatically the use of these agencies is increasing. Many large full-service agencies now have a direct marketing or digital subsidiary working mainly on a fee basis.

◆ *Below-the-line agencies.* Below-the-line agencies specialise in trade and consumer promotions, pack design, logo design and all functions where classical media are not involved and the focus is not on image-type advertising.

An agency's ability to provide advertising services throughout the world is very often crucial to its success in winning significant new business and retaining old accounts. As clients grow and market their products in more and more countries they often feel the need for the services of a worldwide agency. Many account switches have been made almost solely because the new agency could provide worldwide service whereas the old one could not.

■ *How are Ad agencies compensated?* Up to the late 1980s agency compensation was standardised all over the world. In America and Europe it was 15 per cent commission; in South Africa, 16,5 per cent. Since then, however, it has been a mixture of commission, fees, incentives linked to the success of the advertising, etc. However, there are still only two basic forms of ad agency compensation – media commission and fees.

◆ *Media commission:* 16,5 per cent on most media billings and cost plus 19,76 per cent on production work. Most media pay only 15 per cent commission, or even less.

◆ *Fees:* Lately marketers and ad agencies prefer fees rather than commission. Sometimes the commission is not enough for the ad agency to make a fair profit (for example, when handling a small client). A management fee is then arranged for specific types of work, such as strategic plans, research, pack designs, artwork, etc. It could be a flat fee, a cost plus fee, a project fee or even a commission plus fee. Ad agency profitability has, however, declined since switching over to the fee system.

There is no fixed method prescribed by the marketing or advertising industry. Usually an agreement is established when the ad agency is appointed. The trend in the nineties, however, was to use a combination of commission and fees. The deciding criterion was a 'reasonable margin' for the work done by the ad agency.

■ *The future of the ad agency.* The trend of the full-service agency unbundling is likely to continue. There are few full service agencies left. Direct marketing, digital, promotions, public relations, research and especially electronic media coordination will become even more important. Media agencies will grow stronger. It is predicted that a burst of creativity will be required to cope with the new media opportunities and media technology.

Trends with regard to the future of ad agencies are:

◆ *Recruiting* will become very important as an agency will function with fewer levels in every department. The streamlined agency of the future will have a layer of 'thinkers' and a layer of 'doers'. Staff will also need to understand an array of mediums as well as have some technical skills.

◆ *Creativity.* Only the agencies that can come up with the award-winning ideas will survive. This is the reason why creatives are by far the highest-paid staff in the agency. This trend will accelerate.

◆ *Account planners* will be needed. They will be researchers, media, creative or account service experts. Agencies will have to rely more heavily on account planners, who will have to be articulate, persuasive and compatible with the creative people. There will be more focus on consumer insights.

◆ *Research responsibilities* will narrow. Clients are seizing this area. They also appoint their own consumer insights experts and agencies are relinquishing this as well as strategic planning. The agency's research role will be limited to that of a methodology consultant and a bit of advertising research.

◆ *Media planning* will have considerable clout. The computer has made media planners the whizz-kids of today and tomorrow they will be even more influential. The plethora of media, with their high cost and complexity, will dictate this.

◆ *Performance-based incentives* will become a key component of agency compensation. People do what they are paid to do; that's why management-by-objective, tied to incentives, works. Sophisticated clients and agencies will work together to establish base service compensation on a reward system for high performance.

◆ The *position of financial or administrative manager* will emerge because a powerful internal operations executive will be needed to facilitate the return of top agency talent to hands-on client involvement. This person's responsibilities will relate to internal efficiency. Many CEOs will be CAs.

◆ *Top agency talent* will work directly on the business – once again. People who enjoy doing the work rather than administering the bureaucracy will head the agency of the future.

◆ *The successful ones* are those who make themselves relevant by adding value and help in building brand equity for the marketer.

■ *Development of a good client-agency relationship.* There are four prerequisites for a good client-agency relationship: all expenditure on the client's behalf should be approved in advance (by signing a quote); the client should pay agency invoices by the agreed deadline; the agency should avoid handling a competitive client; all information on brands, markets, etc received from the client should be treated confidentially by the agency.

Engel, Warshaw, Kinnear and Reese (2000) make the following suggestions for developing a productive working relationship between the client and the ad agency:

◆ *Maintain good liaison.* Top-level executives from both parties must communicate regularly to air issues arising in day-to-day operations. Most junior staff do not have sufficient background or status to modify operating policies or to put out fires. Minor misunderstandings can easily develop into major difficulties.

◆ *Evaluate promotion in a marketing context.* When sales drop, the blame all too quickly (and perhaps legitimately) is aimed directly at advertising. Then a fairly common next step is to fire the agency – and repeat the entire process a year or two later. But advertising cannot maintain market share for long when the product lags competitively, prices are out of line, distribution is insufficient and so on.

Part of the problem here is the inappropriate application of sales objectives. Although sales are a valid objective under certain conditions, advertising should generally be evaluated in terms of legitimate communications goals, which should be agreed on in advance by all parties. Then it is possible to determine if the agency has accomplished what it set out to do.

◆ *Do not abandon a campaign prematurely.* One of the greatest pressures is to stop a productive campaign because executives (or their wives or husbands) are tired of seeing the ads. Every agency has its stories of how trivial preferences have led to the abandonment of a great campaign. It is necessary to recognise that everyone involved with a company quickly gets sick of the advertising because of sheer familiarity. But please note – agency people are not typical of the average consumer. Abandonment is appropriate only when there is a downturn in productivity.

◆ *Do not be carried away by creative execution.* Many years ago David Ogilvy said, 'Don't ask for great ads; insist instead on great campaigns'. Anyone can argue with details of execution and overlook the most important consideration in the process – consumer benefit must be communicated clearly and memorably. Nothing else really matters. Fortunately, this issue can be clarified by pre-testing the advertising.

◆ *Emancipate the agency from fear.* Some companies are known as 'agency hoppers', making a change every year or two. What kind of output can they expect from an agency? They certainly will not get innovation. Why should the agency take the risk? They will give them what they want. And that, most likely, will be mediocrity.

Also, it is important to note that all agencies will fail at times, so evaluation should be based on the overall batting average. Any group will do its best when it realises that a misstep will not necessarily be fatal.

This does not mean that an unproductive agency should be tolerated. That would make no sense. But it also must be recognised that an agency change is not necessarily a lasting solution. No one has a surefire formula; all mature marketing people are fully aware of this and will take steps to make sure that the charge of poor agency performance has been verified before taking any drastic action.

◆ *Simplify approval.* Avoid 'nit-picking to death' a campaign that pre-tested well and looked promising. First one client executive and then another adds personal touches until the final output is nothing more than you would expect from a committee – bland advertising that has lost its cutting edge. The coup de grâce is added by the chairperson of the board when a family member is added as one of the actors in the TV commercial.

◆ *Permit the agency to make a profit.* The operating margin is so small that most agencies will cut costs and avoid utilising top talent if a client demands too much for what it pays. With no incentive to offer its best the agency will most likely resign the account. It, too, has a right to make a reasonable return on investment (see Figure 3.6).

CHECKLIST – 27 WAYS TO BE A BETTER CLIENT

Relationships

1. *Cultivate honesty.* Be truthful in your meetings and in your ads.
2. *Be enthusiastic.* When you like the ads, let the agency know.
3. *Be frank when you don't like the advertising.* Always cite a reason when turning down an idea.
4. *Be human.* React like a person, not a corporation. Laugh at funny ads even if they won't work.
5. *Be willing to admit you're unsure.* Don't be pressured. Let your agency know when you need time.
6. *Allow the agency to feel responsible.* Tell the agency what you feel is wrong, not how to fix it.
7. *Care about being a client.* Creative people work best for clients they like.

Management

8. *Don't isolate your top people from creative people.* Agency creative people work best when objectives come from the top, not filtered through layers.
9. *Set objectives.* For timely and quality service from your agency, establish and openly share your marketing objectives.
10. *Switch people, not agencies.* When problems arise, agencies often prefer to bring in fresh talent than lose you as a client.
11. *Be sure the agency makes a profit on your account.* Demanding more services from your agency than covered by fees or commissions can hurt relationships.

→

Production

12. *Avoid nit-picking last-minute changes.* Perfection is important, but waiting until the last moment to make minor changes can damage the client-agency relationship. Agencies see such behaviour as indecisive and/or arrogant and lose respect for the client.
13. *Be aware of the cost of changes (both time and money).* The costs of making major changes at the production stage may be five times greater than in the earlier stages.
14. *Don't change concepts during the production stage.* Late concept changes can inadvertently change product positioning and personality.

Media

15. *Understand the economics (and economies) of media.* Be prepared to deal with CPMs, CPPs, and other key elements of media planning and buying so that you can properly understand, evaluate, and appreciate your agency's media strategy.
16. *Understand the importance of lead time.* Early buys can eliminate late fees, earn discounts, make yourself eligible for special promotions, strengthen your agency's buying position and reduce anxiety.
17. *Avoid interfering with the agency's media relationship.* The stronger your agency's buying position, the greater the discounts available to you. Refrain from cutting deals with media reps directly and plan media well in advance.
18. *Avoid media arrogance ('they need us').* Some media will deal with clients and some won't. Misinterpret this relationship and you may either pay more than you should or be too late to get into a medium you need.
19. *Avoid insularity.* Be willing to let your mind travel beyond your immediate environment and lifestyle.
20. *Suggest work sessions.* Set up informal give-and-take sessions with creatives and strategists.
21. *Keep the creative people involved in your business.* Agency creatives do their best work for you when they're in tune with the ups and downs of your business.

Research

22. *Share information.* Pool information to create new and bigger opportunities.
23. *Involve the agency in research projects.* An agency's creative talent gets its best ideas from knowledge of your environment.

Creative

24. *Learn the fine art of conducting the creative meeting.* Deal with the important issues first: strategy, consumer benefits and reasons why.
25. *Look for the big idea.* Concentrate on positioning strategy and brand personality. Don't allow a single ad – no matter how brilliant – to change the positioning or personality of the product.
26. *Insist on creative discipline.* The creative process stimulates concepts and actions. Discipline helps maintain focus on those that count the most.

27. *Don't be afraid to ask for great advertising.* Agencies prefer the high road, but as the client you must be willing to accompany them. If the agency slips, be strong and ask it to try again.

Figure 3.6: Arens, W.F., Weigold, M.F. and Arens, C. (2008).

3.3   DEVELOPING THE ADVERTISING CAMPAIGN

Advertising is a people business. When an advertising campaign is created the advertiser and the advertising agency should not hold out on each other in any way. The role of the advertiser cannot be underestimated in providing the brief while the agency, a unique factory producing unique products, should realise that the quality of the advertising produced is totally dependent on the strategic or strat plan, the creative brief and the calibre of the people involved in its creation. These people include the advertiser.

The following steps should be taken to ensure that the advertising produced will be successful in achieving the desired objectives. The steps will be outlined with reference to Figure 3.7, which illustrates the total involvement method.

The total involvement philosophy and methodology are designed to counteract the feeling that 'fifty per cent of my advertising money is wasted, but I don't know which fifty per cent'. Broadly, this method involves the following steps to minimise the risk of a campaign not being successful: the campaign is planned in a structured way, the necessary information (brief) is gained from the advertiser and outside sources, a total communications plan is created, the campaign is reviewed against objectives, pre-testing is carried out among the target audience and production of the campaign is of a high standard.

In today's marketing environment it is essential that every communication reinforces brand personality in the same manner. Advertising, public relations, packaging, display, sales merchandising and promotion must all be managed to build the brand's equity by communicating the same brand message to consumers.

3.3.1 STEP 1: THE CLIENT BRIEF

This brief identifies the competitive brands, the strengths of the brand, the marketing factors that have a significant impact on it and the marketing objectives so that the most effective communication strategy can be developed.

The client usually provides the following information:

■   *The market.* The existing situation and trends regarding the market and the consumer are examined. What is the brand's market? What other brands or product categories do we compete with? What segments is the brand in?

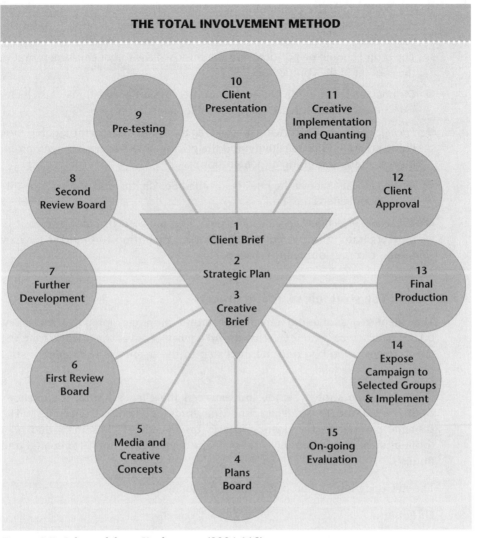

Figure 3.7: Adapted from Koekemoer (2004:119).

Is the product bought on impulse? Do they tend to be brand loyal? The sole purpose here is to set the scene. The market is examined from varying angles and only the ones relevant to building brand equity are selected.

■ *The competition.* The client could outline a SWOT analysis done; an analysis of competitive positions (eg Debonairs Pizza: SA's Favourite versus Scooters Pizza: We deliver. Hot. Tasty. Fast.), competitors' offerings (current and future), competitive advantages of various brands (eg low cost leadership, differentiation, etc) and competitors' promotional activities and budgets.

■ *The brand.* Its history, sales trends, market shares and important information like brand awareness, brand support, brand sensitivity, assumed leadership, brand usage and loyalty.

- *The positioning.* The positioning of the brand *vis-à-vis* its competitors forms the basis of all above- and below- and through-the-line communication. The positioning could be done on benefit/s, value, image even on type of user. The brand should be positioned in the minds of the target consumers and in the context of the competitors.

- *Distribution.* Distribution channels, channel support or resistance. Also issues like channel requirements, merchandising, logistics, etc.

- *Pricing.* The price. The pricing method (eg mark-up, target return, going rate, value pricing). Price sensitivity and the pricing objective (eg survival, profit, market share, skimming or penetration).

- *Promotion.* Past above-the-line, below-the-line, digital and through-the-line promotional efforts and budgets.

- *Marketing objectives.* Specific objectives like increase in sales, increase in market share, filling a gap in the market, preparing the market for new things to come, launching a brand, etc.

3.3.2 Step 2: The strategic planning process

The client (eg marketing director or brand manager) prepares the client brief. Client service who represents the ad agency, receives the briefing from the client, opens a job bag and the next step in the agency is to prepare a strat plan.

The advertising strategy is the link between the client's brand, the agency's creative and media strategies and the target audience (consumers). The strategic planner in the agency focuses on the target consumers and goes through a strategic planning process before the creative brief is prepared and finalised.

The strategic planning process involves the following:

- *Research:*
  - ◆ consumer research (quantitative and qualitative);
  - ◆ consumer insights identification;
  - ◆ pre-campaign concept testing;
  - ◆ during and post-campaign testing; and
  - ◆ desk research (trends).

- *Competitor and brand reviews:*
  - ◆ analysis of competitor activity in the market;
  - ◆ analysis of their strategies, brand communications (above and below the line campaigns) and their positioning;
  - ◆ strategic input on the brand and it's future; and
  - ◆ brand equity measurements.

- *Communication strategies:*
  - ◆ The strategist writes the communication strategy, which needs to be approved by client before creative briefing or campaign development takes place and forms the basis of all brand communications. It serves to provide integration and synergy between all communication elements.
  - ◆ The communication strategy aims to give the brand a specific and differentiated positioning and ideally, the strategy should fit in with the brand plans and marketing strategy for the brand.

The following steps are followed by the strategic planner in the ad agency to prepare the communication strategy.

- *Step 1: Define the business problem or opportunity*

  Every advertising strategy starts as a business issue which may be positive (an opportunity) or negative (a problem). This can be identified by the client, agency or both parties. Not every business problem has an advertising solution, so the role of brand communication in solving a problem or grabbing an opportunity must be understood. The strategist needs a good understanding of the client's business context and needs to be able to see the 'bigger picture'.

- *Step 2: Background (macro-, market- and micro-analysis)*

  This involves obtaining the necessary information – it is the process of sifting through all information to find a few key insights. Usually you will need information about the client's business (industry, markets, four Ps), the brand (brand analysis), competitors (competitor analysis), consumers and media. Research is vital (new research, existing research, desk research).

  The client's business is affected by the external environment including the industry, the market/s in which the product exists, the environmental forces (eg legal, socio-economic, technological and political forces) as well as the internal environment, eg SWOT analysis, company's current strategies relating to product, price, distribution, promotions and the company's approach to business.

  The competitor analysis includes an analysis of the direct competitors, indirect competitors, other brands that consumers see as competitors but that the company may not regard as competitors, competitor's business and marketing strategies, an analysis of their positioning in the market, an analysis of their brand communication, the driving forces in the market and elements in the category that drive consumer's decisions, competitive advantage and point of difference in comparison to competitors, the competitors' media strategies and who they are talking to as well as the various market shares.

- *Step 3: Analyse the brand*

  Figure 3.8 outlines the issues that the stratplanner will consider to focus on the brand's equity and brand value.

- *Step 4: Analyse the target consumer or customer*

  Clearly define the target market – we need to know who we are talking to before we can decide what we need or like to say. Evaluate, segment and target each group carefully to avoid wasting money. The target market could be very broad (eg for Coca-Cola) or very narrow (eg teenagers with pimples). It is vital to do this on a continuous basis as people and the environment change constantly and competitors will capitalise on the changes or gaps in the market. Then relate the communication objectives back to the customer.

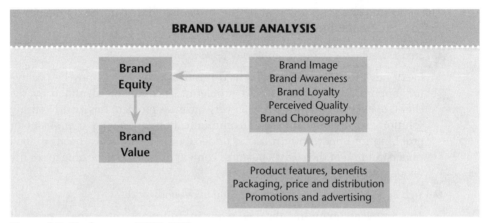

Figure 3.8: Koekemoer (2004:123).

What do we need to know about the consumer? We need to know:

◆ General information, eg demographics, media habits, psychographics, lifestyle, a day in the life of my consumer and consumer trends.

◆ Insights specific to brand information, eg consumer behaviour and decision-making process, consumer mindset (beliefs, values, rituals, perceptions), consumer needs, wants, desires and preferences in a product category, consumer interaction with brands and consumer perceptions of your brand versus competitor brands.

Some key questions to ask are therefore:

◆ Who is the customer?

◆ What do they think?

◆ What do we want them to think/feel?

◆ What should the communications tell them in order for them to be motivated to change their behaviour?

◆ How do we want the brand to be perceived by them?

◆ What is the emotional bond between my brand and my consumer?

◆ What are the rational and emotional reasons why consumers like/ purchase my brand or, alternatively, why they don't?

◆ Is there consumer loyalty or are they using my brand habitually?

◆ How likely is it that there will be brand switching? Why?

■ *Step 5: Define the consumer promise/s*

The consumer promise should be based on the brand positioning and should be a clear, concise, single-minded promise that is motivational to the target audience. For example, Mercedes Benz positioned itself against BMW and Audi as a luxury car offering a driving experience unlike any other. The consumer promise for the M-Class is refined power, for the SL-Class Roadster it's mind-blowing technology and for the CL-Class it's luxury.

■ *Step 6: Set communication objectives*

In setting communication objectives, the role that advertising and other IMC tools will play in solving the business (or brand) problem or capitalising in the business (or brand) opportunity should be considered. Communication objectives should be clearly distinguished from business and marketing objectives. Communication objectives could be to create or increase awareness, to change perceptions, to build brand image, to re-position a brand in the minds of the consumers, to get consumers to talk about the brand, etc. All of the above may be necessary to achieve the business objective 'to grow the business' and the marketing objectives 'to increase sales by 10 per cent during the campaign period' and 'to increase market share by five per cent over the next fiscal period'.

3.3.3 Step 3: The creative brief

In this step, the first two steps are synthesised into an action plan for the development of all communications for the brand: advertising, promotion, public relations, direct marketing and so on. The creative brief consists of three elements, ie the strategy, the desired brand equity and the creative guidelines:

■ *Strategy.* This is a one-page statement that clearly defines the target audience; how its members think, feel and behave; what the communication is intended to achieve and the promise that will create a bond (link) between consumers and the brand. The strategy consists of:

◆ *Key observation.* The most important market/consumer factor that dictates the strategy.

◆ *Key communication objective.* The primary goal the advertising aims to achieve.

◆ *Key consumer insight.* The consumer 'hot button' that the communication will trigger.

◆ *Consumer promise.* The link between the consumer and the brand: what the brand should stand for in the consumer's mind.

◆ *Support.* The reason the brand gives the consumer permission to believe.

◆ *Audience.* Whom are we speaking to? How do they think and feel about the brand?

■ *Desired brand equity.* This is the list of rational and emotional components that describe how we want consumers to think and feel about the brand in the future.

■ *Creative guidelines.* The creative guidelines are a simple list of do's and don'ts giving the creative team clear direction about the attitude, approach and tone the advertising should take in order to create the desired brand equity.

The creative brief is a very important document prepared by the client and/ or the account director. Unilever recommends a brief that answers these eight important questions:

◆ Why do we want new advertising?

◆ To whom are we talking?

◆ What effect should the advertising have on the consumer?

◆ What is the single most persuasive benefit we can offer?

◆ Why should the consumer believe it?

◆ What are the executional considerations?

◆ What are the practical considerations?

◆ Who has the authority?

Let's see what is involved in each question (Koekemoer, 2004:125).

■ *Why do we want new advertising?* The reason for the brief could be a launch, re-launch, need for a new theme campaign or new treatment in an existing campaign, etc. Describe any opportunities or problems to be overcome, backed by relevant information, such as market/brand trends or developments.

■ *To whom are we talking?* Give a pen-picture of the intended target of the advertising, whether it is made up of buyers or users. The picture will include demographics and psychographics if relevant.

■ *What effect should the advertising have on the consumer?* Express the objective of the advertising in terms of consumer buying behaviour. For example, to generate trial, to maintain or increase the brand's share of purchases, to get the product used in a different, additional way. Try to describe what the target consumer thinks about the brand at the moment (using the consumer's words) based on knowledge gained from research. Then describe what the advertiser would like the consumer to think and to do after seeing the advertising.

■ *What is the single most persuasive benefit we can offer?* This should be the appropriate version of the brand benefit from the Brand Positioning Statement (BPS) and it should be capable of influencing the consumer in the way described in the last point. It should be no more than a sentence and should contain no more than a single thought. It should be expressed in consumer language but not be a copy line; turning the benefit into advertising copy is the job of the agency.

■ *Why should the consumer believe it?* This should be based on the 'reason to believe' from the BPS. It may also contain other convincing elements, such as support from a relevant personality.

■ *What are the executional considerations?* Often this section may be left blank, since no or few constraints should be imposed on the agency. However, it is acceptable to ask the agency to consider the use of specific devices such as an advertising property or music.

■ *What are the practical considerations?* Which medium is to be used? In the case of television, if more than one time length is required this should be specified in the brief. Budgets, where known, should be specified. This includes the production budget, especially if it is necessary to fix a maximum figure. Timing constraints, such as launch dates, etc should be noted, as well as the evaluation plan (normally pre-testing at least).

■ *Authority.* The brief should be approved by the project leader and by the person who takes the final decision on advertising, if different. Attachments covering relevant market research or technical evidence, written in straightforward language, may be included with the advertising brief.

Once the briefing document (prepared by the client and agency in steps one, two and three, above) has been given to the advertising agency and discussed with the client, the following steps could be followed by the agency to ensure the creation of a successful advertising campaign.

3.3.4 Step 4: The strategy/planning board

During this stage various departments within the advertising agency, including the creative department, the media department, the sales promotion department and the direct response experts, devise a total communications plan while attention is also given to public relations, Internet, digital and online opportunities, merchandising and product considerations.

Too often advertising is created without considering media aspects or a striking advertising campaign is designed without due attention being paid to sales representatives, merchandising, sales promotion, competitions, point-of-sale material, Internet, give-aways, etc. All of these factors should work together to achieve the desired and stated objectives.

3.3.5 Step 5: Media and creative concepts

The media choice depends on the advertising concept or theme, the target market, the size of the budget and the characteristics and benefits of the various media. It is vitally important that money is invested in the best media and not just spent in all of the media. Creativity in media planning is called for.

When the decision is taken on which media to use, these factors should be considered:

■ cost per thousand;

■ reach versus frequency;

■ the quality of certain media;

- the need for promotional support in certain media; and

- the change in media selection during certain stages of the product's life cycle.

The creative department develops a number of concepts (various ways of how to say what should be communicated) based on the advertising brief. At the same time, the creative department formulates spin-offs, for example, promotions, competitions, give-aways, point-of-purchase material, in-store promotions, direct response ideas, Web pages, mobile media messages, digital ads etc.

3.3.6 Step 6: The first review board

At this stage all initial plans and concepts are presented to members of the review board, which normally includes a campaign planner, a market researcher, the creative director, the media director and often (such as in the case of a major campaign) the managing director of the advertising agency. Each department submits its plans and has to defend its actions. It is necessary to play the 'why' game, to check plans against objectives and to ask: 'What has not been done that should have been done?'

It is now appropriate to bring in another account director who has not yet been exposed to the advertising brief and present the plan to him or her. By playing the 'why' game and checking proposed strategies against objectives it is easier to get out of a situation in which we cannot see the wood for the trees. Particular questions that could be asked by this neutral executive at this stage are: Do the creative ideas fit into the media selected? Will the concept work in digital media? Will the promotional ideas work? Are these ideas practical and cost efficient? Is the television commercial simple, credible, original, relevant and something that the target audience will enjoy looking at? Is the advertisement completely believable? Is the advertisement likeable? Is the theme one that will last or does it have a very short life? The client could be informed about the concepts at this stage.

3.3.7 Step 7: Further development

More often than not the various departments go back after the review board and start all over again. Some agencies even take a campaign that survives the review board, put it in the cupboard and say, 'We now have a reasonable campaign, let's see if we can do a better one'. Strategies are rethought, plans redone and it is probable that the various departments will work and improve on one of the selected advertising and promotional concepts and the media planner will prepare a semi-final media plan. It is essential that everyone involved is confident in what is selected. This time the departments will go to the second review board prepared with answers to that nagging question: 'Why'?

3.3.8 Step 8: Second review board

In the second review board stage the revised plans and concepts are presented to the same team and the neutral senior executive who will act as final devil's advocate. It is often found that the most viable concept has been achieved at this stage and enthusiasm for the campaign is mounting. The client is informed about revised concepts.

3.3.9 Step 9: Pre-testing

It is ideal to pre-test every campaign. The late George Gribbin (ex-president of Young & Rubicam) suggested the following alternatives. The first internal checklist is for television:

- Simplicity (is the message simple?)
- Credibility (is it credible?)
- Originality (is it fresh, original, different?)
- Relevance (is it relevant to the brand?)
- Empathy (do I like it?)

The second is for print advertising:

- Is the advertisement a stopper?
- Is the product the hero?
- Is the advertisement completely believable?
- Is the advertisement likeable?
- Is the theme one that will last?

Sometimes it is necessary to pre-test two concepts among the target audience when there is doubt at the agency or uncertainty about the interpretation of the message. It is absolutely necessary to pre-test all campaigns to assess interpretations, perceptions, etc in order to ensure that the best concept is the one that is used. Pre-testing also enables the agency to check whether the right message is being communicated, whether the advertising communications are credible and whether the image of the product will be enhanced.

Unfortunately, very few ad agencies pre-test campaigns and a commonly made mistake is to take a campaign designed for one cultural group and modify it slightly for use in another. Very few such campaigns work and often they cause more harm than good.

3.3.10 Step 10: Client presentation

Some agencies do not involve the client with steps three to eight and 'surprise' the advertiser with the advertising campaign at this stage. It is, however, preferable to follow a policy of 'no surprises', where the client is involved constantly. In practice this means that the marketing director or brand manager is involved, but presenting a major campaign to a client frequently involves the board of directors. These directors will probably ask the same questions that the devil's advocate and/or the client asked during the second review board stage. The presentation can, therefore, be made with confidence to those who are responsible for making the final decision. The presenters know in advance what fears the client may have and what questions they might be asked. Approval of the campaign should be obtained at this presentation.

3.3.11 Step 11: Creative implementation and quoting

Unfortunately, the advertiser sometimes forces the creative experts to change certain creative ideas, but at this stage everybody should agree on exactly what the campaign will comprise. The TV storyboards are finalised, final scripts are written for digital media and radio, type mark-ups are prepared for print advertising, final copy is prepared for print advertisements, model selection and voice selection (for radio and television) is done, photographers are briefed and production houses and printers are briefed in order that costs may be ascertained.

With regard to quotations, it is necessary to obtain quotes from three suppliers who have been briefed in detail. Once the quotes have been obtained they should be checked against the budget and it should be ensured that all expenses are taken into consideration. Unexpected costs at a later stage, which could result in unpleasant feelings between the advertising agency and the advertiser, should be avoided. The agency then prepares written quotes and presents these along with the final media schedules to the advertiser for final approval.

3.3.12 Step 12: Client approval

At this stage it may be necessary to re-present the whole campaign, the final quotes and the media schedule. Written approval for the campaign and the quotes must be obtained and the media schedules must be approved and signed.

3.3.13 Step 13: Final production

This is the critical stage for the advertising agency when the TV commercials, radio spots, print advertising, point-of-purchase material, promotional items, outdoor posters, Web pages, etc are produced. From the agency's point of view, it is essential to control the production and to ensure that certain standards are met. From the advertiser's point of view, it is essential to be involved in the production process: to supervise what is being done, attend the shoot of a TV commercial, attend the recording sessions of the radio commercials, etc. It is often necessary to make an on-the-spot decision whilst producing a TV commercial, recording a radio spot or producing a print advertisement. Advertisers should not expect the advertising agency to take such decisions if it means that a dispute could arise at a later stage when 'it did not work'. Sometimes additional expenses are incurred that were not budgeted for and these should be approved on the spot by the advertiser.

3.3.14 Step 14: Present campaign to selected groups and implement

It is necessary for the senior executives, the sales representatives, branch managers, dealers, etc to have a preview of the campaign before it breaks. It is essential to get their blessing and cooperation and to avoid surprises. Unless you have the wholehearted cooperation of the branch managers, dealers, sales representatives, etc the campaign does not have a hope of being implemented successfully.

3.3.15 Step 15: Ongoing evaluation

The object at this stage is to build in a measure of efficiency. This begins with the pre-campaign research and continues through pre-testing to the final post-campaign testing (efficiency versus objectives). For example, awareness tests, image shifts, usage tests, etc could be conducted on a continuous basis and compared with pre-test results and objectives. A date and activity chart plotting sales over a specified time period can be prepared so that the advertiser can see what has worked and what has not. This chart could also be used to indicate competitive reactions and activities and the effect thereof on the product's sales. Nielsen data, like out-of-stock situations, should also be included in this chart to reflect a true picture.

A simple way to conduct an ongoing analysis is to measure the effect of the advertising over time at various levels of advertising expenditure. The effect could be the awareness level, the image, the positioning, even sales in the case of direct response advertising (see Figure 3.9 on the following page).

Figure 3.9 indicates that:

- between expenditures o and x there is no effect because there is a certain noise level in the market;
- Figure A: as ad spend increases, so does the effect – the advertising is working;
- Figure B: the advertising is working for a while but after level a, advertising is wasted because more ad spend does not give more or better effect;
- Figure C: more ad spend leads to a proportionally smaller increase in effect; and
- Figure D: a small increase in ad spend leads to a proportionately high increase in effect – the advertising is really working well.

Many advertisers and ad agencies change the advertising simply because they are bored with it and often long before they should, because they do not plot the ad spend and effect on graphs as illustrated in Figure 3.9. To be able to plot the effect, ongoing research (or tracking) is necessary to assess awareness levels, images, brand positioning, sales, etc.

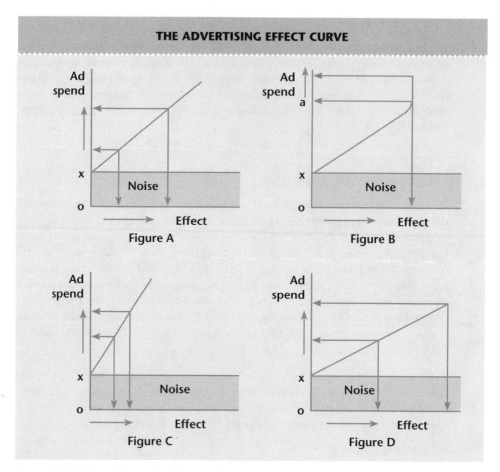

Figure 3.9: Adapted from Koekemoer (2004:130–131).

REFERENCES

Arens, W.F., Weigold, M.F. and Arens, C. 2008. *Contemporary Advertising*, 12ed McGrawHill: Homewood, Illinois.

Belch, E.D. and Belch, M.A. 2004. *Advertising and Promotion*, 6ed Irwin: Homewood, Illinois.

Engel, J.F., Warshaw, M.R.,Kinnear, T.C. and Reese, B.B. 2000. *Promotional Strategy*, 9ed Pinnaflex Educational Resources.

Koekemoer, L. (ed) 2004. *Marketing Communications*. Juta: Cape Town.

Koekemoer, L. 1991. *Profit from Effective Advertising*. Juta: Cape Town.

O'Guinn, T.C., Allen, C.T. and Semenik, R.J. 2009. *Advertising & Integrated Brand Promotion*, 5ed South-Western Cengage Learning: Mason, Ohio.

Shimp, T.A. 2010. *Integrated Marketing Communication in Advertising and Promotion*, 8ed South-WesternCengage Learning: Asia.

4 Advertising Media and Media Planning

AIM OF THIS CHAPTER

The focus in this chapter is on the media of advertising, media planning and media buying.

LEARNING OUTCOMES

After studying this chapter you should be competent in:
- outlining the role of media in advertising and marketing
- describing the various budgeting approaches (top-down and bottom-up)
- describing the main characteristics, strengths and weaknesses of the above-the-line media types
- defining media planning and outlining the main media planning considerations
- describing the media planning process
- discussing media buying

4.1 INTRODUCTION

The ultimate aim of advertising is to persuade customers to purchase the advertiser's product or use the service. The ultimate test for advertising lies in the marketplace – Does it work? Does it convince people to buy? Has it changed attitudes?, etc.

This is not to say that creativity in advertising is not important, in fact, creativity may just be the thing that convinces people to buy a product. Media planning, however, is the heart of the advertising process that ensures the circulation of that lifeblood and ultimately the ongoing health of the advertising campaign.

Media is an integral part of not only the advertising process but also the marketing decision process. Specific media are used to reach specific target markets to communicate specific, designated creative messages. This is shown in Figure 4.1.

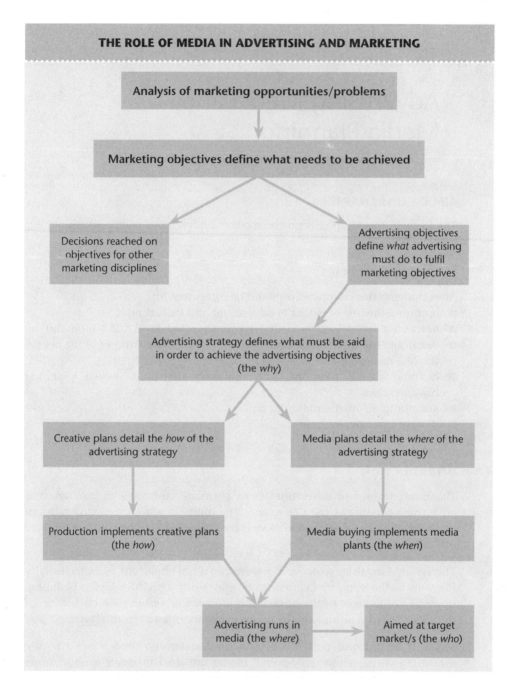

Figure 4.1: Koekemoer (2004:186) and Muller (1999:21) adapted from Leahy's Media Planning Model.

It is clear from Figure 4.1 that the process starts with an analysis of marketing opportunities or problems. Marketing objectives are set, then advertising objectives are defined and advertising uses creativity in media to reach specific target markets (often called target audiences). In order for the creative work to appear in the media two basic functions need to be performed: media planning and media buying.

4.2 THE ADVERTISING BUDGET

In the overall marketing budget there will usually be an advertising budget as well. A certain percentage of the marketing budget is allocated to marketing communication and within that budget a certain percentage is allocated to advertising and the rest is split between public relations, direct marketing, sales promotion, personal selling, sponsorship and digital marketing.

The amount of money budgeted for the various components of the marketing budget serves as indication of the emphasis given by the marketer to, for example, marketing communication and to advertising within the marketing mix. This level of expenditure is important because it determines what the company is prepared to spend. A R500 000 budget will only go so far in a short budget period and will probably not be enough in most highly competitive markets. A budget of R20 million, on the other hand, could really support a brand in all media and in many markets. Certain types of marketers, such as business-to-business marketers, usually operate on smaller advertising budgets, while marketers of FMCG (Fast Moving Consumer Goods) employ substantial budgets.

The main question always is: How much should we spend to achieve a specific objective? In practice there are seven basic considerations in answering this question:

- What are the objectives that the advertising is intended to accomplish?
- What is the envisaged market share objective?
- How much competitive advertising activity is there? In highly competitive markets, advertisers will need to spend a lot of money to maintain market share and more to increase market share.
- What is the market potential for the brand and can the advertising contribute to reaching this potential?
- How much money is available? Management considers advertising expenditure as a cost rather than an investment and it is often difficult to convince them to increase the budget.
- Are there economies of scale in advertising? Brands maintaining a large market share have an advantage over smaller competitors and can spend proportionally less money on advertising and still realise a better return.
- Should we change the advertising strategy? More money is usually made available for such changes or for a re-launch of the brand.

4.3 BUDGETING APPROACHES

Marketers have a variety of budgeting approaches or methods at their disposal. It is, however, common for a marketer to employ more than one method. Large, sophisticated marketers often use different methods from those used by smaller or less sophisticated marketers. Budgeting approaches can be top-down or bottom-up.

4.3.1 Top-down approaches

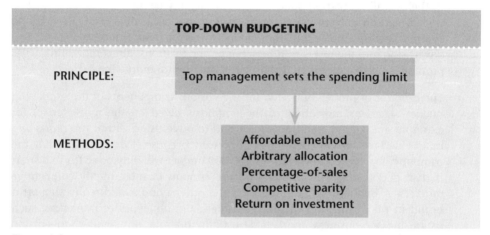

Figure 4.2

The essence of the top-down budgeting method is that top management decides on a budget figure and the spending limit and the budget must stay within this limit. The budget is, therefore, predetermined. Let's briefly review the budgeting methods (Du Plessis et al, 2005:55-58):

- *The affordable method.* In the affordable method (often known as the all-you-can-afford method) the company either determines the amount to be spent in various areas such as production and operations and remaining funds – considered to be the affordable amount – are allocated to advertising and promotion or the allocation is 'what we spent last year plus media inflation (of say 10 per cent)'. The task to be performed by the advertising or promotion is not considered and the likelihood of under- or overspending is high as no guidelines for measuring the effects of various budgets are set.

  The logic for using this approach is that 'if we know what we can afford and we do not exceed it we will not get into financial problems'. While this may be true in an accounting sense, this method does not reflect sound managerial decision-making from a marketing perspective. Very often this method does not result in enough money being allocated to get the product off the ground and into the market. However, overspending and wastage can also occur.

■ *Arbitrary allocation.* Even weaker than the affordable method for establishing a budget, is arbitrary allocation. This approach has no theoretical basis and often the budget amount is set by management solely on the basis of what is subjectively felt to be necessary and/or effective.

The arbitrary allocation approach has no obvious advantages. No systematic thinking has occurred, no objectives have been budgeted for and the essence and purpose of advertising and promotion have been largely ignored. Other than the fact that the manager believes some amount should be spent on advertising and promotion and then picks a number, there is no good explanation as to why this approach continues to be used. However, many budgets continue to be set this way – and often get changed (usually decreased) when circumstances change.

■ *Percentage-of-sales.* Perhaps the most commonly used method for budget setting (particularly in large companies) is the percentage-of-sales method. In this method the advertising and promotion budget is based on past sales of the product with the amount determined in either of two ways: a percentage of the sales or a fixed amount of the unit product cost multiplied by the number of units sold.

A second variation is to use a percentage of projected future sales as a base. Again, this method may use either a straight percentage of projected sales or a unit cost projection. In the straight percentage method, sales are projected for the coming year based on the marketing manager's estimates. The budget is established by taking a percentage of these sales. Often an industry standard percentage will be used to make this determination, say five per cent.

One advantage offered by using future sales as a base is that the budget is not based on last year's sales. As the market changes, these changes and the effect they will have on sales must be built into the next year's forecast rather than relying on past data. As a result the budget is more likely to reflect current conditions and is, therefore, more appropriate.

There are two main advantages to the percentage-of-sales approach. First, it is financially safe and keeps ad spending within reasonable limits as it bases spending on the past year's sales or what the company expects to sell in the coming year. There should be sufficient monies to cover this budget. Second, the method is simple, straightforward and easy to implement. Regardless of which base – past or future sales – is employed, the calculations necessary to arrive at a budget are not complicated.

At the same time, the percentage-of-sales method has some serious disadvantages. The most important is the basic premise on which the budget is established – sales. Using sales as the basis for setting the advertising budget is wrong. This is putting the cart before the horse. Rather than considering advertising as a major factor contributing to sales, the roles are reversed with the level of sales determining the amount to be spent on advertising and promotion. The result is a reversal of the cause-and-effect relationship between advertising and sales.

A second problem with this approach is stability. Only if all companies used a similar percentage would stability be brought to the marketplace. The problem is that this method does not allow for changes in strategy either internally or from competitors. An aggressive company may wish to allocate more money to the advertising and promotion budget. This strategy would not be possible with the percentage-of-sales method.

Unfortunately, this method of budgeting often results in severe misappropriation of funds. If we believe that advertising and promotion have a role to perform in marketing a product, then we should believe that allocating more money to advertising will generate increased sales. Products with low sales will have smaller promotion budgets that in turn will hinder sales progress. At the other extreme, very successful products may have an excessive budget – some of which may be better invested in other marketing communication tools.

The percentage-of-sales method is also difficult to employ for new product introductions. If no past sales figures are available, there may be no basis for establishing the budget. Projections of future sales may be difficult, particularly if the product is highly innovative and/or may have fluctuating sales patterns.

Finally, if the budget is dependent on sales, decreases in sales will lead to decreases in budgets when they may need to be increased. Lower promotion budgets may increase the downward sales trend. Successful companies, however, are often those that have allocated additional funds during hard times or downturns in the sales cycle.

- *Competitive parity.* In the competitive parity method budget amounts are established by matching the percentage of sales expenditures of the competition– if our main competitors spent three per cent of sales, we should do the same. The reasoning here is that setting budgets in this way takes advantage of the wisdom of the industry and takes the competition into consideration. This leads to stability in the marketplace by minimising marketing warfare. If the competition knows that others are unlikely to match their increases in promotional spending, they are less likely to take an aggressive approach to attempt to gain market share.

The competitive parity method also has a number of disadvantages. First, the method ignores the fact that advertising and promotion are designed to accomplish specific objectives by addressing certain problems and opportunities. Second, it assumes that because companies have nearly equal expenditures, their campaigns will be equally effective. Such an assumption obviously ignores the contributions of creative executions and/or media allocations as well as the degree of success or not of various promotions. Further, it ignores the fact that some companies simply make better products than others. Finally, there is no guarantee that the main competitors will not change their strategies. They may launch a new product or re-launch an existing one and spend a lot more on advertising and promotion.

In summary, it is unlikely that a company will employ the competitive parity method as a sole means of establishing the marketing communication budget. This method is typically used in conjunction with the percentage-of-sales or other methods. It is not a wise strategy to ignore the competition. Managers must always be aware of what competitors are doing, but should not just follow them in setting their own goals or developing their own strategies.

■ *Return On Investment (ROI)*. As stated above, in the percentage-of-sales method sales dictate the level of advertising appropriation. This relationship is backward as advertising should rather be seen as a contributor to sales; investment in advertising and promotion should lead to increases in sales. The key word here is investment.

In the ROI budgeting method, advertising and promotion expenditure is considered to be an investment. As with other aspects of the company's investments, advertising and promotion are expected to achieve a certain level of return.

While the ROI method appears to be sound the reality is that it is almost never possible to assess the returns provided by the marketing communication effort – at least as long as sales continue to be the basis for evaluation because there are many other factors that contribute to sales.

4.3.2 Bottom-up approaches

Bottom-up approaches are known as build-up approaches. They are used to avoid the reliance of top-down approaches on judgement, and they mainly focus on the objectives of the marketing communication efforts. Figure 4.3 outlines the bottom-up approach.

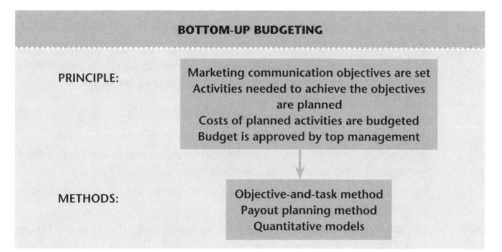

Figure 4.3

Figure 4.3 indicates that the budget decision is an interactive process of setting the marketing communication objectives, planning the strategies and then budgeting in such as way that the strategies can be implemented. Let's briefly review the main bottom-up methods (Koekemoer, 2004:192, Cant et al, 2006:449).

■ *The objective-and-task method*. The objective-and-task method is generally regarded as the most sensible and defendable advertising budgeting method.

When using this method, advertising decision makers must clearly specify the role they expect advertising to play and then set budgets accordingly. The role is typically identified in terms of a communication objective (for example, increase brand awareness by 20 per cent) but is often also stated in terms of sales volume or market-share expectations (increase market share from 15 to 20 per cent).

The following steps are involved when applying the objective-and-task method (Shimp, 2003:250–1):

◆ The first step is to establish marketing objectives such as sales volume, market share and profit contribution.

To illustrate this, let us consider Vodacom as an example. Their marketing objective may be to increase contract clients by 12 per cent during the financial year, to increase the overall contract revenue by 50 per cent and to increase the contribution to profit by seven per cent.

◆ The second step in implementing the objective-and-task method is to assess the communication tasks that must be performed to accomplish the overall marketing objectives.

Vodacom must accomplish, for example, two communication functions in order to realise its overall marketing objective. It must increase consumer awareness of the contracts on offer and persuade consumers that the contracts offer a variety of options in order to use it more.

◆ The third step is to determine advertising's role in the total communication mix in performing the tasks established in step 2.

Given the nature of its products and communication objectives, advertising is a crucial component in Vodacom's mix.

◆ The fourth step is to establish specific advertising goals in terms of the levels of measurable communication response required to achieve marketing objectives.

It is imperative to make realistic goals that are measurable, thus Vodacom's goal will be to increase the contracts by 12 per cent by end of the year.

◆ The final step is to establish the budget based on estimates of expenditure required to accomplish the advertising goals.

For Vodacom to achieve its objectives they for example have to increase their budget by 25 per cent.

The major advantage of the objective-and-task method is that the budget is determined by the objectives to be attained. Thus, rather than being established at the top and passed down, the managers closest to the marketing effort will be involved and specific strategies will be considered in the budget-setting process.

The major disadvantage of this method is that determining which tasks are required and the costs associated with each, is not always easy. While these decisions may be relatively easy for certain objectives (for example, estimating the costs of sampling required to stimulate trial in a defined market area) it is sometimes not possible to determine exactly what is required and/or how much it will cost to complete the job, especially in the digital arena.

■ *Payout planning.* The first months of a new product's introduction typically require heavier-than-normal advertising and promotion appropriations to stimulate higher levels of awareness and subsequently trial. With respect to promotion, spending for a new entry should be approximately twice the amount normally required for the desired market share.

To decide how much to spend, marketers will often develop a payout plan. This plan determines the investment value of the advertising and promotion allocation. The basic idea is to project the revenues the product will generate over two to three years, as well as the costs that will be incurred. Based on an expected rate of return, the payout plan will assist in determining what advertising and promotion expenditures will be necessary and at what time this return might be expected. Typically, a new FMCG product would lose money in year one, almost break even in year two and finally begin to show substantial profits by the end of year three. The advertising and promotion figures are then higher in year one and decline in years two and three. The budget must also reflect the company's guidelines for new product introductions, as companies generally have established time periods in which the products must begin to show a profit. Finally, it should be kept in mind that building market share can be more difficult than maintaining it. Therefore, the drop-off in expenditure in the later years.

■ *Quantitative models.* Many attempts to apply quantitative models to budgeting have met with limited success. Most often these methods have employed computer simulation models involving statistical techniques such as multiple regression analysis to determine the relative contribution that the size of the budget has on the sales response to advertising. Because of problems associated with these methods their acceptance and use have been limited.

Unfortunately, the value of quantitative models has yet to reach the promised potential. Perhaps in future, better computer models will be forthcoming. The discussion of these models is beyond the scope of this text. Such methods do have merit but may need more refinement before achieving widespread success.

4.4 ADVERTISING MEDIA

This section will focus on the main above-the-line media, that is television, print, radio, cinema and outdoor.

Print media lost market share consistently every year between 1978, when commercial television was launched in South Africa, and 2003. Since then it has improved in spite of on-line news. In the mid-1990s the revival of print media was encouraged by the vigorous launch of a number of new newspapers and magazines. Radio also grew during this period as marketers and media experts moved away from television advertising but declined again between 1998 and 2010. Cinema and out-of-home advertising showed no growth. Table 4.1 outlines the 2005 and 2009 ad spend percentages by medium.

Table 4.1	**SHARE OF TOTAL AD SPEND BY MEDIUM 2005 AND 2009 (%)**	
	2005	**2009**
Newspapers	29,8	27,3
Magazines	13,3	12,5
Television	37,8	37,2
Radio	8,6	8,0
Cinema	0,4	0,5
Outdoor	5,4	5,9
Internet	4,7	8,6
Total	100	100

4.4.1 Participants in the media process

There are three professional participants in the media process, namely the advertiser, the advertising agency and the media owner. The fourth participant is the target audience. The advertiser wants to satisfy the needs and desires of the target market. In order to communicate product benefits, the ad agency will be briefed accordingly. The ad agency will recommend which media to use, how best to use them, book the media schedules, check appearance and charge the advertiser. The media owner will accept the booking made by the ad agency, place the advertising as negotiated, charge the agency and publish or broadcast the advertising. See Figure 4.4 on the following page and note the importance of the target audience.

The target audience is crucial in this process as the advertising message in the media is directed at it. The advertiser aims the product or service at the target audience. The ad agency creates advertising that will influence the target audience and books media that will reach the selected target audience. If the target audience does not respond to the advertising, it means that either the creative message is not working or the media is not reaching the target audience or the product is over-priced or doesn't live up to expectations.

4.4.2 The media of advertising

For the student of advertising it is important to get to know the media alternatives, to understand their characteristics, strengths and weaknesses. This discussion will briefly outline current and new media opportunities and some trends. There are four major categories of advertising media, namely print, electronic/broadcast, out-of-home and digital interactive media. Due to recent media trends, there is some overlap. Let's review the main above-the-line types (Koekemoer, 2004:196; Du Plessis et al, 2005:58–60).

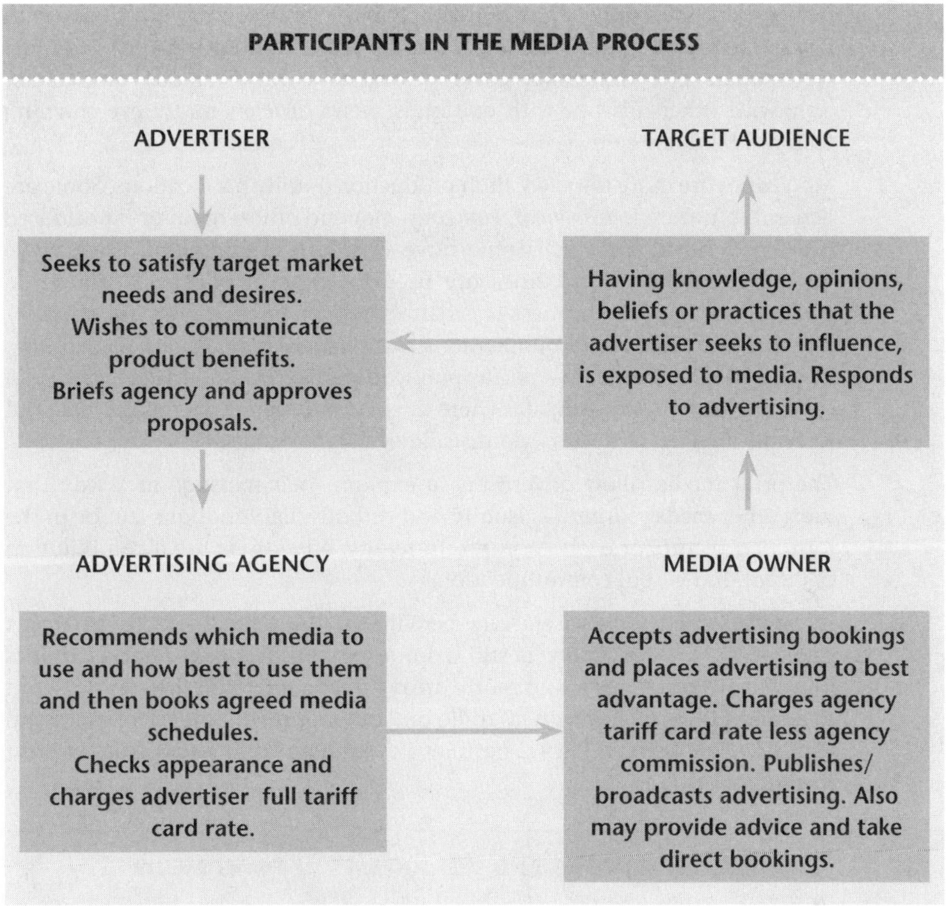

PARTICIPANTS IN THE MEDIA PROCESS

ADVERTISER

Seeks to satisfy target market needs and desires.
Wishes to communicate product benefits.
Briefs agency and approves proposals.

TARGET AUDIENCE

Having knowledge, opinions, beliefs or practices that the advertiser seeks to influence, is exposed to media. Responds to advertising.

ADVERTISING AGENCY

Recommends which media to use and how best to use them and then books agreed media schedules.
Checks appearance and charges advertiser full tariff card rate.

MEDIA OWNER

Accepts advertising bookings and places advertising to best advantage. Charges agency tariff card rate less agency commission. Publishes/broadcasts advertising. Also may provide advice and take direct bookings.

Figure 4.4: Adapted from Koekemoer (2004:195).

- *Print media.* As mentioned earlier, of the total expenditure on advertising across all media approximately 40 per cent is spent on the printed word. Newspapers and magazines are the two main types of media in this class. They attract advertisers for a variety of reasons, but the most important is that print media are very effective at delivering a message to the target audience.

Most people have access to either a newspaper or a magazine. They read to keep up to date with news and events or as a source of entertainment. People tend to have consistent reading habits and buy the same print media regularly. For example, most people read the same newspaper/s each day and their regular choice of magazine reflects either their business or leisure interests. This means that advertisers, through marketing research, are able to build a database of the main characteristics of their readers. This in turn allows advertisers to focus on those media that will be read by the type of people they think will benefit from their product or service.

The essence of newspapers is news. There are national Sunday newspapers (for example, *Sunday Times* and *Rapport*), regional Sunday newspapers, daily newspapers that appear on a regional basis and country and suburban newspapers. Newspapers use lower quality paper and have a very short life. Newspapers offer immediacy, coverage and news. However, ads compete not only with other ads but with editorials, news articles, many eye-catching editorial headlines, etc.

Magazines are more targeted, high production quality publications. Some are general in nature (*Huisgenoot*, *Fair Lady*, etc) and others are more specialised (*Garden & Home*, *Car*, etc). Some have very large circulation, others have limited circulation. Magazines are used to create a particular image, to position the brand. Business-to-business magazines are playing a major role in South Africa with publications like *Financial Mail*, *Finansies & Tegniek*, *Finance Week* and industry-specific publications like *Transport Management*, *SA Coal*, *Gold & Base Minerals*, etc. There are also a large number of professional journals directed at doctors, dentists, lawyers, marketers, etc.

The print media allow advertisers to explain their message in a way that most other media cannot – visually and verbally. Explanations can be in the form of a picture or a photograph. In reality, advertisers use a combination of visual and verbal communication.

In South Africa, advertisers rely heavily on print media to reach target audiences. However, there is still a large proportion of the market that is illiterate or semi-literate and many are a-literate, meaning they do not want to read. In these circumstances radio and outdoor media are more successful vehicles than print. Table 4.2 outlines the strengths and weaknesses of print media.

Table 4.2 **STRENGTHS AND WEAKNESSES OF PRINT MEDIA**

MEDIA	STRENGTHS	WEAKNESSES
Newspapers	• Provide illustrations and explanations • Suitable for high frequency • Adaptable to change • Relatively cheap per reader • Geographically selective • Buyers use it as a guide • A good news medium • High coverage	• Poor reproduction • Short lifespan • Is read selectively • Reaches a general audience • Many advertisers and little chance of dominating • Clutter • Low attention getting

→

Magazines	• Good reproduction • Longer lifespan • Reaches specific market segment • Usually loyal readers • National coverage • Good image creator	• Limited flexibility due to long lead time • Many advertisers and little chance of dominating • Not geographically selective • Short time to convey the message

Adapted from Koekemoer (2004:197) and Cant et al (2006:453–454).

■ *Electronic/broadcast media.* The electronic media are relatively young in comparison with the printed word. Advertisers use electronic media because they can reach mass audiences with their messages at a relatively low cost per person.

In South Africa, many people have access to a television set and almost everyone to a radio. The majority of viewers use television passively as a form of entertainment. Radio demands, through theatre of the mind, active participation, but can reach people who are in and out of the home environment.

Electronic media allow advertisers to add visual and/or sound dimensions to their messages. The opportunity to demonstrate or to show the benefits or results that a particular product can bring gives life and energy to an advertiser's message. Television uses sight, sound and movement, whereas radio can only use its audio capacity to convey meaning. Both media have the potential to tell stories and to appeal to people's emotions when transmitting a message. These are dimensions that print media find difficult to achieve.

Advertising messages transmitted through the electronic media use a small period of time, normally 15, 20, 30 or 60 seconds. The cost of different time slots varies throughout a single transmission day and according to the popularity of individual programmes. The more listeners or viewers that a programme attracts, the greater the price charged for a slice of time to transmit an advertising message.

People are often unable and perhaps unwilling, to become actively involved with electronically transmitted advertising messages, especially radio. There may be too many distractions. Time is expensive and short, so advertisers do not have the opportunity to present detailed information. The result is that radio is most suitable for low-involvement messages. Where the need for elaboration is low, radio seeks to draw attention, create awareness, remind listeners and improve levels of interest. TV has more impact and is more visual. It can demonstrate, create image and persuade people. Seeing is believing.

Electronic media are often used by retailers and FMCG companies because of their ability to reach mass audiences. The strengths and weaknesses of electronic/broadcast media are outlined in Table 4.3.

Table 4.3 **STRENGTHS AND WEAKNESSES OF ELECTRONIC/
BROADCAST MEDIA**

MEDIA	STRENGTHS	WEAKNESSES
Radio	• Is a personal medium • Geographically selective in regional services; national coverage with certain transmissions • Can reach specific audiences at certain times • No literacy necessary • Listening sometimes habitual • Offers theatre of the mind • Low cost	• Limited availability • No reference back to message • No illustration possible, audio only • Only short message • Is a background medium demanding attention – low attention getting
Television	• Involves most of the senses • Viewer is unlikely to ignore the message • Good for demonstrations • Programming allows for a degree of psychographic targeting • Wide coverage • Prestige value • Can involve the entire family • High impact	• Limited availability of quality time • No reference back to message • Relatively expensive medium • Reaches a general audience • Relatively lengthy preparation • Repetition can irritate the viewer • Only national • High production and flighting costs

Adapted from Koekemoer (2004:198–199) and Cant et al (2006:454–455).

■ *Out-of-home media.* Out-of-home media include outdoor media and cinema. Outdoor media consist mainly of billboards (hoardings), signs and poster sites. These include 96-sheeters, 48-sheeters, bus shelters, buses, sports stadium signs and scoreboard ads, aerial signs (hot-air balloons), public waste paper bins, etc. They are large, mainly stationary media used by national advertisers for detergents, liquor, cars, etc. These media are expensive to produce, offering high impact (if used creatively) and not very versatile. Advertising on the company's own trucks and on buses (public transport) has become quite popular and is often referred to as moving media.

Another 'out-of-home' medium is cinema. There has been an effort to revive the cinema as an advertising medium. Due to the large number of prestigious shopping centres appearing in the urban areas and the cinemas in these centres, nearly a million people attend the cinema every week.

Advertising messages transmitted in a cinema have all the advantages of television-based messages. Audio and visual dimensions combine with darkness in the cinema to provide high impact. However, the audience is more attentive because the main film has yet to be shown and there are fewer distractions in the auditorium or less 'noise' in the communication system. This means that cinema advertising has greater impact than television advertisements. This impact can be used to heighten levels of attention, and because the screen images are larger than life and appear in a darkened room, the potential to communicate effectively with the target audience is strong.

The strengths and weaknesses of out-of-home and cinema are outlined in Table 4.4.

Table 4.4	**STRENGTHS AND WEAKNESSES OF OUT-OF-HOME AND CINEMA**	
MEDIA	STRENGTHS	WEAKNESSES
Out-of-home	• Cost per passer-by is low • Suitable for high frequency • Geographically selective • Offers support and serves as a reminder of other advertisements • Large product presentation • High impact	• Necessarily a short message • Reaches the general passerby • Relatively limited space available • High production cost • Local restrictions • Urban clutter
Cinema	• Involves most of the senses • Viewer can't ignore the message • Good for demonstrations • Geographically selective • Individual films provide a high level of psychographic targeting • Viewer receives message in a relaxed atmosphere • High-quality reproduction • Reaches A income and 16 to 24 year-old audience • Very high impact	• Relatively expensive medium • Limited message • Relatively lengthy preparation • Expensive to produce

Adapted from Koekemoer (2004:200) and Cant et al (2006:454).

■ *Digital interactive media.* The advent of the information superhighway has brought a new media form. Digital interactive media are channels of communication with which the audience can participate actively and immediately. They are changing the way advertisers and agencies do business.

With a computer keyboard, consumers can now view and order products directly. They can also participate in game shows. In addition, they can manipulate images to better view a scene and can find information about a product or service on the Internet. They can discuss products on Twitter and Facebook. They can even receive special offers on their cellphones.

This presents a challenge to advertisers and agencies to learn new forms of creativity. They have to deal with a whole new environment for their ads. It's a virtual environment where customers may spend 20 minutes or more, not just 30 seconds and where advertising is a dialogue, not a monologue. And on the Internet, they risk getting 'flamed' (receiving harsh criticism by email) if the 'techies' don't like their ads (Arens, 2002:123 and Du Plessis et al, 2005:415).

4.5   MEDIA PLANNING

What is media planning? For the purpose of this text, media planning is defined as follows (Muller, 1999:22 and Du Plessis et al, 2005:130–131):

Media planning is the development of a specific and detailed process of reaching the right number of appropriate people, the right number of times, in the right environment at minimum cost, to achieve the advertised brand's marketing objectives.

The strength of this definition lies in its focus on the several levels of decision making, which collectively make up the process of media planning. The study of media planning makes it necessary to study the constituent elements. Media planning remains, however, a cohesive process, goal-directed towards the achievement of clearly articulated and tangible advertising and marketing objectives.

The core elements of this definition can be put into six specific questions that the media planner must answer in the process of developing a media plan:

- How many prospects (for purchasing a given brand or product) do I need to reach?
- In which medium (and vehicles) should the advertisements be placed?
- How many times should the prospect see each ad?
- In which months or season should the ads appear?
- In which markets or regions should the ads appear?
- How much money should be spent in each medium?

Although these are only some of the questions that the media planner should ask, each of them must be specifically answered in the resultant media plan.

The media plan itself exhibits many of the components of a model, not least of all in its efforts to give tangible and quantifiable value to the process whereby an advertising message is exposed to and consumed by target consumers.

4.5.1 Media planning considerations

In making both the macro- and micro-decisions there are four primary elements that are central to the media planning process. These are time, reach, frequency and impact.

Let's briefly review the four concepts:

■ *Time.* Of these four key concepts, time is the most easily dealt with and refers simply to the proposed duration of the campaign or, more specifically, the period over which the stated objectives of the campaign will be realised or maintained.

■ *Reach.* Reach refers to the number of persons within the target market who are exposed to the advertiser's message at least once. This is usually reflected as a percentage. Sometimes this is also referred to as coverage.

■ *Frequency.* Frequency refers to the number of times, on average, that a person within the target market is supposed to have been exposed to the advertiser's message.

■ *Impact.* Impact refers to the relative degree of awareness or measured ad noting, achieved by a particular creative execution in any given medium.

All media types offer varying degrees of impact, reach (coverage) and frequency within the confines of a given budget. Some media are high impact but expensive and can, therefore, allow the advertiser to buy only limited frequency. Others are low-impact media but exposure can be purchased very cheaply and high frequency can be maintained for long periods of time.

4.5.2 The media planning process

The media planning process could be described by focusing on four basic steps (Koekemoer, 2004:207):

■ *Step 1: The brief*

◆ Can advertising help, or is there a better way (perhaps direct marketing, public relations or promotional activity)?

◆ Are the advertising objectives realistic?

◆ Is the target achievable? Can it be improved? Must it be redefined for media purposes?

◆ Is there enough, too much or too little money to do the job? How big is the media budget?

◆ Can media exposure do the job in the time set?

◆ Is the creative team missing any tricks? Can media help to do it better?

It is impossible to over-estimate the value of a good brief to the media planner and there exists one overriding principle that should always be applied in developing the brief. This principle is GIGO, which stands for Garbage In

Garbage Out. The media plan can only be good if the brief is comprehensive and meaningful.

The media brief must be distinguished from the broader advertising and creative brief, which in essence creates the foundation for media decision-making but lacks the specific marketing and demographic detail which is the hallmark of the complete media brief. The media strategy cannot be divorced from the total marketing plan and the starting point for any media brief must be the marketing plan itself.

■ *Step 2: The media objectives*

In step two, the media planner considers the advertising and media objectives.

The media strategy is developed directly as a response to a set of objectives, but more often than not these objectives tend to be the creative or advertising objectives rather than a set of specific media objectives.

The crux of the media strategy is the selection between the media – the inter-media decision – and the following two levels of media objectives are relevant:

◆ The broad strategic inter-media objectives, which deal more specifically with the choice between media types.

◆ The detailed schedule of intra-media performance objectives, which outlines more specifically reach and frequency performance parameters by media type, budget allocation and timing of media activity and sets the benchmark for post-campaign media performance evaluation.

■ *Step 3: The media strategy*

This is the prescribed means, the how of attaining the objective. It will outline what media are to be employed, how much, where and when. The crux of the media strategy is the selection between the media – the inter-media decision.

In step three, the media planner selects the media to be used.

At the heart of the media plan lies the inter-media decision, the actual recommendation to use one media type in preference to another. A number of criteria are used to make this decision and these are listed below:

◆ *Creative compatibility and media qualities.* The media plan exists to give direction and form to the creative message and to create an environment that will enhance the probability of the consumer noting and comprehending the creative message.

◆ *Target market exposure.* Regardless of the qualitative aspects of the medium, if the target market is not actually exposed to it, the medium cannot make a contribution to the advertising plan. If the target market is teenagers in LSM (Living Standard Measures) 1 & 2, cinema would be an inappropriate media selection.

◆ *Timing of exposure.* The need to link media exposure to the actual purchase decision is often a critical element of the media plan. In many product categories seasonal sales patterns are applicable. Point-of-sale advertising such as point-of-purchase stands or trolley advertisements provide a final reminder to the consumer at the time and at the point of purchase.

◆ *Track record.* Although media plans are prepared for twelve-month periods, the consumer is completely unaware of this parameter. What the consumer experiences is a continuous communication programme directed towards the achievement of some objective. The media planner must always refer back to previous planning activity in order to assess and build upon those features that proved successful.

◆ *Practical constraints.* There are many instances where the choice of a medium is restricted by practical problems. For instance, the longer booking lead times for magazines (four to six weeks) eliminate them from snap tactical campaigns, which tend to go into newspapers because of the shorter deadlines (24 to 48 hours). Availability of commercial time can be a problem with television, particularly when popular programmes are selected.

◆ *Budget constraints.* The high cost of utilising some media types makes them an inappropriate option for small-budget advertisers. Often it is the high cost of production (such as producing a TV commercial) rather than the flighting of the advertisements themselves that is the restricting factor.

◆ *Competitive frame.* The media activities of competitors create the frame within which the media strategy must be developed. The need to match the media activity of competitors, for instance, will suggest a strategy that mirrors their current media selection.

However they are stated, media selection criteria must inevitably reflect the specific objectives outlined for the media plan. If the objectives include the need to create a push effect in the retail trade, then the medium most likely to create this effect must be chosen (usually TV). If the campaign includes sampling or pamphlet distribution, the ability of the medium to facilitate this is a crucial consideration. In this instance, radio would be excluded.

■ *Step 4: The media plan*

Now the specifics of each medium recommended will be planned. Finally, an overall plan will be calculated and compared with the objectives set in step two.

In the final step, the details of each medium are planned. The media will be listed, the frequency indicated, the dates recorded, the costs added and the overall plan performance calculated. The performance of the media plan will then be compared with the objectives set in step two. The final media plan could consist of the following list on the next page:

1. INTRODUCTION

1.1 Advertiser (client)

Date and client's budget year

1.2 Nature of the campaign

Background to the campaign

2. THE BRIEF

2.1 Marketing strategy

2.2 Advertising strategy

2.3 Creative strategy

2.4 Creative physical parameters

2.5 Target market definition and details

2.6 Budget for media

3. MEDIA OBJECTIVES AND STRATEGIES

3.1 Objectives

3.2 Weighing

3.3 Deployment

3.4 Timing

3.5 Specific strategies

4. SPECIFIC MEDIA PROPOSALS

4.1 Choice of primary medium

4.2 Choice of support medium

4.3 Comments on media rejected

4.4 Outline schedule and budget

5. TOTAL MEDIA COSTS

6. PERFORMANCE EVALUATION

4.5.3 Media buying

Traditionally, media departments have been divided into two clear and complementary functions – media planning and media buying (Koekemoer, 2004:214–215). In the heavily regulated and oligopolistic media environment that has characterised South Africa for the last five decades, the function of media buying has consisted largely of the scheduling, booking and administration of the media plan. The media plan was developed, often to the point of a detailed schedule, by the planner and then passed along to the media buyer for implementation. Pre-campaign and post-campaign performance analyses were the exclusive responsibility of the media planner.

Over and above the smooth administration of the approved media plan, there are a number of areas in which the media buyer can make a direct impact on the content and direction of the actual media plan:

■ *Rate negotiation.* Evaluation of media performance, whether magazines, radio or newspapers, tends to be based on historical data, which are commonly published on an infrequent basis.

■ *Budget and rate monitoring.* Volume discount rates are usually negotiated upfront on an annual basis.

■ *Campaign monitoring.* Provided the media planner has given the media buyer specific measurable objectives, it is the buyer who is in the best position to monitor the actual campaign delivery.

■ *TV scheduling.* Individual TV bursts are initially planned in the form of proposals known as buying briefs. Very often, it is the media planner who sets the broad parameters of these buying briefs by outlining, in addition to the specific reach, frequency and GRP objectives, the basic TV buying strategy. By outlining the parameters in this way the media planner leaves the media buyer free to make decisions about the specific placement of individual spots, for example, does the commercial go into 'Binneland Sub Judice' or '7de Laan', and at what cost?

The final media plan, decorated and presented in the unique individual style of the media planner or media independent, will be a well-reasoned and well substantiated plan to bring the media strategy to fruition.

4.5.4 Monitoring the plan

In many respects it is only after the plan has been booked that the real work begins (Koekemoer, 2004:215–216). It is essential that the media planner monitor all aspects of the media plan and report back not only to the client, but to other members of the agency team. In particular, five aspects need constant scrutiny:

■ *Budget.* It is the planner's responsibility to ensure that the media plan remains within the set budget parameters. During the course of the campaign additional production costs or ad hoc media placements may lead to budget overruns and the media plan must be adjusted accordingly.

■ *Performance.* Every media plan has a clear set of objectives and the media planner must ensure that these objectives are being met.

■ *Environment.* All communication takes place against the framework of competitive marketing activity. The media are also never static and are constantly evolving in terms of both editorial content and readers/viewers/listeners.

■ *Creativity.* The creative work should also be reviewed. If certain assumptions about the creative impact of the advertising have been made, are they being realised?

■ *The brand.* All media objectives and activities flow from the brand's marketing and sales objectives and it is crucial that the media planner monitors very closely the overall effect of the media exposure on the brand's performance.

THE TEN COMMANDMENTS OF MEDIA

Thou shalt not plan without objectives.

Thou shalt tailor thy plan to thy client's marketing needs.

Thou shalt consider thy competitors.

Thou shalt direct thy plan to the right target audience.

Thou shalt take into thy reckoning the strategy of the creative demons.

Thou shalt not bow down before either of the idols Numbers or Gut-feel ... but shalt observe their dictates with discretion and care.

Thou shalt follow with understanding the strategy of the media square.

Thou shalt honour the principle of KISS (Keep it simple, stupid!).

Thou shalt honour thy common sense and clear logical thought.

Thou shalt not plan with undue haste.

Koekemoer (2004:216).

REFERENCES

Arens, W.F. 2002. *Contemporary Advertising*, 8ed Irwin: Homewood, Illinois.

Belch, G.E. and Belch, M.A. 2004. *Advertising and Promotion*, 6ed Irwin: Homewood, Illinois.

Cant, M.C., Strydom, J.W., Jooste, C.J & Du Plessis, P.J. 2006. *Marketing Management*. Juta: Cape Town.

Dunn, S.W. 1969. *Advertising, Its Role in Modern Marketing*, 2ed Holt, Rinehart and Winston: New York.

Du Plessis, F., Bothma, N., Joordan, Y and Van Heerden, N. 2005. *Integrated marketing communication*. New Africa Books: South Africa.

Du Plessis, F., Bothma, N., Joordan, Y and Van Heerden, N. 2003. *Integrated marketing communication*. New Africa Books: South Africa.

Koekemoer, L. (ed) 2004. *Marketing communications*. Juta: Cape Town.

Muller, G. 1999. *Media Planning – Art or Science?* 2ed MASA: Johannesburg.

Shimp, T.A. 2002. *Promotion Management and Marketing Communication*, 6ed The Dreyden Press: Orlando, Florida.

Strydom, J., Jooste, C. and Cant, M. 2000. *Marketing Management*, 4ed Juta: Cape Town.

Principles of Advertising

AIM OF THIS CHAPTER

In this chapter a number of aspects regarding advertising is discussed. These include what advertising is, the classifications of advertising, theories of how advertising works, the role of advertising in marketing, specific tasks of advertising, advertising objectives, models for setting advertising objectives and the role of advertising in building brand equity.

LEARNING OUTCOMES

After studying this chapter you should be competent in:
- defining advertising and explaining the implications of the definition
- outlining the classifications of advertising
- explaining how advertising works by outlining some relevant advertising models
- discussing the role of advertising in the marketing programme
- discussing the nature and importance of advertising objectives
- outlining the models for setting advertising objectives
- discussing the role of advertising in building brand equity

5.1 ADVERTISING DEFINED

We can simply define advertising as

a way of telling the market what we want to sell or want to buy, a means of informing existing and potential customers about a product, its special features and benefits and a means of persuading them to buy the product.

More generally the purpose of advertising is to induce potential customers to respond favourably to the offerings of a firm.

Kumar et al suggests the following definition: 'a paid and nonpersonal form of presentation and promotion of ideas, goods or services by an identified sponsor' (Kumar, 2002:1).

Arens (2005:7) defines advertising along similar lines: 'Advertising is the structured and composed nonpersonal communication of information, usually paid for and usually persuasive in nature, about products (goods, services, and ideas) by identified sponsors through various media.'

Advertising is a mass communication process whereby verbal and non-verbal symbols are transmitted through a channel to a receiver with the objective to communicate an idea, change or reinforce an attitude or provide important information about a particular product or service. The advertising process can be explained with Figure 5.1 below.

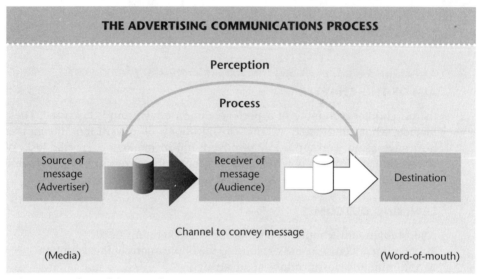

Figure 5.1: Adapted from Aaker (2006:60).

As can be seen from the figure, advertising communication always involves a perception process and four of the elements shown in the model: the source, a message, a communication channel and a receiver. In addition, the receiver will sometimes become a source of information by talking to friends or associates. This type of communication is termed word-of-mouth communication and it involves social interactions between two or more people and the important ideas of group influence and the diffusion of information. An explanation of some of the key terms are given below.

■ **Source**

The source of a message in the advertising communication system is the point of which the message originates. There are many types of 'sources' in the context of advertising, such as the company offering the product, the particular brand or the spokesperson used. The source of the information or message is known as the advertiser. This could be a manufacturer, retailer, service organisation or even the government in some cases. They are of obvious importance in deciding how best and through whom, to communicate the advertising message.

■ **Message**

The message refers to both the content and execution of the advertisement. It is the totality of what is perceived by the receiver of the message. The message can be executed in a great variety of ways and can include for example, the use of humour and fear.

■ **Channel**

The message is transmitted through some channel from
receiver. The channel in an advertising communication
one or more kinds of media, such as radio, television, newspa,
billboards, point-of-purchase displays, Internet, cellphone and so
impact of communication can be different for different media. Word-o
mouth communication represents another channel that is of special interest
because it can sometimes play a key role in an advertising campaign. It
should be noted that any communication system has a channel capacity.
There is only so much information that can be moved through it and only
so much that the receiver will be able to receive and capable of processing.
When the message is transmitted it is picked up or decoded and adopted. The
ultimate goal is to create a positive perception. This depends on attitudes,
values and the experience of the receiver who is known as the audience.

■ **Audience**

The audience is also known as the target market, which is derived through
a segmentation process or exercise based on variables such as geographic,
demographic, psychographic factors, lifestyles, behaviour, etc. Of particular
interest might be the receiver's involvement in the product and the extent to
which he/she is willing to search for and/or process information.

■ **Destination**

The communication model does not stop at the receiver but allows for
the possibility that the initial receiver might engage in word-of-mouth
communication to the ultimate destination of the message. The receiver
then becomes an interim source and the destination becomes another
receiver. The reality is that for some products the absence of word-of-mouth
communication can be fatal. It is only the word-of-mouth communication
that has the credibility, comprehensiveness and impact to affect the ultimate
behaviour of a portion of the audience.

Noise is something that happens all over in this process and it is any external
factor or factors which interferes with the reception of the message and distort
the intended meaning. Examples include the use of contradictory words or
inappropriate illustrations, poor printing quality or fuzzy audio reception
(Engel et al, 1994:32).

Here, then, is the definition of advertising that underlies this text:

> Advertising is 'any paid form of mass presentation of ideas, products and services
> by an advertiser, addressed to selected target audiences with the objective of
> creating awareness, informing, reminding, influencing, and persuading them
> to buy the product or service or to be favourably inclined towards these ideas,
> products or services' (Koekemoer, 2004:67).

From the above definitions, it is clear that the following factors are involved:

◆ *Paid form.* This says exactly what it means – it is paid for and is not free as
in the case of publicity. It is a medium which offer a method of bringing a
message to the market but in order to use it, it must be paid for. Advertising

is a deliberate and sponsored message disseminated through a medium such as TV, radio, print or digital for which payment is made.

◆ *Low-cost mass communication.* Advertising is a means of communication that enables advertisers to deliver a message to a large number of potential customers at the lowest possible cost.

◆ *Ideas, goods and services.* Advertising is concerned with ideas (potential, economic, social), tangible goods (FMCG, durables, etc) or services offered by institutions such as banks, garages and hotels.

◆ *Advertiser.* In advertising, the advertiser is known to the market or their name is made known. This means the market will know who is sending the message to them. The source could, inter alia, be a company, non-profit organisation, political party or an individual.

◆ *Selected target audience.* The reason why a company segments its market or do research to identify needs and wants is to focus their product offering on this selected audience. It is therefore not aimed at everybody. Each advertisement has a target audience it is intended to reach. The advertising message is, therefore, tailor-made to address and influence the selected target audience.

◆ *The objective of the advertisement.* The specific objective varies from one advertisement to another. The ultimate aim of every advertisement is having to persuade the target audience to buy or to be favourably inclined towards the product, specific objectives could be to create awareness, to inform the target audience about the features and benefits of the product, to remind them, to establish a particular, desirable image, to position the brand *vis-á-vis* competitive brands, etc.

5.2   CLASSIFICATION OF ADVERTISING

The classification of advertising can be done in different ways and means, but the four main criteria are its purpose, target audience, geographic area and medium (see Table 5.1). Each of these classifications includes a number of categories that will be discussed briefly.

Table 5.1   **CLASSIFICATION OF ADVERTISING**

PURPOSE	TARGET AUDIENCE
▪ Primary and selective demand	▪ Consumer advertising
▪ Brand advertising	▪ Business-to-business advertising:
▪ Corporate image advertising	- industrial advertising
▪ Commercial/non-commercial advertising	- professional advertising
▪ Action/response advertising	- trade advertising
▪ Retail advertising	

→

GEOGRAPHIC AREA	MEDIUM
▪ National advertising ▪ Regional advertising ▪ Local advertising ▪ International advertising	▪ Print advertising (newspapers and magazines) ▪ Broadcast/electronic advertising (radio, cinema and television) ▪ Outdoor advertising (fixed sites and transit) ▪ Internet

Source: Koekemoer (2004:68).

5.2.1 Classification by purpose

The categories normally covered here are primary and selective demand advertising, product advertising, idea, corporate image, commercial, non-commercial, action/response and retail advertising.

■ *Primary and selective demand advertising.* Primary demand advertising is designed to stimulate demand for the general product class or entire industry, whereas selective demand advertising focuses on creating demand for a particular manufacturer's brand. Most of the advertising for various products and services is concerned with stimulating selective demand and emphasises reasons for buying a particular brand.

Advertisers might concentrate on stimulating primary demand in several situations. When a company's brand dominates a market, its advertising may focus on creating demand for the product class as it will benefit the most from market growth. For example, the Hartbeespoort potato growers want to increase demand for their potatoes. They form a growers' association to promote Hartbeespoort potatoes. However, a member of the potato growers' association, Tri-Me Potatoes, may also want to advertise its company's potato product, 'Tri-Me Potatoes'. In the first instance, the potato growers' association is trying to stimulate primary demand. In the second instance, Tri-Me is trying to stimulate selective demand.

■ *Brand advertising.* Brand advertising is primarily aimed at consumers, but it could also be aimed at the trade and industrial customers. Successful brand advertising creates a demand among consumers so that retailers will put pressure on suppliers (wholesalers and manufacturers) to supply more of the brand in order to meet the demand.

Building demand through brand advertising is not easy. A company must have a brand that both the trade and consumers recognise and they must be convinced that it is better than other brands.

■ *Corporate image advertising.* This is often called non-product or institutional advertising. Corporate image advertising promotes the organisation's mission or philosophy rather than a specific product. For example, Kulula.com airlines is initiating their Project Green to help reduce carbon loads and green house gases released by their aircrafts and increase bio-diversity and conservation of the natural ecosystem. This initiative is to educate people on how to live greener and improve the quality of life and environments for South Africa. A company website is also often considered to be corporate advertising.

■ *Commercial and non-commercial advertising.* While commercial advertising seeks profits, non-commercial advertising is used around the world by governments and non-profit organisations to seek donations, volunteer support or change consumer behaviour (Arens, 2005:17).

Commercial advertising, therefore, includes selective demand, product, direct response, national and retail advertising, while non-commercial advertising includes idea and corporate image advertising.

■ *Action/response advertising.* Some ads are intended to bring about immediate action by the advertisement's audience, others have a longer-term goal. The objective of *awareness/image advertising*, for example, is to create awareness, create interest in and an image for a product and to influence readers or viewers to select a specific brand the next time they shop.

A direct-response ad, eg direct mail however exemplifies action advertising because it seeks an immediate, direct response from the reader.

■ *Retail advertising.* Retail advertising is advertising by large, medium and small retailers that attempts to bring consumers in their target area into their store(s) to buy the merchandise that the store carries or to buy specific brands on special offer.

Retail advertising is usually selling not only individual brands but also the retail establishment as the place to buy a number of brands.

Retail advertising often includes price information, service and return policies, location of the store and hours of operation. Often retailers include a number of brands in a single advertisement to show or promote the range of merchandise available.

5.2.2 Classification by target audience

Two broad categories exist here: consumer advertising and business-to-business advertising (Belch & Belch, 2009:21).

■ *Consumer advertising.* Consumer advertising is aimed at people nationally or locally who buy the brand or service for their own or someone else's use (for the husband or wife, for the family, etc).

One of the fastest growing tools of marketing communications is that of direct marketing. Direct response advertising is a method of direct marketing whereby a product is promoted online or through an advertisement that offers the customer the opportunity to purchase directly from the manufacturer or retailer. Direct response advertising has become very popular in recent years owing primarily to changing lifestyles, particularly the increase in dual-income households. This has meant more discretionary income but less time for in-store shopping. Thus, the convenience of shopping through the mail, by telephone or online has led to the tremendous increase in direct response advertising.

■ *Business-to-business advertising.* For many companies, the ultimate customer is not the mass consumer market but rather another business, industry or profession. Business-to-business advertising is used by one business to advertise its products or services to another.

The target for business advertising is people who either use a product or service or influence a firm's decision to purchase another company's product or service. Three basic categories of business-to-business advertising are industrial, professional and trade advertising.

◆ *Industrial advertising.* Advertising targeted at individuals who buy or influence the purchase of industrial goods or other services is known as industrial advertising. Industrial goods are those products that either become a physical part of another product (raw material, component parts, etc), are used in the manufacture of other goods (machinery, equipment, etc) or are used to help the manufacturer conduct business (office supplies, computers, copy machines, etc).

◆ *Professional advertising.* Advertising that is targeted at professional groups – such as doctors, lawyers, dentists, engineers or ad agencies – to encourage them to use or specify the advertiser's product for others' use, is known as professional advertising. For example, pharmaceutical companies advertise in medical journals and in sales aids to doctors to encourage them to prescribe their products to patients.

Professional advertising should not be confused with advertising done by professionals. In recent years, advertising by professionals such as dentists, lawyers and doctors has been growing in popularity as legal restrictions have been removed and competition has increased.

◆ *Trade advertising.* Trade advertising is advertising directed at wholesalers, retailers and agents to convince them to carry (or push) certain national brands in their inventory or to list them and sell them to consumers. Before consumers have an opportunity to purchase a product it must be available in retail stores. Manufacturers use trade advertising to promote their products to wholesalers and retailers. Trade advertising tends to emphasise the product's profitability and the consumer demand that will create high turnover of the product for the retailer.

Trade advertising can be used to get initial trial for a product, increase trade support and announce consumer promotions. Ultimately the aim is to get the trade to stock the product and become regular buyers of the products. If they tried it and liked it they will buy it again.

5.2.3 Advertising by geographic area

Depending on the supplier, available resources and the target audience the advertising can be national, regional, local and even international (or global).

The term national advertising refers to advertising by multinational marketers or the owner of a trademarked product (brand) or service sold through different distribution outlets, wherever they may be. It does not necessarily mean that the product is sold nationwide, but in all major centres.

National advertising is usually image-creating and the most general in terms of product information: aspects such as price, retail availability and even service and installation are often omitted from national advertising. Since each retailer will play a major role in the final sale of the product, national ads for companies such as Lever Brothers, Colgate, Procter & Gamble, etc cannot be extremely specific. National advertising seeks to establish demand for a brand, especially one sold through self-service outlets. Ideally the customer comes into the retail store already presold on a certain brand because of its national advertising. Sometimes a marketer prefers to focus on a particular region and uses regional media. Normally the advertising will say 'only in Gauteng' or 'only in the Western Cape', etc.

Local advertising is done mostly by retailers or local merchants in local newspapers or radio stations to encourage consumers to shop at a specific store or to use a local service such as a restaurant or fitness club or hairdressing salon, etc. While national advertisers focus more on the brand, local advertisers focus more on giving customers a reason to patronise their particular outlet. Therefore, aspects like trading hours, credit facilities, expertise, service, store atmosphere, variety of products, etc are stressed. International advertising is mostly used by multinational marketing companies like L'Oreal, Nestle, Colgate, Coca-Cola, etc to promote their brands to the trade and to consumers. In many cases the brands are well-known all over the world and the advertising approach is the same, although the execution may allow for different models, different languages, cultural issues, etc.

5.2.4 Advertising by medium

Most of the advertising we see every day appears in mass media. The media could be split between print media (newspapers and magazines), broadcast or electronic media (radio and television), cinema and outdoor media (hoardings, transit media, etc). These are popularly known as above-the-line media. Sales promotions and direct marketing efforts (including the Internet) are known as below-the-line media. These also include digital media (social, mobile, etc). Through-the-line efforts are integrated efforts cutting across all media.

5.3   HOW ADVERTISING WORKS

We have looked at what advertising is and the types of advertising, but now we need to look at how it actually works. Simply put, the aim of advertising is to 'turn people's minds around'. This is achieved through six stages: exposure, attention, comprehension, acceptance, retention and action.

- *Exposure*. This refers to exposing the target audience to the advertising message. Since consumers tend to be selective in their demand for products they need to be exposed again and again to get the persuasion process in motion.

- *Attention*. The first job of advertising is to create awareness or grab attention. This is achieved by choosing something unique or different from the norm – by being obviously different.

- *Comprehension*. Noticing an advertisement initially does not mean you understand the message. Comprehension deals with meaning. It involves the clear understanding of the message by the target audience as intended by the sponsor.

- *Acceptance*. This is where the target audience accepts the message because it is credible and conforms to their existing beliefs and attitudes. The activities, image, models, etc in the advertising message must be acceptable.

- *Retention*. Retention deals with long-term memory. By means of reminder advertising, the competitive urge for a product could be entrenched.

- *Action*. The ultimate purpose of all advertising is to persuade customers to buy. However, most advertising is created to inform the target audience, create preference, build image and eventually lead to patronage by the target audience.

For an advertising message to be communicated successfully it should, therefore, be targeted at the right audience, capable of gaining attention, understandable, relevant and acceptable. For effective communication to occur, messages should be designed that fit the cognitive capability of the target audience and follow the model of how advertising works. Unfortunately, there is no such single model despite years of research and speculation by a great many people.

But what is the fundamental premise by which advertising is thought to work? Fill (1999:269-71) says that there are two polarised views of this subject: the first is referred to as the *strong theory of advertising* and the second as the *weak theory of advertising*.

- *The strong theory of advertising*. The strong theory of advertising assumes that advertising is capable of effecting a degree of change in the knowledge, attitudes, beliefs or behaviour of target audiences. This theory appears to have been universally adopted as a foundation for commercial activity.

  The theory holds that advertising can persuade someone to buy a product that he or she has never previously purchased. Furthermore, continual long-run purchase behaviour can also be generated. Under the strong theory, advertising is believed to be capable of increasing sales at the brand and the product-type levels. These upward shifts are achieved through the use of manipulative and psychological techniques that are deployed against consumers who are passive, possibly due to apathy, and are generally incapable of processing information intelligently.

■ *The weak theory of advertising.* This theory states that the strong theory does not reflect the real world and believes that a consumer's pattern of brand purchases is driven more by habit than by exposure to advertising. According to the weak theory, advertising is capable of improving people's awareness and knowledge. In contrast to the previous theory, however, consumers are selective in determining which advertisements they observe and only perceive those that promote products that they either use or have some prior knowledge of. This means that in most cases they already have some awareness of the characteristics of the advertised product. It follows that the amount of information actually communicated is limited. Advertising is not potent enough to convert people who hold reasonably strong beliefs that are counter to those portrayed in an advertisement. The space of a print or outdoor ad and the time availability (thirty seconds) in radio or television advertising is not enough to bring about conversion, and when combined with people's ability to switch off their cognitive involvement there may be no effective communication. Advertising is employed as a defence, to retain customers and perhaps to increase their usage. Advertising is mainly used to reinforce existing attitudes.

Unlike the strong theory, this perspective accepts that when people say that advertising does not influence them they are generally correct. It also assumes that people are not apathetic or unintelligent and are capable of high levels of cognitive processing.

Therefore, the *strong theory* suggests that advertising can be persuasive, can generate long-run purchasing behaviour and increase sales. The *weak theory* suggests that purchase behaviour is based on habit, that advertising can improve knowledge and reinforces existing attitudes. These two perspectives serve to illustrate the dichotomy of views that has emerged about this subject. The theories are important because they are both right and they are both wrong. The answer to the question 'How does advertising work?' lies somewhere between the two views and is dependent on the particular situation facing each advertiser. Where elaboration is likely to be high and if advertising is to work, then it is most likely to work under the strong theory. For example, advertising for consumer durables and financial products should urge prospective customers into some form of trial behaviour. This may require further explanation by a sales representative, a demonstration, a contract, etc. The vast majority of product purchases, however, involve low levels of elaboration, where involvement is minimal and where people select brands, often unconsciously, from a number of alternatives. Reminder advertising, confirming attitudes and beliefs, may be sufficient here.

New products require people to convert or change their purchasing patterns. It is evident that the strong theory must prevail in these circumstances. Where products become established their markets generally mature so that real growth is non-existent. Under these circumstances advertising works by protecting the consumer franchise and by allowing users to have their product choices confirmed and reinforced. The other objective of this form of advertising is to increase the rate at which customers reselect and consume products. If the strong theory was the only acceptable approach then theoretically advertising would be capable of continually increasing the size of each market until everyone had been converted. There would be no 'stationary' or saturated markets.

Considering the vast sums that are allocated to advertising budgets, not only to launch new products but also to pursue market share targets aggressively, the popularity and continued implicit acceptance of the power of advertising suggest that a large proportion of resources must be wasted in the pursuit of advertising-driven brand performance. Indeed, it is noticeable that since the early 1980s, organisations have increasingly switched resources out of advertising into sales promotion activities. There are many reasons for this, but one of them concerns the failure of advertising to produce the anticipated levels of performance, to increase market share. In fact, many marketers believe that advertising is unable to actually get the sale: while the effects of advertising in increasing brand awareness and favourable attitudes for the brand are easily believed, effects on sales are less believable. It is thus often useful, after advertising creates such awareness and brand liking, to supplement advertising with sales promotions (both consumer promotions and trade promotions), which are often more effective in actually getting consumers to try the brand. Such sales promotions may be especially required if research shows, during the situation analysis, that target consumers are aware of the brand and think it has the features they are looking for but have not yet tried it.

In summary, then, the strong theory fails to deliver the expected results. On the other hand, the weak theory may not apply to all circumstances. Reality is often a mixture of the two.

5.4 THE ROLE OF ADVERTISING IN THE MARKETING PROGRAMME

Advertising planning and decision-making take place in the context of an overall marketing strategy. The marketing strategy includes a statement of marketing objectives and the spelling out of particular methods and tactics to reach those objectives. The marketing objective should identify the target segments to be served by the organisation and explain how it is going to serve them. The expectations, needs and wants of target market consumers are identified and analysed in preparing a marketing plan.

Once the marketing plan has been prepared the advertising plan can be prepared including aspects like advertising objectives, message strategy and media strategy. Figure 5.2 (on the following page) outlines the above.

The planning process begins with a thorough analysis of the situation facing the advertiser. Situation analysis involves an examination of all important factors operating in a particular situation. In many cases this means that as well as relying on company history and experience new research will be undertaken. The situation analysis should focus on the market issues (size, trends, buying habits,

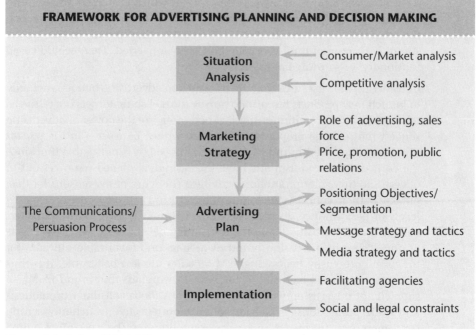

FRAMEWORK FOR ADVERTISING PLANNING AND DECISION MAKING

Situation Analysis ← Consumer/Market analysis / Competitive analysis

Marketing Strategy → Role of advertising, sales force / Price, promotion, public relations

The Communications/Persuasion Process → Advertising Plan → Positioning Objectives/Segmentation / Message strategy and tactics / Media strategy and tactics

Implementation ← Facilitating agencies / Social and legal constraints

Figure 5.2: Aaker (2006:53).

loyal customers, etc), an analysis of the product (features, benefits, competitive advantages, etc) and a competitive analysis (relative strengths and weaknesses, history of competitive moves, advertising expenditure, push or pull strategy, etc).

The advertising plan can never be viewed in isolation. It is always part of the bigger picture, the marketing communications plan or promotional mix. The promotional mix is heavily influenced by whether the company chooses the push or pull strategy to create sales.

The push strategy involves marketing activities (primarily sales force and trade promotion) directed at channel intermediaries to induce them to order and carry the product and promote it to end users as depicted in Figure 5.3. Note, however, that direct marketing is a push strategy directed at final consumers.

A pull strategy involves marketing activities (primarily advertising and consumer promotions) directed at end users to induce them to ask intermediaries for the product, and thus induce the intermediaries to order the product from the manufacturer.

An interesting way of examining the specific tasks of advertising and its role in marketing is to relate them to the various stages of the PLC as well as to consumer behaviour in the relevant stages.

■ *Building awareness.* Generally speaking, it is easy to understand that building awareness is one of the specific tasks of advertising when a new product or service is introduced. It is the act of taking potential customers from a

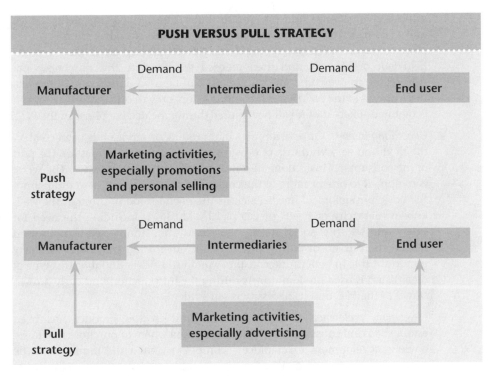

Figure 5.3: Adapted from Koekemoer (2004:82).

state of blissful ignorance to interested awareness. Advertising is focused on getting attention and should, therefore, be creative, bold and aggressive. The relevant consumer behaviour characteristic at this stage is that of extensive problem solving, which means that the consumers are being faced with new concepts, ideas and/or products and, therefore, have to resolve problems that arise in their own minds. There are many forms of awareness-building advertisements, the most common of which is the straight announcement of a new product or service.

■ *Informing the target audience.* Closely allied to the previous task (building awareness), the dissemination of knowledge is, in a general sense, that of 'spreading the gospel'. In other words, this task is a type of missionary work in which the main purpose of advertising is to persuade people to try something new. An example is cellphones: many consumers might have been unsure when this new product was first launched and the manufacturers had to persuade people that it was worth trying by putting out extensive information on the product. This type of advertising is used predominantly in the introduction stage of the PLC and again in the extensive problem solving phase of consumer behaviour.

■ *Overcoming misconceptions.* Often consumers have misconceptions about products or services that prevent them from purchasing these items. Unfortunately, manufacturers may not know of these secret fears, concerns or misconceptions and are, therefore, mystified when their marketing efforts are not successful. Research is the answer for establishing what it is that is inhibiting consumers and preventing them from purchasing such product, and once their misconceptions have been established, advertising is a very powerful medium for overcoming them. Advertising can articulate a secretly-held fear or concern and then proceed to eliminate this misconception. Advertising to overcome misconceptions can be used during any of the first three phases of the PLC that is the introduction, growth and maturity stages. It is highly unlikely that it will be required during the decline phase of the PLC.

■ *Generating interest.* Once awareness of a product or service has been created, the next and very vital task of advertising is to generate interest on the part of the consumer. This is done in a number of fairly obvious ways. The secret is to appeal to one or more of the consumer's basic needs. These range from the basic physiological needs (such as the need for food), through the well-known hierarchy of needs (developed by Maslow), including the need for safety and security, social needs, ego needs and, finally, self-actualisation needs. There is no disputing the fact that advertising plays an extremely important role in generating consumer interest. Understandably, this type of advertising is used predominantly during the introduction and early growth stages of the PLC and its necessity is self-evident.

■ *Developing preference.* Once a basic interest in the product has been established and consumers have been informed where to purchase it, a fairly obvious development takes place – competitors enter the market and the consumer is faced with a different type of problem. The consumer now has to choose between different brands or manufacturers. This behaviour pattern is described as limited problem solving, which is basically choosing between the alternatives offered. In this regard the very important function of building brand preference for a particular manufacturer's product is the challenge facing advertising. Encouraging consumers to switch to a particular brand or to remain with it if they have already purchased it, is the basic task of advertising in this phase of the PLC.

■ *Supporting the sales force.* Marketers expect advertising to lead to sales, to increase consumer demand and to increase market share. Immediate sales may not be possible due to the fact that advertising is just one of many factors contributing to sales and most advertising works over an extended period. However, retailers will list products and even give more shelf space to those brands that are supported by advertising. Advertising can give the sales force confidence in the brand and help them to obtain larger orders, expand the distribution and improve trade relations.

■ *Generating leads.* This is the so-called direct response task of advertising in marketing. It simply means that an advertisement will generate a direct inquiry from a customer that the firm can follow up and, hopefully, convert to a sale. Of course, it is used predominantly during the introduction and growth stages of the PLC, although many firms successfully use this type of advertising throughout the PLC. It stands to reason that the type of product involved will be an important factor here since it is self-evident that a low unit-price product would not use this type of advertising. However, a very sophisticated high unit-price product that would justify an individual follow-up would certainly use this type of advertising.

- *Positioning the product.* This is one of the most important tasks of advertising. It is most commonly used during the growth stage of the PLC when consumers are starting to see competitive products advertised and are, therefore, seeking to establish some position for a particular product in their own minds. The easiest way to get into a person's mind is, of course, to get in first! But if it cannot be first then the company concerned must find a way to position itself against the competitive product that got there first. Porsche, for example, is positioned in the prestige segment of the car market; Duracell is positioned as the longer-life and hence better value battery; brands such as Quicksilver are positioned to appeal to the urban street warrior; while Kulula.com is positioned as a low-cost airline. There is no doubt whatsoever that advertising plays a significant role in product positioning.

- *Building credibility.* Marketers should never underestimate the power of the printed word. If consumers see a product advertised regularly and in a consistent way there is no doubt that the legitimacy of the company and its products is established in their minds. This is particularly relevant during the growth stage of the PLC.

- *Building image.* Once again this task of advertising is particularly relevant during the growth stage of the PLC. Closely allied to product positioning, image building simply means that the marketer attempts to build a unique image for his or her product as compared with competitive products. Advertising is well-known for its ability to create a particular image. An important factor to be taken into consideration when building image is that there should be consistency of the advertising message over a long period.

- *Reassuring purchasers and creating trust.* The task of advertising in reassuring purchasers of a company's product or service is a very important one. It is used in virtually all stages of the PLC, although obviously it has major application during the introduction and growth stages. The phenomenon referred to when a customer has a concern about a purchase is cognitive dissonance. This simply means that after purchasing a product a consumer may fear that he or she has done the wrong thing and question the wisdom of the decision to purchase. For example, Scooters Pizza has been incredibly successful by setting expectations for fast delivery and then beating them. They claim they'll deliver your pizza in 39 minutes or it's free. This service level will make a huge impression on customers, reassuring them of their decision. There are many subtle ways of reassuring purchasers that they have made the right choice. The manufacturers of a particular brand of shirt include in the packaging a note complimenting the purchaser on his or her selection and reassuring him or her that he or she has bought a top-quality garment that will give him or her maximum satisfaction.

- *Reminding consumers.* When a product reaches the maturity stage of the PLC and consumers are no longer attracted by its novelty, they nevertheless have to be reminded about its existence. Advertising plays a significant role in this respect and does a number of very specific things. First, it reminds consumers about the product and their perhaps successful use of it over along period of time. It also reminds consumers where the product is available. It seeks to maintain what is known as 'top-of-mind' awareness of the product so that the moment the consumer requires a product of that category the manufacturer's particular brand will come to mind as a result of the continuous advertising to which the consumer has been exposed over a long period of time.

In this phase of the PLC, consumer behaviour is often referred to as routinised response behaviour. This implies that the consumer makes a purchasing decision as a matter of routine and, therefore, needs constant reminding of what to select. Advertising is the most powerful element of the marketing communication mix with which this can be done.

Advertising can however not be everything. There are some things it can and cannot do and the following are some of these things what can and cannot be done by advertising:

WHAT ADVERTISING CAN AND CANNOT DO

ADVERTISING CAN

- remind the target audience to buy;
- announce a new brand or service;
- create brand awareness;
- stimulate impulse buying;
- expand the market and attract new buyers;
- affect direct sales and encourage enquiries;
- announce a price change;
- announce a pack change or a special offer;
- change attitudes;
- increase confidence in a brand or a company;
- reinforce a buying decision and reduce post-purchase blues (cognitive dissonance);
- remind consumers about products, features, etc;
- fight competition;
- increase sales;
- support stockists; and
- support sales and counter staff.

ADVERTISING CANNOT

- 'sell' an inferior product;
- reach everybody;
- lead to immediate sales (not always);
- fight off better competitors;
- solve all your marketing problems;
- save a dying brand (not alone); or
- persuade everyone.

Figure 5.4: Koekemoer (2004:87).

5.5 ADVERTISING OBJECTIVES

Before we can discuss the types of advertising objectives and the models for setting them, it is essential to focus on the criteria for establishing good advertising objectives.

5.5.1 Criteria for setting objectives

Shimp (2007:162–163) states the following six criteria that good advertising objectives must satisfy:

- *Objectives must include a precise statement of who, what and when.* Objectives must be stated in precise terms. At a minimum, objectives should specify the target audience (who), indicate the specific goal to be accomplished (what, such as awareness level) and indicate the relevant time frame (when) in which to achieve the objective. Objectives must be hierarchical: going from the most important to the least important.

- *Objectives must be quantitative and measurable.* This is important in order to avoid ambiguity. This requirement implies that advertising objectives should be stated in quantitative terms. A non-measurable objective would be a vague statement such as 'advertising should increase consumers' knowledge of product features'. This objective lacks measurability because it fails to specify the particular product features. The objective 'to increase market share' is not as satisfactory a guideline as 'to increase market share by 5 per cent' or indeed 'to increase market share by 5 percentage points within 18 months'.

- *Objectives must specify the amount of change.* In addition to being quantitative and measurable, objectives must specify the amount of change they are intended to accomplish. To 'increase sales' fails to meet this requirement. To 'increase awareness from 60 to 90 per cent' is highly satisfactory because it clearly specifies that anything less than a 30 per cent awareness increase would be considered unsuitable performance.

- *Objectives must be realistic.* It is only too easy for objectives to reflect a degree of wishful thinking; instead they should be developed as the result of a detailed analysis of opportunities, corporate capability, competitive strengths and competitive strategy. Unrealistic objectives are as useless as having no objectives at all. An unrealistic objective is one that cannot be accomplished within the budget or the time allotted to the proposed advertising investment. For example, it is not realistic to expect a small advertising budget to produce an increase to, say, 65 per cent consumer awareness for a brand that has achieved only 15 per cent awareness during its first two years on the market.

- *Objectives must be internally consistent.* It is quite obviously unrealistic to pursue incompatible objectives; as an example of this, to aim for substantial gains in both sales and profits simultaneously is rarely possible. Advertising objectives must be compatible (internally consistent) with objectives set for other components of the marketing communication mix. It would be inconsistent for a manufacturer of packaged goods to proclaim a 25 per cent reduction in the sales force while simultaneously stating that the advertising objective is to increase retail distribution by 20 per cent. Without adequate sales force effort it is doubtful that the retail trade would give a brand more shelf space.

- ■ *Objectives must be clear and in writing.* For objectives to accomplish their purposes of fostering communication and permitting evaluation they must be stated clearly and in writing so that they can be disseminated among their users and among those who will be held responsible for seeing that the objectives are accomplished.

It is also essential that they satisfy the SMART criteria for being Specific rather than general in nature, Measurable, Actionable, Realistic and Timebased.

5.5.2 Types of advertising objectives

There are different types of advertising objectives that can be set. It is also important that every marketing communication plan using advertising must have an objective. Advertising that tries to be all things to all people tends not to be very effective. It is vital, therefore, to develop clear and precise objectives for all advertising. These objectives should describe the target audience and the effect or response that the communicator seeks or aims to have on the target audience. There are three major types of objectives: informational, attitudinal and behavioural.

Table 5.2 on the following page outlines these three types of objectives, the specific task that the advertising is expected to perform and the intended end result. It is clear from this table that the informational objectives of advertising have the task of creating awareness and knowledge with the behavioural end result of trial usage, increased usage or sales leads. The attitudinal objectives have the task of associating the brand with a user type, creating brand attitudes and associating feelings with brand use in order to lead to loyalty. Behavioural objectives, on the other hand, have the task of using awareness, knowledge, brand attitudes, etc to create trial purchase or repeat purchase.

One could also simply say that advertising objectives can be direct or indirect. Direct objectives are those that seek an overt behavioural response by retailers or a direct response from the audience, for example, trial or purchase. Indirect objectives are aimed at communication tasks that need to be accomplished before overt behavioural responses can be achieved, for example, create brand awareness, disseminate information and create knowledge in order to establish a particular image, create brand attitudes, etc.

5.6   THE ROLE OF ADVERTISING IN BUILDING BRAND EQUITY

As an introduction to the discussion of the role of advertising in building brand equity, it may be worthwhile to consider what Aaker, Batra and Meyers (2006: 331–332) say about building strong brands.

Table 5.2 **TYPES OF OBJECTIVES**

TYPE OF OBJECTIVE	SPECIFIC TASK	END RESULT
Informational	Advertising → Brand awareness	→ Trial purchase
	Advertising → Brand awareness → knowledge of brand attributes/ benefits	→ Trial purchase
	Advertising → Knowledge of new application	→ Increase usage
	Advertising → Knowledge about brand and company	→ Sales leads/sales via personal selling
Attitudinal	Advertising → Associate brand with user type	→ Loyalty
	Advertising → Brand attitude/liking	→ Loyalty
	Advertising → Associate feelings with brand use/ positive	→ Loyalty
Behavioural	Advertising → Brand awareness → knowledge of brand attributes → brand attitude	→ Trial purchase/ repeat purchase
	Advertising → Knowledge of brand attributes/ benefits	→ Trial purchase/ repeat purchase
	Advertising → Brand attitude/liking	

Source: Koekemoer (2004:89).

A brand can have high equity, or value as a tradable asset, for many reasons. According to David Aaker, brand have equity because they have high awareness; many loyal customers; a high reputation for perceived quality; proprietary brand assets such as access to scarce distribution channels or to patens; or the kind of brand associations (such as personality associations). A schematic version of Aaker's brand equity framework appears in Figure 5.5 on page 119. As can be seen in the figure, this equity of the brand is 'captured' in the name and symbol of the brand.

Consumers prefer high-equity brands because they find it easier to interpret what benefits the brand offers, feel more confident of it, and get more satisfaction from using it. Because of such consumer preference, the brand can charge a higher price, command more loyalty, and run more efficient marketing programs (eg it can spend less on retailer incentive and it costs less to launch brand extensions). The brand can therefore command higher asset value.

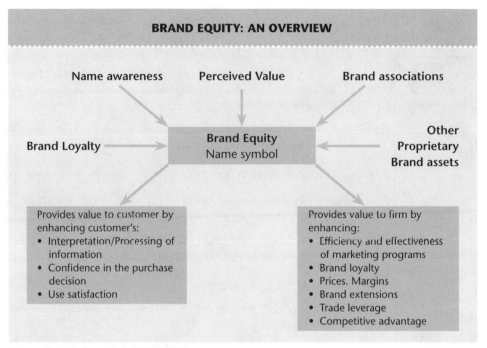

Figure 5.5: Aaker et al (2006:332).

5.6.1 Brand awareness

Brand awareness can produce a lasting competitive advantage (Aaker, 2001:165–166) for the following reasons:

■ Brand awareness provides the brand with a sense of familiarity and people like the familiar. For low-involvement products, such as soap or chewing gum, familiarity can drive the buying decision.

■ Name awareness can be a signal of presence, commitment and substance – attributes that can be very important even to industrial buyers of big-ticket items and consumer buyers of durables. The logic is that if a name is recognised there must be a reason for it.

■ The salience of a brand will be determined if it is recalled at a critical time in the purchasing process, for instance, the initial step in selecting an advertising agency, a car to test drive or a computer system to consider.

Brand awareness is an asset that can be remarkably durable and sustainable. It can be very difficult to dislodge a brand that has achieved a dominant awareness level. Consider the power of the high awareness of Coca-Cola, Sunlight, Omo, Panasonic, Nokia, Toyota, etc.

5.6.2 Brand associations

Aaker (2001:167) defines this as 'the association attached to a firm and its brands'. A brand association is anything that is directly or indirectly linked in memory to a brand. These associations could be linked to the rational elements and/or the emotional elements of a brand. It could culminate in a brand positioning.

Although Brand X cola may win blind taste tests over Coca-Cola, the fact is that more people buy Coke than any other cola, and most important, they enjoy the experience of buying and drinking Coca-Cola. The most common association is that of product attributes or customer benefits, for example, value for money, durability, safety, etc.

A brand's associations are assets that can differentiate, provide reasons to buy, instill confidence and trust, affect attitudes towards a product and provide the basis for brand extensions.

5.6.3 Perceived quality

Perceived quality is the value that customers place on products. Perceived quality affects Return On Investment (ROI) directly because the cost of retaining customers is reduced, and indirectly because it allows a higher price to be charged and enhances the market share. Furthermore, perceived quality does not increase costs. Enhanced quality may lead to reduced defects and lower manufacturing costs.

The conclusion that can be drawn from the above is that brand equity is built via sustained creative communication of a brand's benefits to the consumer and backing it with a product that delivers over time.

5.6.4 Brand reputation

A brand builds a reputation through advertising (its positioning), its performance, its acceptability, its wide usage, its value for money perception, its features, benefits, competitive advantage, etc.

5.6.5 Brand loyalty

Brand loyalty involves faithful use and purchase of a product. A prime enduring asset for some businesses is the loyalty of its customer base. Aaker (2001:168–169) identifies five sustainable competitive advantages derived from an existing base of loyal customers:

■ Firstly, it reduces the marketing costs of doing business since existing customers usually are relatively easy to hold because the familiar is comfortable and reassuring. Keeping existing customers happy and reducing their motivation to change is generally considerably less costly than trying to reach new customers and persuading them to try another brand.

■ Secondly, the loyalty of existing customers represents a substantial entry barrier to competitors. Excessive resources are required when entering a market in which existing customers must be enticed away from an established brand that they are loyal to or even just satisfied with.

- Thirdly, brand loyalty provides trade leverage. Strong loyalty towards a brand will ensure preferred shelf space because stores know that customers include such brands on their shopping lists.

- Fourthly, a relatively large, satisfied customer base provides an image of a brand as an accepted, successful, enduring product with service backup and continuing product improvement.

- Finally, a base of loyal customers provides the time to respond to competitive moves – it gives a firm some breathing space to either match or neutralise the competitor's actions.

REFERENCES

Aaker, D.A. 2001. *Strategic Market Management*, 6ed John Wiley & Sons: New York.

Aaker, D.A. 2002. *Building Strong Brands*. Simon & Schuster, London.

Aaker, D.A., Batra, R. and Meyers, J.G. 2006. *Advertising Management*, 5ed Prentice Hall: Englewood Cliffs, New Jersey.

Arens, W.F. 2005. *Contemporary Advertising*, 10ed Irwin: Homewood, Illinois.

Avery, J. 2000. *Advertising Campaign Planning*. The Copy Workshop: Chicago.

Belch, G.E. and Belch, M.A. 2009. *Advertising and Promotion*, 8ed Irwin: Homewood, Illinois.

Fill, C. 1999. *Marketing Communications. Contents, Contexts and Strategies*, 2ed Prentice Hall: Hertfordshire, UK.

Jones, J.P. and Slater, J.S. 2003. What's in a name. *Advertising and the concept of brands*, 2ed M.E. Sharpe Inc, New York.

Koekemoer, L. and Bird, S. 1998. *Promotional strategy: Marketing communications in Practice*. Juta: Cape Town.

Koekemoer, L. Bird, S. 2004. *Marketing communications*. Juta: Cape Town.

Kotler, P. 2000. *Marketing Management. Analysis, Planning, Implementation and Control*, 7ed Prentice Hall: Englewood Cliffs, New Jersey.

Kotler, P. 2008. *Marketing Management*, 13ed Prentice Hall: Upper Saddle River, New Jersey.

Kumar, N. and Mittal, R. 2002. *Advertising Management*. Anmol Publications: India.

Wilson, R.M.S. and Gilligan, C. 2005. *Strategic marketing management: planning, implementation and control*. 3ed Elsevier: United Kingdom.

Shimp, T.A. 2007. *Integrated Marketing Communication in Advertising and Promotion*. 8ed The Dryden Press: Orlando, Florida.

6 Principles of Personal Selling

....

AIM OF THIS CHAPTER

This chapter highlights the essence of personal selling and demonstrate its advantages over other forms of marketing communication. It also seeks to discuss the promotion rule, the sales communication process, persuasive selling communication, the typical sales tasks, sales positions, the scope and nature of a salesperson's activities, what a salesperson should know, the buying decision, the future of personal selling and some ethical issues in selling.

LEARNING OUTCOMES

After studying this chapter you should be competent in:
- ◼ describing the advantages of personal selling over the other elements of the marketing communication mix
- ◼ explaining the sales communication process and the role of persuasive communication in selling
- ◼ discussing the importance of using questions in selling
- ◼ describing the sales tasks performed by a salesperson
- ◼ describing the scope and nature of a typical salesperson's activities
- ◼ explaining what a salesperson should know in order to improve sales performance
- ◼ describing the steps in the buying decision process
- ◼ describing the modern selling task and the various trends taking place in the profession of selling
- ◼ explaining the various ethical issues that arise in selling

....

6.1 SELLING, SALESMANSHIP AND PERSONAL SELLING

The American Marketing Association defines selling as 'the personal or impersonal process of assisting and/or persuading a prospect to buy a commodity or service and to act favourably upon an idea that has commercial significance to the seller'. Another definition highlights selling as *the art of persuading people to want what the salesperson has – in terms of products, services or ideas*. This basically implies the dual effect of establishing and persuading: establishing people's needs and wants and persuading people to use the company's products or services to satisfy them. The art of salesmanship has also had its share of definitions, one being that *salesmanship is the art of teaching or helping others to buy*. Another definition maintains that salesmanship is *the art of persuading somebody to either accept or follow the ideas of the salesperson and therefore lead them to the action desired.*

For the purpose of this chapter personal selling can be defined as follows:

Personal selling is a person-to-person process by which the seller learns about the prospective buyer's wants and seeks to satisfy them by offering suitable goods or services and making a sale.

Regardless of which definition is preferred, persuasion is ultimately at the core of personal selling and salesmanship.

6.2 ADVANTAGES AND DISADVANTAGES OF PERSONAL SELLING

In many companies, sales personnel are the single most important link with the customer – therefore, the best conceived and executed marketing effort can fail if the sales force is ineffective. Personal selling has the following advantages and disadvantages:

- ■ *Advantages.* These advantages arise from the fact that it involves face-to-face communication with a potential customer. Personal sales messages are usually more persuasive than the other tools of marketing communications. The advantages of personal selling include the following:
  - ◆ *Obligation.* In a face-to-face setting, prospective buyers are more likely to feel obliged to pay attention to the salesperson's message.
  - ◆ *Tailored messages.* Since the salesperson communicates with only one potential customer at a time, she or he can tailor the message to suit the customer's specific needs.
  - ◆ *Immediate feedback.* Communication flows in both directions during the personal selling process. The customer provides feedback in the form of questions, a frown, a laugh, an objection or through positive or negative body language. This enables the salesperson to establish whether a particular sales approach is working. If it isn't, the salesperson can respond immediately with a different approach.
  - ◆ *Complex information.* A salesperson can communicate a greater amount of complex information than can be transmitted with other marketing communication tools.
  - ◆ *Demonstrations.* Products can be demonstrated and visual aids can be used to get the sales message across.
  - ◆ *Customer education.* In many instances, the salesperson is likely to make a number of calls on the same client, thus providing sufficient time to educate the client about the product's benefits and advantages.
  - ◆ *Relationship building.* The salesperson is at the forefront of relationship building. By making regular calls on a customer she or he has the opportunity to build a positive relationship on behalf of the company.

◆ *Qualified prospects.* Personal selling can be specifically directed at qualified prospects, whereas the other forms of marketing communication can be wasted because many people in the audience are not prospective buyers.

◆ *Expenses match requirements.* Advertising and sales promotion often require substantial budgets, whereto the size of the sales force and the attendant expenses can be established to match requirements.

◆ *Closing the sale.* Probably the most important advantage of personal selling over other forms of marketing communication is that it is considerably more effective in closing the sale and getting the signature on the order form.

◆ *Bottom-line responsibility.* While advertising, public relations and sales promotion pave the way for personal selling and act in a supportive capacity, the sales function has direct bottom-line responsibility for obtaining orders.

■ *Disadvantages.* There are not many disadvantages of personal selling, but they are worth noting. These are:

◆ *Small number of contacts.* Sales people only have a limited amount of time to call on prospects. Consequently they can only communicate with a relatively small number of potential customers per day.

◆ *Costs per call.* Expenses, such as travel, are incurred when making a sales call and opportunity costs in terms of waiting time should also be considered. Therefore, the cost per call is usually higher than that of other marketing communication elements.

◆ *Poor selling skills.* A poorly trained salesperson can do more harm than good for the organisation's marketing effort.

6.3 THE PROMOTION RULE

The decision concerning how much emphasis to give personal selling relative to the other tools in the promotion mix depends on the task that must be accomplished. These communication tasks are determined by the company's marketing objectives and strategy, by its resources, the kinds of customers in its target market and by the nature of the other three elements in the marketing mix, namely the product, the price and distribution (or place).

A general rule on promotion (the fourth 'P' in the marketing mix) states that as the complexity of the product increases, the value of the product grows but the number of potential customers decreases (see Figure 6.1 on p124). It then becomes economically feasible, assuming sufficient product value, to incur the necessary time and travel costs to personally visit a prospect.

In contrast, as the value of the product decreases, the number of potential buyers increases, as in the case of Fast Moving Consumer Goods (FMCG) where advertising becomes the more cost-effective way to promote the product (see Figure 6.2 on p124).

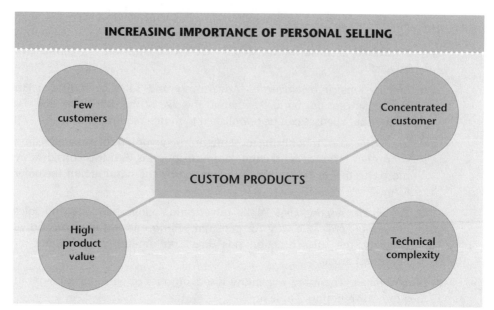

Figure 6.1: Koekemoer (2004:224).

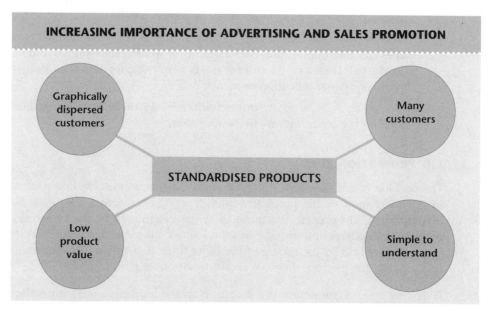

Figure 6.2: Adapted from Koekemoer (2004:224).

6.4 THE SALES COMMUNICATION PROCESS

Communication, in a sales context, is the act of transmitting verbal and nonverbal information and understanding between seller and buyer (Blem, 2003:47). A simple communication model which illustrates how the salesperson or buyer communication process works is shown in Figure 6.3 below.

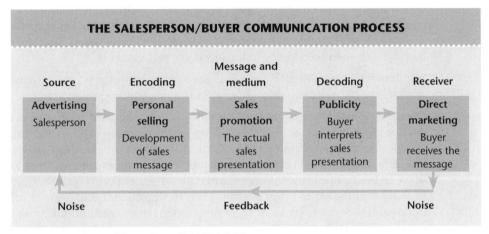

Figure 6.3: Adapted from Futrell (1994:103).

The model can be explained as follows:

- *Source:* The source is the salesperson.

- *Encoding process:* The salesperson converts ideas and concepts into the language and materials used in the sales presentation (such as leaflets).

- *Message:* The message providing the information is conveyed in the sales presentation.

- *Medium:* The medium is the form of communication used. It includes discussion, words, visual materials and body language.

- *Decoding process:* The information is received and translated into meaningful information by the receiver or prospect.

- *Feedback:* Reaction to the communication is transmitted back to the sender. The reaction may be verbal or non-verbal.

- *Noise:* Issues such as differences in perception between salesperson and prospect and disorganised sales presentations, for example, are known as noise and create barriers to effective communication.

A successful salesperson knows how to develop a sales presentation (encode) in such a way that the buyer clearly understands the message (decode). Communication media such as one-on-one discussion and visual aids in the form of pictures, drawings, models or samples all assist in ensuring a successful face-to-face communication.

6.5   PERSUASIVE SELLING COMMUNICATION

In order to be successful, a salesperson must master the art of persuasive communication. This requires the ability to change a person's beliefs, position or course of action.

- *Two-way communication.* Persuasive communication is most effective when both the salesperson and prospect participate. Two-way communication enables a salesperson to receive feedback. If the prospect talks enough, the salesperson will be able to establish her or his needs and wants. The sales message can then be adapted to the prospect's requirements.

  A situation where a salesperson does all the talking, while the prospect listens passively, is not nearly as persuasive since it is one-way communication.

- *Questions.* Also known as probes, questions are an excellent technique for developing two-way communication. By getting a prospect to talk, the salesperson also gets him or her to think. Fortunately, most people like to talk, especially about themselves. Good question techniques are important to uncover needs, to clarify objections and gain agreement on proposals. Bear in mind that the art of using questions is a conversational skill and not an interrogative device. The basic types of questions are closed (or direct) and open questions:

  - ◆ *Closed or direct questions.* This type of question requires a clearly defined answer such as 'yes' or 'no'. For example, 'Do you want to repeat your order?' is a closed question.

  - ◆ *Open questions.* 'I have six honest serving men. They taught me all I knew. Their names were Where and Why and What and When and How and Who.' Rudyard Kipling's famous words illustrate the starting points of effective questioning. Open questions enable a salesperson to obtain much-needed information from the prospect. For example, 'With cost of living escalating annually, what have you done to prepare yourself for retirement?' This thought-provoking question is aimed at establishing the prospect's current situation.

  Questions should be asked sparingly and wisely. Ideally only those that assist the salesperson to establish the prospect's wants and needs should be used. Asking questions is a skill – and it becomes even more effective when accompanied by a pause to allow the prospect as much time as possible to respond. The salesperson must be an intelligent enough listener to turn the feedback received into selling points that guide the prospect to a favourable buying decision. This requires empathy, which is the ability to understand the feelings of the prospect as well as the words the prospect uses.

- *Listening.* Listening is an art that requires concentration and energy. According to psychologists, humans can think about four times faster than they can talk. This provides the salesperson with an opportunity to plan a sales strategy around what the prospect says.

  If the prospect's mind wanders from the topic under discussion, questions can be used to regain attention. But the salesperson must listen intently to what the prospect has to say!

The following listening skills are important:

◆ Listen for key factors.

◆ Look attentive and show interest in what the prospect is saying.

◆ Anticipate what the prospect is trying to get at and what the major issues will be.

◆ Subconsciously summarise what the prospect has said to ensure that every aspect is understood.

◆ Learn from the prospect's words, mannerisms, actions, tone of voice and expressions.

◆ Listen carefully to the prospect's answers and avoid thoughts about the next question until the first reply has been heard and understood. Each question should be constructed from the previous response.

■ *Body language.* Body language is an important part of talking and listening. It can reinforce or detract from the spoken word. Much can be learned from a frown, a raised eyebrow or a smile during a sales presentation and the prospect and salesperson can literally communicate without uttering a word.

The salesperson must be able to recognise non-verbal signals, to interpret them correctly and be prepared to alter the sales strategy if necessary by slowing down, changing or even stopping the presentation whenever a difficult situation arises.

■ *'Magic' words.* Image-packed words should be used to give a mental picture of how the product or service will benefit the customer. These include 'magic' words such as 'savings', 'winning', 'profits', 'free', 'now', etc. In addition, the technical terms of the industry in which the salesperson and the prospect operate should be used with maximum effect and words should be pronounced correctly.

■ *Total communication skills.* A successful salesperson is adept at using all the skills of communication – words, voice, eyes, face and body. She or he should be able to speak clearly, with enthusiasm and at a steady pace that is understandable. Pitch, tone of voice and speed of speaking should be varied and eye contact maintained as much as possible. Eyes can transmit enthusiasm and sincerity. The face can register happiness, confidence and conviction while the whole body position should convey confidence and interest.

6.6   SALES TASKS, SALES POSITIONS AND SALESPERSON'S ACTIVITIES

This section provides an outline of the tasks, positions and activities of salespeople and is important to take into account in the management of sales.

■ *Sales tasks.* Salespeople can be classified by the sales tasks they perform (Figure 6.5 on p128).

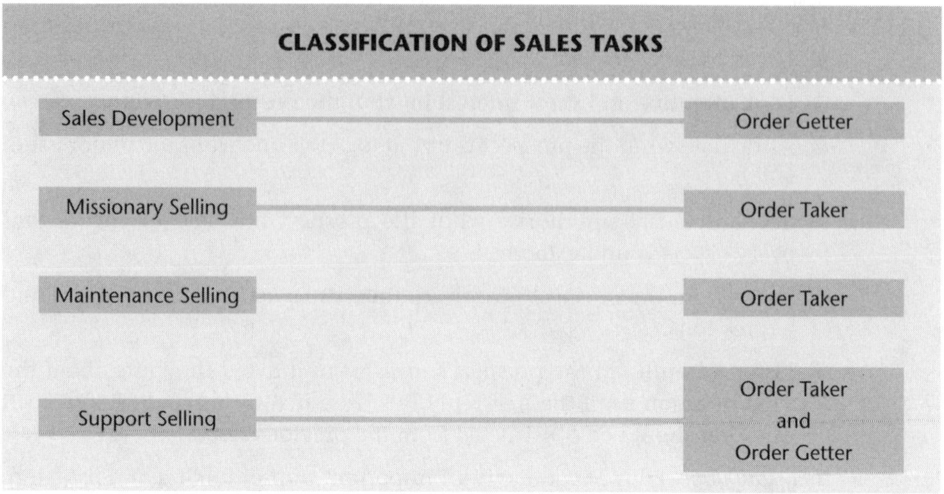

CLASSIFICATION OF SALES TASKS

Sales Development	Order Getter
Missionary Selling	Order Taker
Maintenance Selling	Order Taker
Support Selling	Order Taker and Order Getter

Figure 6.5: Koekemoer (2004:229).

According to Figure 6.5 the following sales tasks are performed:

◆ *Sales development.* Sales development involves the generation of new customers by encouraging a change of supplier or use of a new product or service.

◆ *Missionary selling.* Missionary salespeople help pull the product through the marketing channel by providing low-key personal selling assistance, such as ensuring that sufficient stocks are held in the channel outlets. They are sometimes called merchandisers.

◆ *Maintenance selling.* Maintenance selling involves the generation of sales volume from existing customers.

◆ *Support selling.* This type of salesperson provides continuing service to the customer. In addition, they may sell directly by suggesting a replacement rather than repairing an old product.

Some salespeople are order takers (such as a clothing salesperson sitting in the men's department waiting for a customer to walk in) while others are order getters (a fertiliser salesperson visiting farmers to get orders). Let's briefly look at the two approaches:

◆ *Order getters.* People who spend most of their time on sales development are known as order getters because they create sales. Their sales strategy requires a high degree of creativity that must be matched by a professional sales presentation. They usually call on customers, and this requires planning and organising.

Typical order getters are insurance and capital equipment salespeople.

◆ *Order takers.* This task entails accepting orders. It tends to be more reactive than proactive, ranging from asking what the customer wants to waiting for the customer to order. Many telemarketers take orders from loyal customers ordering goods such as office supplies, etc. Order takers rarely have a sales strategy and seldom use a sales presentation.

■ *Sales positions.* The title 'salesperson' embraces a variety of selling positions and activities, which include the following:

◆ *Product delivery salesperson.* For example, the Coca-Cola salesperson who not only delivers the product to the cafe or supermarket but takes orders from customers.

◆ *Inside order taker.* A cafe owner is an inside order taker, as is a waiter at a restaurant.

◆ *In-the-field order taker.* This type of salesperson usually takes fill-up orders for FMCG when regular stocks are low or when a high-demand period (such as a long weekend or holiday) is approaching.

◆ *Goodwill builder.* These people call on clients to build goodwill and where possible to educate them in the use of certain products. For example, a pharmaceutical or medical sales representative who makes regular calls on doctors to promote prescription medicines or medical equipment.

◆ *Technical expert.* Here the major emphasis is placed on technical knowledge, such as an engineering salesperson who acts as a consultant to the client. The object is to provide technical backup service or advice or to work with the client to solve a particular problem.

◆ *Creative seller of tangible goods.* In this case the salesperson could be dealing with sales of capital equipment to industrial buyers. The total cost is usually high and technical specifications, output and technical backup and service become important.

◆ *Creative seller of intangibles.* This is probably one of the most difficult selling positions. An insurance salesperson is a typical example. Selling intangibles demands an analysis of the ENPs (expectations, needs and problems) of the client and, in the case of insurance, for example, an analysis of the current and required insurance portfolio.

◆ *Key account selling.* Very large customers with branches throughout the country usually require a special selling effort, particularly if the buying is centralised at a head office. Key account selling is usually the responsibility of more senior salespeople or even the sales manager. Relationships are very important, and the salesperson should be a skilled negotiator.

◆ *Telemarketing.* The telephone is used to call on customers. This form of selling has many of the benefits of a personal visit while saving time and money.

◆ *Team selling.* Some companies have different people handling different sales tasks when dealing with a specific account or high ticket items. It is known as team selling and could include the sales person and technical staff working together.

Irrespective of this diversity of roles, a trend common to all sales positions is the increasing emphasis on professionalism in selling.

The contemporary salesperson faces more intense competition, a more sophisticated buyer and has to perform a variety of activities including the following:

◆ *Selling.* The task of selling includes servicing established accounts and prospecting for new accounts. Additionally, the salesperson is frequently called on to provide consulting services. For example, it may be necessary to demonstrate how a product will combine with the design and operational aspects of the prospect's product.

◆ *Maintaining relationships.* The salesperson must maintain cooperative relationships with the various distribution channel members. One of the tasks is to deal with channel conflict such as late deliveries, bad service and incorrect invoices. Salespeople sometimes have to help their customers with managerial problems ranging from administration to the recruitment, motivation and retention of staff.

◆ *Planning.* In view of the intense competition in most types of business selling these days, salespeople are now spending a major portion of their time on planning their activities. Effective sales planning involves the following:

-   scheduling and routing of sales calls;

-   determining the frequency of contact with established accounts;

-   assigning the appropriate amount of time to prospecting for new accounts;

-   analysing the response or visits to the website;

-   evaluating tapped and untapped sales potential within a sales territory;

-   assisting the sales manager on budgeting and forecasting for a sales territory over a specific period of time; and

-   participating in the decision-making process of establishing goals, objectives, strategies and techniques for a territory so that it can be profitably operated.

It is obvious from the above that time management is important. The salesperson must know how much time to devote to which activity and to which customer or prospective customer.

6.7   WHAT A SALESPERSON SHOULD KNOW

Much of the information about a company is taught in company sales training courses, while the rest is usually gleaned from diligent study and personal observation. The professional salesperson should have an understanding and/or knowledge of the following matters:

■ *Company history.* Studying the history of the company will help the salesperson to develop pride in the company and its products. She or he should know when the company was founded, how it got its name, what activities it is involved in and what contribution it makes to society.

■ *Executives and key personnel.* The salesperson should know who the top executives in the company are and to whom they are accountable.

- *Marketing policy.* An understanding of the company's marketing policy will help highlight the fact that selling is only a part of the salesperson's duties. A great deal of time is spent servicing customers, answering questions and solving problems.

- *Pricing and credit policy.* Detailed knowledge of the company's pricing and discount policies and procedures is essential for successful selling. Price objections are constantly raised and have to be handled. A high price may need to be justified by superior quality or greater profit potential and discounts must be understood and carefully explained.

  A sale is not complete until it is paid for, so the salesperson has to know how to avoid all possible credit problems by writing down all the terms of sale, explaining them carefully and obtaining the buyer's signature.

- *Customers and competitors.* A salesperson constitutes the eyes and ears of the company and as such should be trained in intelligence gathering. Salespeople normally are closer to customers than other staff members and are usually the first to see or hear about a new competitor or a new product launch. Such information should always be fed back to the sales manager.

  Apart from knowledge of the competitors, their products and policies, the salesperson should have knowledge of the different types of customers that have to be dealt with, as well as their needs, buying motives and buying habits.

- *Buying centre and gatekeepers.* The salesperson plays an important communication role in the link between customer and supplier. Typically, a salesperson selling to industry may have contact with an entire buying centre in the customer's organisation. A buying centre can consist of buyers, the managing director, the production manager, the financial director and various other interested individuals or groups. To reach many of these decision makers, the salesperson may have to penetrate the barriers erected by the various company gatekeepers such as receptionists, secretaries and telephone operators. Gatekeepers control the flow of information and people to others in the organisation. In some companies the secretary has the authority to prevent salespeople from seeing the decision maker. In many companies the financial director, who is responsible for the profitability of the company, can influence buying decisions.

- *Selling skills.* Every salesperson should be taught how to make effective sales presentations at company and other selling skills workshops. Features, advantages and benefits must be explained for each product. Some companies go so far as to develop scripts or planned sales presentations which are then reinforced through role playing – the salesperson does a practice sale to a colleague who plays the part of a customer in a simulated sales situation.

- *Product knowledge.* As a 'problem solver', the salesperson has to have a thorough understanding of the company's products to be able to show prospects how and why they will benefit from buying them. Product knowledge is essential to successful selling and the salesperson must know how the company's products are produced, how they function, how they are different from competitor's products and what makes them unique.

■ *Field procedures and responsibilities.* A salesperson has to know how to divide her or his time between active and potential customers and to utilise time properly, planning each call accordingly.

It is important to know that approximately a third of a salesperson's day is made up of travel from one call to the next, making appointments, indulging in small talk and waiting to see the right person. Improved planning and better routing of trips from home base could help improve productivity.

6.8   THE BUYING DECISION

The buying decision is influenced by the customer's expectations, needs, wants or problems. People's buying decisions can also be affected by internal and external forces. These could include buying power (internal) or peer pressure (external). These forces could be rational or emotional. Buyers go through various steps when making a buying decision. The salesperson's job is to translate the prospect's needs into the action of a buying decision. This often involves a series of steps, as illustrated in Figure 6.6.

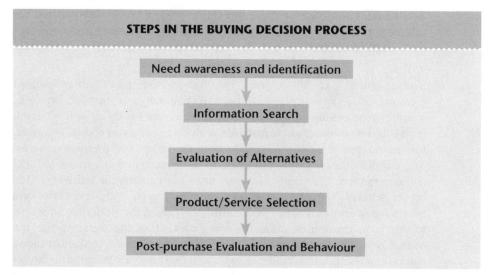

Figure 6.6

As illustrated, a need is identified by the buying unit. For example, a family's first small car bought five years ago may break down (need awareness). The prospective buyer then seeks information by either shopping around for a new vehicle or establishing the price of having the existing one repaired (information search). As the information is processed, alternative options are evaluated (evaluation of alternatives). Finally a purchase decision is made. Assuming the decision is to purchase a new vehicle, post-purchase evaluation will leave the buyer with a certain level of satisfaction or dissatisfaction.

The salesperson must be aware of the steps in the buying decision process since she or he can play a vital role in each one of them. For example, by pointing out that a prospect's car is beyond repair, a sales person can influence the need awareness and identification stage. By the same token, once the prospect has bought a new vehicle it makes sense to maintain contact through the post-purchase stage by reassuring the purchaser that she or he has made the correct decision. See Figure 6.7 for the 28 steps in the four stages applicable in buying a new car.

CUSTOMER ACTIVITIES IN BUYING A NEW CAR	
STAGE 1	1. Awareness of need for a new small car 2. Mental process: evaluating alternatives based on image and reputation 3. Decide to consider Corsa and Fiesta

STAGE 2	4. Speak to friends and relatives
	5. Read motoring magazines
	6. Ask owners (if possible)
	7. Telephone dealers for information
	8. Visit dealers:
	  • examines the appearance of tangibles
	  • surveys the availability and friendliness of sales staff
	  • views the models available on the floor
	  • studies the actions of other customers at dealers (positive or negative)
	  • asks: 'Do I feel important; wanted?'

STAGE 3	9. Decide to further pursue the Corsa 10. Visit dealers again 11. Demonstration by salesperson 12. Price and interest rate, extras required (what is included; what is not?) 13. My trade-in? (offered a good price or not?) 14. Payment terms and length of contract 15. Model and colour available or not. If not, how long is the waiting list; what is the delivery time? 16. Decide to buy and sign the contract 17. Deposit required, finance and insurance to be arranged

→

STAGE 4	18. Car is prepared for delivery (pre-delivery service), fitting of extras, etc.
	19. Customer takes delivery (demonstration given, everything explained by salesperson)
	20. Customer drives the car and experiences it
	21. Follow-up by the salesperson and/or the dealership
	22. Customer brings the car in for a few minor adjustments or a problem
	23. Speed and accuracy of fixing the problem, attitude of the dealership after the event (follow-up activity)
	24. Customer books the first service
	25. Customer brings the car in for the first service
	26. The way in which the first service is done (friendly, efficient, the cost, what is communicated, etc.)
	27. Follow-up on the first service
	28. Other after-sales-service activities

Figure 6.7: Koekemoer (2004:239).

6.9 THE FUTURE OF PERSONAL SELLING

Selling has changed over the years. Originally seen as the task of getting a product sold, whether the customer wanted it or not, the modern approach emphasises the philosophy that selling means helping customers to buy products or services that satisfy their needs. The new breed of salesperson is educated, computer literate and able to absorb a vast amount of information about products and customers. In many instances the salesperson is likely to have technical training and be backed by a top-flight team of engineers and market researchers. The salesperson of tomorrow will focus on quality, prompted by the following issues:

■ *Sophistication of consumers.* Consumer education is creating a more commercially aware, sophisticated and discerning purchaser.

■ *Professionalisation of the buying function.* This occupational group has made great progress towards enhancing professionalism in their ranks. Buyers attend courses and know that good buying saves money and improves profits.

■ *Better sales training.* Companies are also providing salespeople with better training. They know that buyers do not buy features, they buy benefits. They are trained in product knowledge, selling skills, adding value and building long-term relationships.

■ *Improved telecommunications.* As technology advances, the application of telecommunications to selling is emerging as a valuable cost-cutting and revenue-generating selling method. Although a phone call lacks the personal contact benefits of a face-to-face sales call, telemarketing is proving to be useful in selling industrial products and services. It is a cost-effective way of increasing sales by expanding market penetration and introducing new products and services.

A major difference between telesales and face-to-face salespeople is that the latter are generally expected to be creative problem solvers whereas telesales people usually sell from a prepared script.

■ *Technology.* Technological advances have resulted in a new breed of salesperson who sells market problem-solving systems designed for specific customer needs. Many buyers prefer a total solution to their purchasing problems rather than a number of separate buying decisions. Modern salespeople are trained to begin with a needs analysis which assesses the prospective buyer's business and mode of operation. This is followed by a written and verbal presentation. In the case of products such as computer systems the salesperson is often supported by a team of technical experts.

Computer programs are becoming increasingly effective tools for the salesperson. Elaborate analyses of territories, products and customer performance become available. Mathematical sales models for both established and new products can forecast likely sales responses and guide sales and production. Computer programs can assist in determining a salesperson's call standards as well as planning an effective call routing schedule.

■ *The Internet.* Salespeople can now be contacted by email and cellphone. They can advertise on a webpage, interact with customers via the Internet and offer interactive online shopping or ordering opportunities. This can be done even if the salesperson is not available. The website will provide product and ordering information at all times.

6.10 ETHICAL ISSUES IN SELLING

Because salespeople are at the forefront of the interface between the company and the customer, certain ethical issues can arise that pose a dilemma. For example, should the salesperson make a delivery promise even though she or he knows it cannot be kept? Other ethical issues include:

■ *Gifts.* These are usually acceptable but care should be taken to ensure that they are not seen as a bribe.

■ *Trade information.* Customers usually see sales people as a useful source of trade information. The ethical dilemma facing the salesperson is how much information should be passed on.

■ *Expense accounts.* Not all expenses can be quantified to the last cent, eg parking. However, many of these expenses are allocated on trust.

■ *False reporting.* This is referred to as 'ghost calling'. Reports are submitted although a call was never made. This is regarded as stealing time from the employer.

■ *Vehicle use.* Some companies provide sales staff with cars and an allowance is made for private use. However, it is not intended that the salesperson should do more private than business mileage.

- *Moonlighting.* Having two jobs may interfere with a salesperson's performance, particularly if the second job requires working late at night.

Other ethical issues such as bribery, running down the competition, and falsifying orders are also closely associated with the task of selling. However, the salesperson's value system, if based on integrity, should not have problems.

REFERENCES

Blem, N. 2003. *Achieving Excellence in Selling, A South African Approach.* 2ed Oxford University Press: Cape Town.

Futrell, C. 1994. *ABC's of Selling.* 4ed Irwin: Homewood, Illinois.

Koekemoer, L. 1997. 'VAAM – Value Added Activity Management'. The SA Journal of Marketing and Sales, 3(4).

Koekemoer, L. (ed) 2004. *Marketing Communications.* Juta: Cape Town

7 Principles of Sales Promotion

....

AIM OF THIS CHAPTER

The aim of this chapter is to describe the nature and scope of sales promotion, to outline some sales promotion objectives and activities, to discuss when to use sales promotion and the effects thereof, to state what sales promotion can and cannot do and to provide a framework for planning the sales promotion strategy.

LEARNING OUTCOMES

After studying this chapter you should be competent in:
- defining sales promotion and discussing the nature and scope of sales promotion
- outlining the objectives of sales promotion
- describing the types of sales promotion activities
- discussing the development and trends in sales promotion
- debating why consumers respond to sales promotions
- discussing when a marketer should use sales promotion
- indicating how sales promotion affects sales
- outlining what sales promotion can and cannot do
- discussing how a marketer should go about planning a sales promotion

....

7.1 THE NATURE AND SCOPE OF SALES PROMOTION

Many people incorrectly think that sales promotion is anything that a marketer does to 'promote' sales. Not so. As pointed out earlier in this text, marketing has its own unique terminology and it is, therefore, essential to use it correctly. Sales promotion is one of the elements of the marketing communication mix and there is no shortage of definitions for this important element.

Sales promotion is part of the promotion mix and is a below-the-line communication tool. Below-the-line communication is basically the communication with the market by means of media that is not regarded as the traditional media such as print, radio and television. It includes point of sale material, coupons as well as competitions. We can define sales promotion as those means used by marketing management to enhance the efforts of advertising, public relations, and direct marketing in order to achieve the set goals of the company (Du Plessis et al, 2005:226).

According to Koekemoer (2004:13), sales promotion is a marketing activity aimed at offering incentives for consumers in order to achieve organisational short-term objectives. Sales promotion is a short-term strategy that is measurable and provides for accountability. It is mostly adopted in the maturity stage of a product life cycle to increase sales of the products or services.

The 'official' definition of sales promotion was given in the American Marketing Association's first formal *Dictionary of Marketing Terms*, edited by Peter Bennett (1988:179): 'Sales promotion: media and non-media marketing pressure applied for a pre-determined limited period of time at the level of consumer, retailer, or wholesaler in order to stimulate trial, increase consumer demand or improve product availability.'

Most definitions, however, are deficient in that they do not incorporate one vital group of people or audience, as they will be referred to collectively – the marketer's own salespeople. We will illustrate just how important this group is in the marketing communication strategy.

From the aforementioned discussion, it would seem that five main factors emerge as being important considerations in defining sales promotion. We will examine these factors briefly in order to arrive at our own definition of sales promotion.

First, there seems to be no doubt that sales promotion is action focused. While advertising may be designed to build a brand image and personal selling may be designed to build long-term relationships, it would seem that most sales promotions are designed to elicit a *specific* action or response from the target audience in the short term.

Second, sales promotion is generally planned as a specific marketing event. In other words, it is a 'stand-alone' activity which, although incorporated into the marketer's overall marketing communication strategy, is planned as a unique event.

Third, sales promotion very often has a tangible component, or specific sales promotion materials. These can range from the inexpensive 'giveaways' mentioned earlier, to in-store display materials, elaborate booths and displays at trade shows.

Fourth and this is a key issue, sales promotion can be targeted to three distinct audiences. The first is internal and is usually the marketer's own salespeople. There may, however, be other employees targeted such as technical sales support people or telemarketers. The second audience is the intermediaries in the channel of distribution and the third is the marketer's final customers or consumers. Fifth, sales promotion is designed to achieve short-term results. Time is one of the key elements of sales promotion and may range from a 'one-time-only' offer, which calls for an immediate response from the customer or consumer, to a limited time offer stretching over a few days.

With these points in mind, the definition of sales promotion that underlies this text is as follows:

> *Sales promotion is a blend of marketing communications activities and materials designed to intensify the efforts of the marketer's sales force, induce intermediaries to stock and sell the marketer's product offering, and/or persuade consumers to buy the product offering within a specified, limited time period.* (Koekemoer, 2004:267)

Let's now examine the objectives of sales promotion. It is important to point out that all sales promotion activities should be planned within the context of an IMC strategy, as outlined earlier in this text. It bears repeating that no single element of the marketing communication mix is likely to produce the optimum result in a marketer's strategy. It is thus important for a marketer to know the advantages and disadvantages of each element and when and how to 'use' them.

7.2 SALES PROMOTION OBJECTIVES

Good marketing practice suggests that a detailed set of objectives should be determined prior to the development of an overall marketing strategy. Indeed, a good way to remember the sequence is to use a simple acronym, MOST, where M stands for mission (the corporate mission, often defined in a formal mission statement), O stands for objectives, S stands for strategy, and T stands for tactics. These objectives will, in turn, 'drive' the sub-objectives, which are the detailed, operational objectives for each element of the marketing communication mix. Thus, the sales promotion objectives are derived from the marketer's overall marketing communication objectives.

Objectives have characteristics which serve as an indication that they are good. Firstly it goes without saying that an objective must be stated in precise terms. This means that it must be expressed in quantifiable or measurable terms. For instance, it would be pointless to say: 'Our objective is to get more consumers to try our new deodorant'. For this 'objective' to be realistic and effective, it must specify how many consumers should try the new deodorant. Typically, this would be specified in terms such as a percentage of the target market.

As important as it is to express an objective in quantifiable or measurable terms, this is not sufficient for it to be operational. A timeframe for the accomplishment of the objective must be specified. In the area of sales promotion, it would typically be a rather short period of time. Some sales promotion activities may be designed to achieve results in as little as one day. An example would be a one-day sale at a retail outlet. Others may be of longer duration, but it is unusual for a sales promotion campaign (as they are often called) to last for much longer than, say, three months. This is fairly common with contests, which typically run for a quarter.

All sales promotion objectives should be realistic. How we define tenacities is important, of course. Generally, this is taken to mean that objectives should be challenging, yet achievable. It would be unrealistic, for example, to expect to double the number or demonstrations of a new car to prospective customers within a week.

Furthermore, sales promotion objectives must have clearly assigned responsibility for their accomplishment. This would normally he spelled out in the job descriptions of the various sales and marketing executives in the organisation. However, when there are varying targets (objectives) for each of the salespeople, for example, it is important to detail these appropriately.

Finally, a general requirement for all objectives is that they be clear, unambiguous and in writing. This is simply good management practice and eliminates unnecessary confusion and even acrimony.

Some examples of generalised sales promotion objectives are given below. These broad objectives would have to be stated in specific terms in order to be effective.

- Encourage salespeople to intensify their efforts to sell a 'slow-moving' product in the range.
- Challenge salespeople to sell more of a certain product to existing customers.
- Encourage salespeople to locate and qualify more prospects.
- Encourage salespeople to set up more in-store displays.
- Encourage salespeople to train more distributor salespeople.
- Induce wholesalers to carry a particular product line.
- Persuade distributors to promote (push) a particular brand in their promotional activities.
- Persuade retailers to give a particular brand shelf space.
- Encourage retailers to support a sales promotion campaign by carrying more inventory of a particular product.
- Encourage retailers to sell old stock before the brand is re-launched.
- Persuade retailers to participate in a contact-operative in-store promotion.
- Induce product trial by consumers.
- Encourage existing consumers to buy more of the product.
- Minimise brand switching by consumers.
- Build consumer goodwill.
- Encourage repeat purchases.
- Enhance IMC efforts and build brand equity.

As will be noted, these are examples of generalised sales promotion objectives for salespeople, intermediaries and consumers.

7.3 FACTORS INFLUENCING THE SALES PROMOTION STRATEGY

The specific type of sales promotion activity chosen will depend on a number of factors and, in particular, on the sales promotion objective being pursued. Marketers must also take into consideration product-related, customer-related, organisation-related and situation-related factors when developing their sales promotion strategy. Let's review these factors:

■ *Product-related factors*

◆ *Product type.* Generally speaking, certain types of products lend themselves to sales promotion more than others. In the main, sales promotion is frequently used by marketers of Fast Moving Consumer Goods (FMCG) such as groceries and personal care products. However, this does not mean that other types of products, such as consumer durables, are excluded. In fact, in recent years more and more consumer durables, from household appliances to cars, have been the subjects of very heavy use of sales promotion. Consider personal care products, for example: Unilever would offer their Lux beauty soap and provide an incentive to the consumers by providing the second one for free, a buy-one-get-one free strategy. Another example will be that of Cadbury's special edition slab chocolates that are only available for a limited period.

◆ *Price.* Depending on the price elasticity of a particular type of product, sales promotion will be more effective or less effective. Sales promotion will generally be more effective with products that have a very elastic demand curve (a reduction in price will lead to increased sales) and less effective with products that have a very inelastic demand curve (for example, consumers are unlikely to buy more salt when the price of salt is reduced).

◆ *Brand image.* Marketers can basically pursue two types of brand image strategies, although it must be recognised that there are many variations between these two 'extremes'. The first is an exclusive brand image and the other is a value-oriented brand image. A greater focus on sales promotion would certainly harm an exclusive brand's image while it may enhance that of a value-oriented brand.

◆ *Product's stage in its life cycle.* It will readily be appreciated that the promotional strategy used by a marketer will vary significantly in the different stages of the Product Life Cycle (PLC). The objectives in the introductory stage are to introduce the product to the market and generate initial interest and product trial, whereas the objectives in the maturity stage are to remind consumers of the product and to maintain market share. Very different types of sales promotion activities will therefore be used to achieve these objectives.

■ *Customer-related factors*

◆ *Characteristics of the target market.* It should be clear that the profile of the individuals that make up the target market will be a significant factor in developing the sales promotion strategy, if the target market selected is made up of, say, young people between the ages of 16 and 24, the type of sales promotion strategy used will be very different from that used for a target market of senior citizens over 60.

◆ *Type of buying decision involved.* In consumer behaviour terms there are different types of buying decisions. If a consumer is buying a product that is regularly and frequently used (such as toothpaste), the type of buying behaviour is most probably routinised response. On the other hand, if the consumer is buying a product that is purchased very infrequently (such as a family car), then the consumer will most probably engage in what is called extensive problem solving.

◆ *Involvement level.* There is a 'range' of consumer involvement in a purchase decision, from low involvement to high involvement. In a low-involvement product purchase decision the consumer attempts to maximise benefits rather than minimise risk. As the purchase frequency rises, the performance risk associated with any one purchase falls and the consumer looks more towards getting the most value for money, in general, therefore, sales promotion is best suited to low-involvement products that are purchased frequently.

◆ *Psychological risk level.* High-involvement products and the associated purchasing decisions imply that consumers will focus on minimising their exposure to economic, psychological and performance risk. This implies a very different set of criteria that will be considered in the overall purchase decision. And this in turn means that the marketer must consider very carefully which, if any, sales promotion activities will be appropriate.

■ *Organisation-related factors*

◆ *Overall marketing communication strategy.* Since sales promotion is but one of the elements of the marketing communication mix available to a marketer, it must be used in strict compliance with the company's overall corporate and marketing communication strategy.

◆ *Resources available.* Resources, both human and financial, are, essential to conduct business, and since even the largest organisations do not have infinite resources, prudent management dictates that the selected marketing activities should be within the company's means.

■ *Situation-related factors*

◆ *Prominence of the company in its environment.* Depending on how prominent a company is in its environment it may well have to indulge in a certain amount of sales promotion activities simply because its target market expects it to. If a company however wants to maintain a low profile it would certainly not participate in any sales promotion activities.

◆ *Competitors' activities.* Whether marketers like it or not, in certain situations they have no alternative but to respond to the actions of their competitors.

7.4 TYPES OF SALES PROMOTION ACTIVITIES

As will probably have become apparent by now, sales promotion activities fall into three broad categories: internal, to the 'trade' and to the targeted consumers or end-users. A straightforward way to represent this is shown in Figure 7.1.

Figure 7.1 on the following page, illustrates the sequence of sales promotion activities and the respective audiences involved. First, the company's own sales

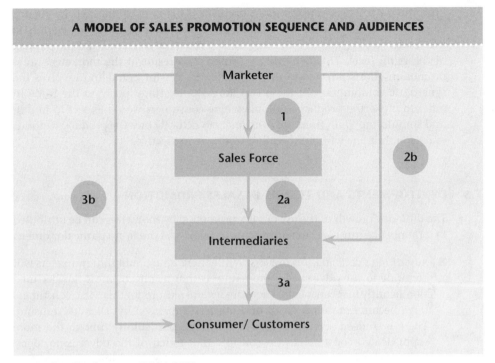

A MODEL OF SALES PROMOTION SEQUENCE AND AUDIENCES

Figure 7.1: Koekemoer (2004:273).

force is targeted (1). It stands to reason that if the sales force is to be spurred on to intensify its selling efforts it should be given the appropriate motivation to do so. This may range from simply briefing the sales force on an upcoming sales promotion campaign aimed at the intermediaries to a sophisticated sales competition with significant incentives.

Next, it will be noted that there is one line (2a) from the sales force to the intermediaries and another (2b) from the marketer directly to the intermediaries. (Note: The 'generic' term intermediaries (plural) is used here, although this could be a single large retailer, or the more 'conventional' wholesaler-retailer combination.) This simply means that the second step in sales promotion activities is directed to the intermediaries and if the sales force is involved, their efforts come first, if the sales force is not involved, the marketer's efforts are aimed at the intermediaries directly, as indicated by line 2b. A variety of sales promotion activities is used to induce intermediaries to participate. Finally, marketers will target consumers or customers either directly, as indicated in line 3b, or, more usually, via the intermediaries, as indicated by line 3a. It is important to follow this sequence, particularly in view of the pivotal role the intermediaries usually play in any sales promotion campaign.

The implications of the model in Figure 7.1 are that there are 'push' and 'pull' activities taking place to effectively increase sales. 'Push' implies a forward thrust whereby the marketer encourages channel members or intermediaries ('the trade') to stock and promote products. This is accomplished by means of personal selling, trade advertising and trade-oriented sales promotion to wholesalers and retailers. 'Pull' suggests a demand by consumers for the product at the retail level. This demand, or 'pull' is the result of the marketer's sales promotion efforts directed to the consumer. Successful marketing involves the synergistic combination of these two 'forces' – exerting 'push' to the trade in order to make the product available where consumers would expect to find it, and stimulating 'pull' from the consumers to actually buy the product. It stands to reason that one without the other would be ineffective.

7.5   DEVELOPMENTS AND TRENDS IN SALES PROMOTION

The dramatic growth in the use of sales promotion by marketers can be attributed to a number of causes. These are discussed below and are in no particular order:

- *Advertising's declining effectiveness.* While there is no doubt that marketers will continue to use advertising, the reality is that its effectiveness has declined significantly in recent years. There are several reasons for this. First, consumers have become more educated and are less impressed by 'slick' advertising. There is, indeed, even a degree of cynicism, particularly among the more sophisticated consumers who consider that much of the advertising today is an insult to their intelligence. Second, the sheer volume of advertising has led to a level of advertising clutter that militates against consumers being able to give appropriate attention to the hundreds (if not thousands) of advertising messages with which they are confronted each day. For a single advertisement to stand out and be remembered by a consumer is an increasingly rare occurrence these days. Third, the technological capability consumers now have to 'mute' television advertisements simply renders them ineffective. Much advertising, for example on radio, is simply 'tuned out' by listeners who apply selective perception. And the fact that we are living in an increasingly 'visual society' in which consumers are reading less means that print advertising is simply not reaching the target audience as it did some years ago. Young people also spend a huge amount of time on social media and the Internet.

- *Balance of power shift.* Until fairly recently, marketers of consumer packaged goods were generally more powerful and influential than the intermediaries in the distribution channel. Indeed, marketers were almost exclusively the 'channel captains'. The reason was twofold. First, marketers were able to generate consumer 'pull' for their products by means of heavy mass media advertising, particularly television. This effectively required retailers to carry the marketer's brands whether they wanted to or not. Second, retailers did very little marketing research of their own and were, thus, dependent on marketers for information on how successful a proposed new product was likely to be. Retailers could, therefore, be convinced by a marketer's sales representative that it would be a good idea to stock up on a new product because test market results (or some other research) indicated favourable consumer response to the product.

■ *Consumers have become more price sensitive.* Price has taken on a more important role in the consumer's decision-making process specifically since the worldwide recession of 2008 and onwards. Ironically, as more and more marketers turned to various forms of price reduction to stimulate sales these actions made consumers even more price-conscious. There is also a significant number of consumers who only purchase a particular type of product (invariably consumer staple goods) when it carries a special offer. Further, these consumers are no longer brand loyal and will purchase whichever brand happens to be on sale.

■ *Many products are mature.* Many products are in the maturity if not even the early decline stage of the PLC. In many product categories there is almost market saturation. Hence marketers find themselves having to fight harder and harder to maintain their existing market share, let alone gain market share. It is generally conceded in the marketing literature that as products enter the maturity stage of the PLC marketers compete more on price than on product attributes or qualities.

■ *Undifferentiated commodity products are offered in many product categories.* As products and markets have matured and the pace of technological capability has accelerated, many product categories have several brands within a particular price bracket that are virtually indistinguishable from one another.

■ *Reduced brand loyalty.* Consumers generally have become much less brand loyal than they once were. It is no secret that a competitor can 'reverse engineer' a new product and produce a similar product, even bypassing patent constraints, within a very short space of time. Consumers find it easy to switch among brands, especially cheaper substitutes, since they all offer similar features and benefits.

■ *Sales promotion is now 'politically correct'.* The extensive use of sales promotion by marketers of FMCG has taught consumers two valuable lessons. First, there are definitely significant rewards for 'shopping smart'. For a very small (if any) increase in shopping effort consumers are able to realise significant savings. Second, the brands on promotion are not of lower quality. In fact, many 'top-of-the-line' brands are regularly offered on promotion.

■ *Short-term orientation.* Increased competitiveness, coupled with pressure from shareholders to produce results, and the internal reward structures of many companies have made marketing managers much more short-term in their outlook.

■ *Forecasting demand has become more difficult.* As a result or the proliferation of new brands marketers (and retailers) find it increasingly difficult to forecast consumer demand. This is not surprising since most of these 'new' product offerings are simply displacing existing products or even cannibalising sales of the marketers' own products.

■ *Expectations of price decreases.* Particularly in the consumer durable goods category, prices of many products have decreased in both absolute and real terms, thanks largely to technological advances. Many consumers have been quick to realise this and often delay purchasing in the expectation that the price of a particular product will come down. This is particularly so when technology advances very rapidly. A good example is the mobile industry. When a new Nokia phone is introduced, for example, many consumers tend to delay their purchases as the cellphone technology advances rapidly which makes the value of a new model decrease within a short period of time. Also, better models of the same phone will soon be available.

■ *Emphasis on sales volume and market share.* As marketers learned how to 'use' and benefit from the experience curve and market share strategies, it was inevitable that there would have to be an emphasis on sales volume. And since sales promotion is a proven sales volume generator, marketers have naturally resorted to sales promotion programmes to achieve sales volume.

■ *The 'prisoner's dilemma' or 'vicious circle' problem.* Somewhat akin to a price war, many marketers find themselves locked into a defensive, reactive escalation of sales promotion expenditures. If a marketer cuts sales promotion spending, a loss of market share will almost certainly follow. If a marketer increases sales promotion spending, there will most likely be an increase in market share. But this is soon whittled away by competitors responding with matching or even better sales promotion programmes. This induces the marketer to use even more sales promotion, thus perpetuating the cycle.

As we consider the foregoing list, however, it must be said that the growth in sales promotion will not continue ad infinitum. The decrease in advertising effectiveness will possibly bottom out and even start to turn around when interactive advertising becomes more widespread (Koekemoer, 2004:276). Mergers and acquisitions among manufacturers may start to counteract the power of retailers. And inefficient marketers simply won't be around forever.

7.6   WHY CONSUMERS RESPOND TO SALES PROMOTION

To understand why consumers respond to sales promotion we have to consult the field of consumer behaviour, which provides a rich collection of concepts and theories that shed light on this question.

■ *Classical conditioning.* Perhaps one of the best-known examples of classical conditioning is that of Pavlov's experiments with dogs. Pavlov observed that dogs would always salivate when food was present. He then coupled a previously neutral stimulus, the ringing of a bell, with the presentation of food. Eventually, the dog would salivate whenever the bell was rung whether food was present or not. In conditioning terminology the food serves as the unconditioned stimulus, salivation is the response and the ringing of the bell is the conditioned stimulus.

Applying this concept to sales promotion, it can be said that an in-store display offering some incentive to purchase the product is the conditioned stimulus, in that the consumer associates it with the brand and an incentive to purchase. The unconditioned stimulus, of course, is the special offer and the response is to purchase the product. The basic rationale of classical conditioning as it applies to sales promotion is that the consumer can be induced to form positive feelings towards a conditioned stimulus, such as the sales promotion display by associating that stimulus with an unconditioned stimulus (such as a special cents-off offer that naturally generates positive feelings that ultimately lead to a response such as a purchase).

- *Operant conditioning.* The basic principle of operant conditioning is that a reinforced behaviour is more likely to persist. Skinner experimented with small animals and birds, placing them in what became known as the 'Skinner Box', which was equipped with a small lever connected to a food hopper. If the animal or bird pressed the lever, reinforcement for this behaviour was provided in the form of food. As this response-reinforcement sequence was repeated, the animal or bird became more and more likely to press the lever in any given period of time.

As applied to sales promotion in the marketing context, purchasing the product is the behaviour the marketer wishes to teach consumers and a sales promotion incentive of some kind is the reinforcement provided. A good example of operant conditioning would be an in-pack coupon that specifically rewards the behaviour of purchasing a product (Rothschild & Gaidis, 1981).

- *Attribution theory.* The basic concept of the attribution theory is that it describes how consumers explain the cause of an event. These explanations are called 'attributions', which result directly in attitude change rather than behavioural change. However, to the extent that attitudes are the antecedents of behaviour, the theory is very relevant. According to Mizerski et al (1979) three types of attribution theories can be distinguished: self-perception, object perception and person perception. These differ in terms of the object about which the attribution is being made. Attributions about one's motives relate to self-perception (the 'why-did-I-buy' question). Attributions directly about products relate to object perception (the 'why-is-brand-X-on-promotion' question) and if an attribution is made about another person the relevant theory is person perception (for example, the salesperson).

The self-perception theory is most readily applicable to repeat purchasing after a promotion. According to the theory, if the promotion is sufficiently strong and effective, the consumer will attribute the purchase to an external cause (the promotion) and not to his or her own possibly favourable attitude towards the brand.

The attribution theory provides a useful framework for studying how the use of sales promotion affects the consumer's attitude towards a brand. These attitudes are influenced as the consumer seeks to explain his or her actions (self-perception theory), the actions of others (person-perception theory) or the reasons behind the promotion of particular brands (object-perception theory).

- *Price perception theories.* Since an 'adjustment' to the full price of a product like a price reduction, either direct or indirect, is implicit in a majority of sales promotion strategies, it is important to examine the process by which consumers perceive prices. This perception is critical for determining the appropriate size and presentation of price decreases. Let's examine two of the better-known theories.

◆ *Weber's law.* Sometimes referred to as the 'Just noticeable difference' concept, Weber's law addresses the question of how much of a stimulus change is necessary in order for it to be noticed. This law postulates that this 'just noticeable difference' is proportional to the absolute magnitude of the original stimulus. Algebraically, it can be expressed as follows:

Let ΔS = size of stimulus change that will be noticed

$\quad$ S $\:$ = original magnitude of the stimulus

$\quad$ K $\:$ = constant of proportionality

Weber's law is then:

$$\frac{\Delta S}{S} = K$$

Expressed in pricing terms, if a R1 price decrease on a R10 item is the minimum price decrease that will be noticed then k = 0,1 (10 per cent).

Two important concepts emerge from Weber's law. First, price cuts that are less than the 'just noticeable difference' may be completely ineffective and, second, a base price or reference price is important for determining the effectiveness of a price reduction. This second concept will now be elaborated on.

◆ *Adaptation-level theory.* The adaptation-level theory proposes that perceptions of new stimuli are formed relative to a standard or 'adaptation level'. The adaptation level is determined by previous and current stimuli to which a person has been exposed and thus changes over time as a person is exposed to new stimuli. The adaptation level for judging the price of a particular item is called the 'reference price'. It can readily be appreciated, therefore, just how important it is to establish in consumers' minds a 'reference price' for a particular product.

In developing an effective sales promotion programme, marketers must appreciate that a price promotion is compared by consumers to a perceived benchmark – a reference price – and that the comparison must yield a perception of savings to the consumer. Marketers often 'remind' consumers what the reference price is in their promotional literature, advertising and in-store displays. Prominent statements such as 'Regularly priced at R10', 'Now only R8 for this week only', or simply 'Was R10, Now R8', make comparison easy and help the consumer calculate the savings.

■ *Consumer decision-making process.* No discussion of the reasons why consumers respond to sales promotions would be complete without reference to the consumer decision-making process. A number of comprehensive consumer behaviour models have been developed which attempt to integrate all the factors involved in how and why consumers arrive at a particular decision.

The very first step in the consumer decision-making process is 'problem recognition'. It is in this area that sales promotion is very effective since a promotion such as a special display can trigger 'problem recognition'. The display either reminds consumers that they require the product being promoted or stimulates the latent demand for the product category. Later on in the decision-making process, when the consumer has reduced the choice to two competing brands, sales promotion may play a decisive role in tipping the scales in favour of the brand being promoted. Since many of the products concerned are low-involvement, low-unit -price, low-psychological-risk items, the consumer is unlikely to be willing to expend a great deal of time and energy searching for additional information in order to make the purchase decision. The stimulus and incentive produced by the sales promotion offer is, therefore, often all that is required to induce the consumer to purchase the brand being promoted.

Vodacom and Cell C have entered the price war started last year by MTN. Cell C made a big splash with its new 'Woza Wheneva' campaign. Cell C's Woza Wheneva offers 20 free extra airtime minutes for every R10 spent on recharging. For example, a R10 recharge notches up R10 airtime and 20 minutes of free Cell C-to-Cell C calls. A R25 recharge earns you 50 minutes, a R30 investment provides a full hour of free talktime. The promotion allows a subscriber to earn a maximum of 100 extra free minutes per SIM per week. Vodacom reacted by announcing its price promotion via a full page advertisement in the Sunday press. Billed as March Madness, Vodacom offered its prepaid subscribers 20 per cent free airtime when they recharge.

7.7   WHEN TO USE SALES PROMOTION

Deciding when to use sales promotion may be the difference between being successful or not. As the saying goes: 'Timing is everything!' This is particularly relevant in developing sales promotion strategy. Timing in this context actually relates to a number of situations. First is what may be referred to as 'calendar timing'. As this implies, it has to do with the season, day of the week, time of the month or other special dates. Intuitively, we would realise that there are sales promotion strategies that lend themselves to association with the seasons of the year. The fashion industry, for example, is especially attuned to the seasons and sales promotion programmes must be carefully planned to synchronise with the relevant season. There are many other products, from gardening supplies to sporting equipment that are closely associated with the seasons of the year.

In the shorter term, day of the week and time of the month have special significance in terms of planning sales promotion programmes. Clearly, if the likelihood that consumers will respond to a sales promotion offer if it is made on a certain day of the week or at a certain time of the month is high, then it will benefit the marketer to factor this into the planning. Many marketers, and especially retailers, plan their sales promotion programmes very carefully around significant days or times, for example, many marketers of food products will plan their in-store product-sampling promotions for a Friday afternoon and

Saturday morning when they know there is likely to be higher than normal store traffic. Other promotions are planned for the end of the month presumably when most consumers are paid.

There are clearly a number of special days in the year which lend themselves to a variety of sales promotion opportunities. Naturally, the product and/or services associated with the particular date will dictate the type of sales promotion programme that would be appropriate. Starting with Valentine's Day in February to Easter to Christmas in December, these 'special dates' are effectively exploited by many marketers. Again, since they are unique in terms of their position on the calendar it is essential to plan all the necessary sales promotion activities and/or materials well in advance. If a date is missed for any reason, the marketer effectively has to wait another year before being able to do anything relating to that particular date. Point-of-sale display materials for a special Mother's Day offer on sweets or flowers are simply no good whatsoever if they only arrive at the retailers on the Monday after Mother's Day!

The second timing-related situation is that associated with the PLC. The major marketing texts generally suggest different promotion strategies for the different stages of the PLC. Clearly, it is inappropriate to generalise, but there are some basic principles that can be applied. In the introduction stage of the PLC, the marketer's basic objective is to build primary demand for the product category. The basic promotion strategy is to inform the target market of the product's existence and to induce the innovators to try it. Specifically, sales promotion can be used very effectively to accomplish part of this objective. Depending on the type of product a number of sales promotion strategies could be implemented to coax consumers to try the product, ranging from giving free samples of a new food item to offering prospective luxury car buyers the free use of a demonstration model for a weekend. Note that sales promotion will almost always be used in conjunction with advertising in this phase.

In the growth stage of the PLC when competition begins to be a major threat, the marketer starts to emphasise building selective demand. The main promotional objective is to persuade the target market to buy the marketer's product instead of that of the competitor's. A variety of sales promotion strategies is available to the marketer to assist in accomplishing this objective. Once again the specific sales promotion strategy selected would depend on the product. Promotions could range from a simple on-pack premium to 'reward' the consumer for buying the brand to an elaborate 'frequent buyer' programme to 'reward' the customer for staying with the brand.

In the maturity stage of the PLC, product differentiation becomes increasingly difficult to maintain, competition intensifies and profit margins come under severe pressure. The marketer is now faced with having to continue efforts to build selective demand, maintain market share and intensify distribution. Although the main promotion strategy is still persuading, there is a distinct move to the target market of the product, particularly if it is a low-unit price, low-involvement, low-psychological-risk staple good. It is probably in this stage of the PLC that sales promotion strategy is more intensively applied than in any of the other stages. When many competitive products become virtually homogeneous, sales promotion is extensively used at the retail level to maintain sales volume. Typical sales promotion strategies range from simple price-off coupons, to two-for-the-price-of-one, to significant manufacturer rebates.

In the decline stage of the PLC, some competing brands start to drop out of the market and the marketer's strategy has to do with whether or not it is still profitable to stay in that product market. Depending on which way the decision goes (to stay in or exit the market), sales promotion is often a significant factor in the marketer's strategy. If the marketer decides to stay in the market, for example, a product upgrade and re-launch is often undertaken. Sales promotion can play a major role in this situation. If the decision is taken to exit the market, however, sales promotion is frequently the only marketing communication element used to liquidate the remaining inventory of the product.

The third, and probably the most intriguing, timing-related situation is associated with the stages of the consumer's purchase decision. This is illustrated in Figure 7.2 below.

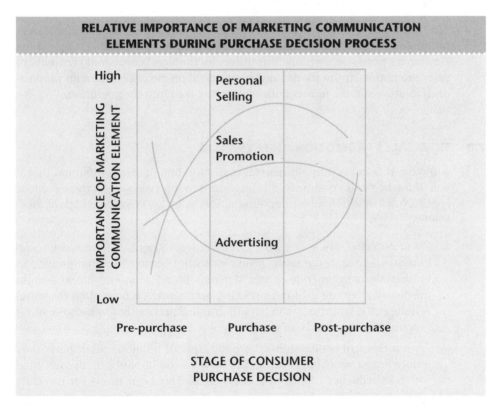

Figure 7.2: Koekemoer (2004: 284–285).

It will be noted in Figure 7.2 that there are three stages in the consumer's purchase decision – pre-purchase, purchase and post-purchase. In the pre-purchase stage, advertising plays a significant role, informing the consumer of the existence of the product and where to get it, but sales promotion, for example, in the found of free samples, can also play an important role in obtaining low-risk trial. Indeed, depending on the type of product, sales promotion may be considerably more effective than advertising.

During the purchase stage, advertising falls off dramatically in terms of its effect on the consumer's decision whereas personal selling comes to the fore. Sales promotion now becomes very useful and is manifested in a variety of forms – from coupons, to point-of-purchase displays, to samples, to rebates, all of which can stimulate specific demand at the retail outlet.

In the post-purchase stage, advertising regains some of its importance, mainly to reassure the buyer that the right purchase decision was made. Personal selling (where applicable) is also important since the customer appreciates personal contact after the sale. Should there be any hint of cognitive dissonance ('buyer's remorse') it is, in fact, essential for the salesperson to maintain contact until the customer is completely satisfied. The main role of sales promotion in this stage is to encourage repeat purchases from satisfied first-time 'triers'. Coupons or other special offers are often used in this instance.

The most interesting observation about this model is the fact that sales promotion maintains a fairly high level of importance in all three stages of the consumer's purchase decision. This illustrates the significance and versatility of sales promotion in the marketing communication strategy, although product- and situation-specific factors must always be taken into consideration.

7.8 HOW SALES PROMOTION AFFECTS SALES

Although it is implicit in our general understanding of sales promotion that it will 'influence' sales positively, it is important to understand that there are four specific ways in which sales promotion affects sales. Let's examine each of these briefly.

■ *Brand switching.* There is a distinction between 'aggressive' and 'defensive' brand switching. 'Aggressive' brand switching occurs when the promotion induces the consumer to buy a different brand from the brand bought previously. 'Defensive' brand switching occurs when a promotion for brand A induces the consumer who bought brand A previously to purchase brand A again (in other words, to remain loyal to brand A).

From a classical conditioning viewpoint, special promotional displays may induce brand switching because they serve as conditional stimuli associated with price reductions. Remember, the consumer has been 'trained' to associate special promotional displays with price reductions. Consumers will respond to the display even if a price reduction is not also present. This probably explains the phenomenon that occurs when a retailer, for example, sets up a special promotional display of a slow-moving product, which consumers then purchase in larger quantities than when it was merely placed in a 'regular' shelf spot.

■ *Repeat purchasing.* There are two types of repeat-purchase effects associated with sales promotion. The first occurs simply because any purchase of a brand has implications beyond the immediate purchase decision. The consumer forms a habit towards purchasing the brand, sustains the habit, and learns about the performance of the brand. Because sales promotion can induce purchases that would not otherwise occur, this effect becomes very relevant in the study of sales promotion.

The second repeat-purchase effect involves a change in purchase probability as a result of purchasing the brand 'on promotion'. Purchasing a brand on promotion may, for example, weaken the consumer's attitude towards the brand, which in turn may reduce the probability of a repeat purchase. This is known as the promotional-usage effect and illustrates just how important it is for a marketer to have a 'balanced' promotional strategy. Frequent and inappropriate sales promotion programmes could have an adverse effect on sales. Repeat-purchase effects resulting from a marketer's sales promotion efforts take on a broader meaning with respect to consumer durable products. In this case, repeat purchasing may mean more than repurchasing the same brand. It may influence the consumer to purchase other products in the marketer's product line or to continue using the dealer's service facilities. A simple example would be the purchase of a microwave oven by a consumer who had previously purchased the same brand of refrigerator.

■ *Purchase acceleration.* When consumers are induced to buy in greater quantities or more frequently than they would normally buy, it is referred to as purchase acceleration. It will immediately become apparent that while this may produce more sales in the short term, it is possible that sales promotion programmes aimed at purchase acceleration may simply 'cannibalise' future sales and thus result in no net gain. The marketer's objective, therefore, should be to induce the consumer to use more of the product, thus leading to a higher consumption rate in the same time period.

■ *Category expansion.* Strongly related to the concept of increasing primary demand, that is, demand for the general product category, the basic objective of category expansion is to shift the demand curve to the right. Marketers can achieve this in two ways. The first is by creating a new purchase occasion or reason. This is when a marketer actively encourages consumers to buy and use the product on an occasion or for a reason other than the generally accepted one. An example is that of Royal baking powder which was initially for baking cakes and biscuits. It is now used in addition to baking, for cooking, it is added in pumpkins and to cook potatoes.

The second way marketers can achieve category expansion is by increasing the usage or consumption rate. This is a common objective for many FMCG manufacturers. However, although it might be relatively straightforward to persuade consumers to purchase a larger quantity of a particular product, the real challenge is to get the consumers to actually use or consume the product at a higher rate than before. Marketers of many food products have achieved some success by using promotions, such as offering a free recipe book that is designed to show consumers more and different ways to use the product. What the marketer wants to avoid is that the sales promotion programme merely results in a purchase acceleration situation. This can perhaps best be illustrated in Figure 7.3.

It will be seen in this figure that what happens with many sales promotion programmes is that there is a temporary increase in sales as a result of the programme. This is illustrated in Figure A. However, not long after the sales promotion programme, sales return to the 'normal' level. In Figure B, on the other hand, sales level out at a higher level than before the sales promotion programme.

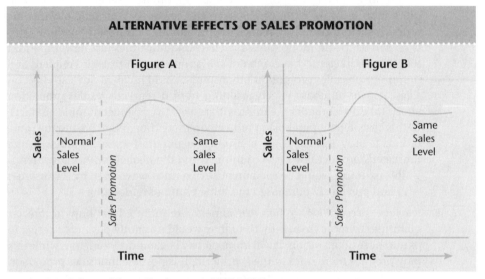

Figure 7.3: Adapted from Koekemoer (2004:288).

In this case the marketer has indeed been successful in achieving greater usage or consumption. It is thus clear that marketers have to 'teach' consumers how to consume or use more of the product it they are to effectively achieve category expansion. A 'new', higher sales level could also be attributable to a gain in market share, which, of course, is a very desirable situation for any marketer. In order to determine which of the two factors led to the increase in sales, the marketer would have to undertake the appropriate marketing research.

7.9 WHAT SALES PROMOTION CAN AND CANNOT DO

Despite what some marketers may think or hope, sales promotion is not a cure-all, magic formula that will solve a multitude of marketing problems. There are some tasks that sales promotion simply cannot perform, and it is important to understand this.

Sales promotion cannot solve the following problems:

- Compensate for a poorly trained sales force.
- Compensate for insufficient or inadequate advertising.
- Give the trade or consumers any compelling reason to continue purchasing a brand.
- Permanently stop an established product's declining sales trend or improve the acceptance of an undesired product.

Specifically, sales promotion can have the following effects:

- Stimulate sales force enthusiasm for a new, improved or even a mature product.
- Rekindle sales of a mature product.
- Facilitate the introduction of new products to the trade.
- Increase on- and off-shelf merchandising space.
- Neutralise competitive advertising and sales promotion.
- Obtain trial purchases from consumers.
- Retain existing users by encouraging repeat purchases.
- Increase product usage by 'loading up' consumers.
- Pre-empt competition by 'loading up' consumers.
- Reinforce advertising.

7.10 PLANNING THE SALES PROMOTION STRATEGY

Given that sales promotion strategy will be planned as part of the overall marketing strategy and will conform to the principles of IMC, it is essential that a systematic plan be followed. A simple model illustrating the sequence and components of a sales promotion strategic plan is shown in Figure 7.4.

Figure 7.4: Adapted from Koekemoer (2004:291).

■ *Define the target audience.* The sales promotion target audience is the group at whom a particular sales promotion is directed. As stated earlier in this chapter, sales promotion can be directed to the marketer's own salespeople, to the intermediaries and their sales forces and to consumers.

■ *Define the objectives.* The sales promotion objectives are derived from the overall marketing communication objectives. Earlier in this chapter, a list of general sales promotion objectives was given. Naturally, these objectives would be stated more precisely to fit the marketer's specific situation.

■ *Set the budget.* The sales promotion budget is part of the overall marketing communication budget. However, since the overall budget is an aggregation of the budgets for the individual marketing communication mix elements, it stands to reason that we would at least start with each component. In practice, it is inevitable that adjustments will be made before the final budget is established. The 'objective-and-task' method of budgeting will result in a much more realistic budget. In essence, this simply means determining the tasks required to achieve each objective and then 'costing out' each task.

■ *Develop the strategy.* A number of decisions are necessary to develop an effective sales promotion strategy. Basically, however, they all fall under the following headings:

  ◆ what to offer or the incentive;

  ◆ the size of the incentive to be offered;

  ◆ the means of distributing the incentive;

  ◆ the criteria for participation in the promotion; and

  ◆ the duration of the sales promotion programme.

  It is imperative that all sales promotion efforts are carefully integrated with the other elements of the marketing communication mix.

■ *Select the methods to be used.* A considerable number of sales promotion methods are available to a marketer. Which one/s to use will depend on:

  ◆ the sales promotion objectives;

  ◆ characteristics of the target audience;

  ◆ characteristics of the product;

  ◆ characteristics of the channel of distribution;

  ◆ the legal and regulatory environment;

  ◆ the competitive environment;

  ◆ the economic environment; and

  ◆ the available budget.

■ *Implement the programmes.* In order to implement any marketing programme effectively a detailed plan of action is necessary. In brief it will specify who will do what, when and how it will be done. The 'who,' of course, refers to the assigned responsibility for the achievement of the specific sales promotion objective/s. The 'what' refers to the details of the sales promotion campaign itself. For example, are coupons to be distributed? The 'when' refers to the timing of the sales promotion campaign. The 'how' refers to the tactical implementation specifics of the campaign,

- ■ *Evaluate the effectiveness.* The approach most used in evaluating sales promotion effectiveness involves measuring sales before, during and after the sales promotion event or programme. If the programme is successful sales should increase during the campaign. Although sales may then taper off at the end of the particular programme, it is hoped that they will perhaps 'level off' at a rate slightly higher than they were before the campaign. Needless to say, the evaluation is a crucial step in the whole process, and the results achieved will be used to guide future sales promotion programmes. It would be naive to conclude that all sales increases achieved after a sales promotion programme are exclusively attributable to the effectiveness of the programme. Indeed, if the marketer is applying an IMC strategy it follows that other elements of the mix may well have been used as part of the particular campaign. However, we can evaluate measurable aspects of the sales promotion programme, such as coupon redemption or rebate claims made, for a good indication of the effectiveness of the programme.

REFERENCES

Belch, G.E. and Belch. M.A. 2004, *Advertising and Promotion: An Integrated Marketing Communications Perspective*, 6ed. McGraw-Hill/Irwin: Burr Ridge, Illinois.

Bennett, P.D. (ed) 1988. *Dictionary of Marketing Terms.* American Marketing Association: Chicago, Illinois.

Blattberg, R.C. and Neslin, S.A. 1989. 'Sales Promotion: The Long and the Short of It', *Marketing Letters*, 1(1).

Blattberg, R.C. and Neslin, S.A. 1990. *Sales Promotion: Concepts, Methods, and Strategies.* Prentice Hall: Englewood Cliffs, New Jersey.

Cant, M.C., Strydom, J.W., Jooste, C.J. & Du Plessis, P.J. 2006. *Marketing Management.* Juta: Cape Town.

Coen, R.J. 2002. 'Insider's Report: Robert Coen Presentation on Advertising Expenditures', Universal McCann, *McCann Erickson Worldwide*, December.

Cook, J. 1997. There's Gold in Them There It Brands'. *Sales and Marketing Strategies & News* (March).

Dagnoli, J. 1991. 'Jordan Hits Ad Execs for Damaging Brands', *Advertising Age* (November).

Du Plessis, F., Bothma, N., Joordan, Y. & Van Heerden, N. 2005. *Integrated marketing communication.* New Africa Books: South Africa.

Etzel, M.J., Walker, B.J. and Stanton, W.J. 2004. *Marketing*, 13ed McGraw-Hill/Irwin, Burr Ridge, Illinois.

Koekemoer, L. (ed) 2004. *Marketing communications.* Juta: Cape Town.

Kotler, P. 1988. *Marketing Management: Analysis, Planning, Implementation and Control.* Prentice Hall: Englewood Cliffs, New Jersey.

Luick, J.F. and Ziegler, W.L. 1968. *Sales Promotion and Modem Merchandising.* McGraw-Hill: New York.

Mallory, M. 1994. 'At Coke, Marketing is It', *Business Week* (February).

Mizerski, R.W., Golden, L.L. and Keman, J.B. 1979. 'The Attribution Process in Consumer Decision Making', *Journal of Marketing*, 45(2).

Perreault, W.D., Jr and McCarthy, E.J. 1996. *Basic Marketing: A Global-Managerial Approach.* Irwin: Chicago: Illinois.

Promo. 2002. 'Slow & Steady: Promo's Exclusive Annual Report of the U.S. Promotional Industry, *promo* (April). See www.promomagazine.com.

Rossiter, J.R. and Percy, L. 1987. *Advertising and Promotion Management.* McGraw-Hill: New York.

Rothschild, M.L. and Gaidis, W.C. 1981. 'Behavioral Learning Theory: Its Relevance to Marketing and Promotions', *Journal of Marketing*, 45(2).

Sacks, C. and Fuller, J. 1994. The Store That Cried Sale!' Ad L.A. (February).

Schoell, W.E. and Guiltinan, J.P. 1995. *Marketing: Contemporary Concepts and Practices,* 6ed Prentice Hall: Englewood Cliffs, New Jersey.

Scott, C.A. 1981. 'Forming Beliefs from Experience: Evidence from Self-Perception Theory', in *Perspectives in Customer Behavior*, Harold H. Kassarjian and Thomas S. Robertson (eds) Scott, Foreman: Glen view, Illinois.

Sheth, J.N. and Sisodia, R.S. 1995. 'Feeling the Heat'. *Marketing Management* (Fall).

Shimp, T.A. 1993. *Promotion Management & Marketing Communication.* The Dryden Press: Orlando, Florida.

Sternthal, B., and Craig, C. 1982. *Customer Behaviour: An Information Processing Perspective:* Prentice Hall: Englewood Cliffs, New Jersey.

8 Principles of Direct Marketing

AIM OF THIS CHAPTER

This chapter introduces direct marketing by defining it, looking at the reasons for its growth, comparing it to general marketing and discussing its key variables, its advantages and its integration into seamless marketing.

LEARNING OUTCOMES

After studying this chapter you should be competent in:
- defining direct marketing
- fully discussing the key elements of the definition
- explaining the reasons for the growth of direct marketing
- discussing the difference between general and direct marketing
- discussing the key decision variables of the direct marketing mix
- explaining the advantages of direct marketing
- explaining how general and direct response advertising can be integrated into seamless marketing

8.1 WHAT IS DIRECT MARKETING?

For nearly two decades direct marketing has been the fastest growing form of marketing communication activity in the USA and in most other developed countries. Since 2003 it accounted for well over 55 per cent of the total expenditure on marketing communications in the USA. It has now come of age in South Africa too. Yet there is still much confusion about what direct marketing is.

The generally accepted definition is the following one used by the American Direct Marketing Association:

Direct marketing is an interactive system of marketing that uses one or more advertising media to effect a measurable response and/or transaction at any location (Stone, 1986:1).

Perhaps a more elaborate definition can be used:

Direct marketing is the interactive use of a variety of advertising media, to encourage an immediate planned behavioural response in such a way that this behaviour can be recorded, analysed and stored on a database for future retrieval and use.

To properly understand this definition, it is necessary to examine each of its key elements:

- *Direct marketing is interactive.* The marketer and the customer engage in two-way communication. This makes direct marketing different from many other methods of marketing. For example, general marketing uses mass advertising on TV, radio, in print, etc but it has no precise method of obtaining feedback from those consumers. Direct marketing, on the other hand, allows the marketer and the customer to communicate with each other – directly and immediately. If this communication results in a series of transactions, the direct marketer achieves the ultimate goal of direct marketing: the development of a long-term, one-to-one relationship with the customer.

- *Direct marketing uses a variety of advertising media.* This means that direct marketing activity can be implemented via a wide range of media. These include all above-the-line media used by general advertising, as well as those traditionally associated with direct marketing, such as direct mail and the telephone. In addition new media, such as the Internet and interactive TV, are tailor-made for direct marketing applications.

- *Direct marketing stimulates behaviour.* In fact, the results are measurable. Through the methods of coding and tracking that direct marketers have developed, behavioural response and every sale can be identified with an individual customer and traced back to its advertising source. Thus the financial return on direct marketing campaigns can be calculated down to the last cent. With the exception of personal selling, no other communications activity can be measured with such complete accuracy. For example, a company sells software packages. Each software package costs R100 to produce and sells at R500. The company sends out 50 000 mail packages at R5,00 a package. The campaign achieves a four per cent response and a 50 per cent conversion rate.

Knowing these figures, the company can calculate the following:

Cost of campaign = No. of packages × cost per package
ie 50 000 × R5,00 = R250 000

No. of responses = No. of packages × response rate
ie 50 000 × 4% = 2 000 responses

No. of sales = No. of responses × conversion rate
ie 2 000 × 50% (or one sale for every two responses) = 1 000 sales

Profit margin per sale = Selling price − production cost per software package
ie R500 − R100 = R400

Gross profit = No. of sales × profit per sale
ie 1 000 sales × R400 = R400 000

Net profit = Gross profit − cost of campaign
ie R400 000 − R250 000 = R150 000

Because it's measurable, direct marketing is also testable, namely, a company can use a small part of its budget to test a campaign before it commits itself to using the full budget. As long as the test is valid, the company can closely predict the sales it will generate from the full campaign or 'roll out'.

- ■ *Direct marketing uses a database.* Direct marketing activity follows a cyclical system. At the hub of this cycle is a computer database from which customer information is obtained before each direct marketing activity and to which additional customer information is added after each campaign for future retrieval and use. With each new marketing activity the database becomes richer in relevant customer information. In other words, the database of customers becomes more usable and 'marketable' because it allows the direct marketer to understand, and therefore satisfy, the needs of each customer with increasing accuracy.

The most obvious defining characteristic of any direct marketing communication, regardless of the medium used, is the fact that it affects a response. Therefore, all direct marketing communications, by definition, must provide the prospect with the opportunity and means to respond. Response media include telephone, mail, fax, Internet and personal visits. For a response and/or transaction to occur, the prospect does not necessarily have to visit a store. A request for further information or the exchange of money for goods or services can take place wherever both parties have access to communications media and delivery mechanisms (such as the postal service or on-line).

One last definition could be added to this discussion. The definition focuses specifically on the intended purpose of various forms of direct marketing:

> *Direct marketing includes any direct communication to a consumer or business recipient that is designed to generate a response in the form of an order (direct order), a request for further information (lead generation), and/or a visit to a store or other place of business for purchase of a specific product/s or service/s (traffic generation).* (WEFA Group, 1995:3)

The three types of response action are defined as follows:

- ◆ *Direct order* includes all direct response advertising communications, through any medium, that are specifically designed to solicit and close a sale. All of the information necessary for the prospective buyer to make a decision to purchase and complete the transaction is conveniently provided in the advertisement.

- ◆ *Lead generation* includes all direct response advertising communications, through any medium, that are designed to generate interest in a product or a service and provide the prospective buyer with a means to request and receive additional information about the product or service.

- ◆ *Traffic generation* includes all direct response advertising communications, through any medium, that are designed to motivate the prospective buyer to visit a store or any other business establishment and to buy an advertised product or service.

In order to incorporate the key elements of the above definitions into one definition, it will be necessary to sacrifice brevity for the sake of comprehensiveness. The following definition encompasses all the determining characteristics of direct marketing:

> *Direct marketing is an interactive system of marketing designed to create and keep customers by developing long-term, personal relationships with each of them through increasingly relevant product or service offerings. To achieve this, direct marketing uses one or more advertising media to generate a measurable response in the form of an order (direct order), a request for further information (lead generation), and/or a visit to a store or other place of business (traffic generation)* (Koekemoer, 2004:332).

8.2 THE GROWTH OF DIRECT MARKETING

Direct marketing is still the dominant form of marketing in the USA. In countries where it is not yet dominant it is close to being the fastest growing form of marketing. But the question to be answered now is: Why this phenomenal growth and demand?

The growth of direct marketing is intimately linked to the enormous social and technological changes that have occurred throughout the world last century, but especially since the 1960s.

- ■ *The shattering of traditional social structures.* Fundamental social change is now accelerating at such speed that the future is upon us before we can properly assimilate the present. Alvin Toffler calls this phenomenon 'future shock', which he describes as 'the shattering stress and disorientation that individuals experience when subjected to too much change in too short a time' (Toffler, 1970:12).

  Material goods are no longer considered for their durability, but for the instant gratification they provide. Many new products are valued for their ability to be used immediately and discarded as soon as the next improved version hits the market. More products and services with ever-diminishing life cycles proliferates the world's markets, while advertising clamours for the consumer's attention from every side, promising new lifestyles and creating new aspirations.

  In terms of marketing, rapid social and technological change plays havoc with target markets. No sooner has a company defined its markets and they shatter, change composition or disappear altogether. The traditional market research cycle is too lengthy to be of much use – before the research is complete the market has changed or disappeared.

  In South Africa this problem is particularly acute: social change is accelerating faster than in many other countries. With the abolition of apartheid, racial groups that were kept apart by force in the past are now mixing freely. Given that South Africa has one of the most culturally diverse populations in the world this new-found freedom of social intercourse has turned the country into a crucible of continually changing markets. From the marketer's perspective, South Africa is not so much a 'rainbow nation' as a kaleidoscope of rapidly shifting markets that disintegrate and re-form into new and surprising entities in the blink of an eye.

The challenge lies in developing relationships not with groups of consumers but with individual consumers. This allows the marketer to offer different products and services to individuals as their needs change. And it is direct marketing's ability to target with pinpoint accuracy and to develop long-term customer loyalty that provides the means to achieve this.

■ *The change in consumer lifestyles.* The traditional family structure has been shattered in the last few decades. Before the 1960s it was still meaningful for marketers to define the average family as husband (breadwinner and main decision maker) plus wife (full-time housewife and decision maker or influencer) plus children (users). Today the very notion of an 'average' family is meaningless. Instead we find households of the most diverse composition: singles, single-parent families, unmarried couples, remarried couples with children from previous marriages, communal families, homosexual couples with adopted children, extended families, married couples with foster children – in fact, every type of family structure imaginable.

Even the roles of 'traditional' family members have changed drastically. A combination of the changing role of women and sheer economic necessity has ensured that both parents are likely to be breadwinners. Children, too, now form a significant market possessing both the financial means, the consumer 'know-how' and access to digital technology to be considered decision makers in their own right.

At the other end of the age spectrum, retired people form the most lucrative consumer market in the world. This is a relatively recent development that has resulted from living longer due to medical science, higher discretionary income and reduced financial commitments due to empty nests.

Coupled with these factors, average levels of education and income have increased dramatically in developed countries over the last forty years. This has created a much larger market of consumers with higher discretionary income than ever before.

What does this mean for marketing? It means that mass marketing is problematic because mass markets have splintered into multiple smaller markets each with its own set of needs.

It is direct marketing – with its ability to target individuals according to their unique needs – that can provide the highly personalised service that the modern consumer demands. What's more, direct marketing gives the hard-pressed, time-conscious consumer the most convenient method of purchase. Goods can be ordered from the home for delivery to the home, saving consumers the hours that are otherwise necessary to travel to a store, find parking, stand in a queue and then travel home again.

■ *Advances in computer technology.* The rapidly decreasing cost of storing information on computer has contributed significantly to the growth of direct marketing. Today vast quantities of customer information can be stored on a database for a fraction of what it would have cost a decade ago. This information can be manipulated quickly and efficiently to provide the marketer with accurate customer profiles and buying patterns. With the advancement of laser-printing techniques, the direct marketer has the ability to tailor messages to individual customers based on accurate knowledge of each customer's needs and buying behaviour.

But perhaps the most important innovations have come in the area of computer connectivity and networking. Online database access has revolutionised customer service by giving frontline staff, especially telemarketers, instant access to customer records. Modern technology and the Internet have given customers direct access to company databases for the ultimate in browsing and ordering convenience.

■ *The growth of consumer credit.* The proliferation of bank and store credit cards, together with the widespread use of toll free telephone numbers, has played a major role in the growth of direct marketing. Goods and services can be ordered and paid for by telephone, and monthly debits efficiently transacted by electronic transfer.

■ *More accurately targeted media.* The fragmentation of mass markets has been reflected in the movement towards more accurately targeted media. Mass circulation magazines have been supplanted by specialist publications catering to a diverse assortment of niche markets. Magazine racks are overflowing with magazines that target every imaginable interest group. Because these magazines are accurately targeted at well-defined markets, direct marketers have seized the opportunity to also use the print medium as an exceptionally effective vehicle for response-driven advertising.

8.3 THE DIFFERENCES BETWEEN GENERAL MARKETING AND DIRECT MARKETING

Although there are many similarities between general and direct marketing, there are also important differences that must be taken into account. Only by first understanding these differences can we integrate the two disciplines to ensure synergistic marketing activities. The fundamental differences are shown in Table 8.1.

With a clear understanding of the differences, we can now use the strengths of each discipline to produce a powerful, synergistic marketing effort. This is best illustrated by considering where the strengths of general and direct marketing can be combined in the overall marketing effort.

Table 8.1 **DIFFERENCES BETWEEN GENERAL MARKETING AND DIRECT MARKETING**

GENERAL MARKETING	DIRECT MARKETING
Mass selling. Buyers share common demographic, psychographic and lifestyle characteristics.	Selling to individuals. Customers identified by name, address and purchase behaviour.
Product benefits do not always include convenient distribution channels.	Distribution is an important benefit.
Retail outlet is the market place.	Medium is the market place.

Marketer loose control as the product enters the channel.	Marketer controls the product until delivery.
Advertising used to create awareness, build image and benefit recall. Purchase action deferred.	Advertising used to generate an immediate order or enquiry.
Repetition of advertisements used over time.	Repetition used within the advertisement.
Consumers feel less risk – have direct contact with the product and direct recourse.	Could feel high perceived risk – product bought unseen. Recourse is distant.

Adapted from Koekemoer (2004:338)

8.4   THE CONFLICT BETWEEN GENERAL AND DIRECT MARKETING

Ever since direct marketing came of age a conflict with general marketing has been evident in some form or another. The most damaging antagonism has occurred at the point where the two disciplines most often meet head-on – in the area of advertising.

The following are major causes of conflict:

- *Mutual ignorance.* Both sides have been guilty of ignorance and, even worse, of an unwillingness to understand the nature and purpose of the other's discipline. Although there have always been advocates of integration, ignorance has also bred practitioners from each side who believe that the two disciplines are mutually exclusive – that you can either use general advertising or direct response advertising, but not both.

- *The perceived lack of common objectives.* This arises from the last point, but is particularly applicable to advertising per se. General advertising agencies have tended to focus on long-term objectives such as creating awareness, building the brand and stimulating brand recall. As such, they have viewed direct response advertising, with its emphasis on immediate response and sales through special offers, as a short-term, tactical activity that prostitutes the brand and undermines long-term brand-building activity. However, direct response advertisers have argued that general brand advertising is targeted to wide, cannot be measured accurately and is incapable of efficiently attaining the central business objectives of making sales and creating and keeping customers.

- *The battle for budget.* Understandably, the most serious clashes have occurred over the allocation of budget. For a long time direct marketing was viewed by many mainstream marketers as the 'poor relation' of marketing. Direct marketers were forced to fight for whatever budget allocation they could get. This created a confrontational attitude, especially on the part of direct response agencies towards general advertising agencies. However, over the last decade many businesses have begun to move increasingly larger portions of their budget to direct marketing, especially using digital media.

As a result, general advertising agencies have felt more and more threatened. Clearly, this antagonistic situation is not conducive to integration.

■ *Lack of strategic integration.* Largely because of the above issues, general and direct advertising have not been strategically integrated – they have not been planned at top marketing level as complementary activities aimed at attaining the same overall company objectives. Ironically, lack of long-term planning that integrates general and direct advertising is also the cause of the above conflicts: without strategic direction from top management it is impossible for line managers to achieve effective integration.

These are serious problems but, as more businesses are discovering, they can be solved. The answers lie in understanding the principles and objectives of both disciplines.

8.5   KEY VARIABLES OF THE DIRECT MARKETING MIX

It is a known fact that developing the right marketing mix in general marketing requires the correct combination of the four Ps. In direct marketing, however, the key decision variables are somewhat different. Here we have to combine the right target market (via media, list or database segmentation) with the right offer, the right timing and the right creative appeal. Once again, the 'rightness' or success of these decision variables must be measured in terms of how they satisfy the needs of the selected target market.

■ *Target market: database/list/media.* This is the most important decision area of direct marketing. The choice of media offers a range of alternatives. It includes all the media available to general marketing (TV, radio, print, etc) plus direct mail, telephone and the Internet or digital media that are becoming increasingly important as technology develops. Multimedia units at retail sites, TV shopping channels, interactive TV and virtual-reality computer-shopping technology can also be used. Many of these require lists of actual or prospective customers or names, addresses and other relevant marketing information extracted from a database.

Accurate targeting, however, is one of the key factors that make direct marketing such a powerful and effective form of marketing – it ensures highly efficient use of the advertising budget because there is little or no wastage. The direct marketer avoids spending money on communicating with consumers who have no need for his or her product.

■ *Offer.* The offer is the complete sales proposition made to a prospective customer. It includes the product or service itself, the price at which the product or service is offered, any adjustments to the price (such as 'early bird' discounts and other special price incentives), free gift offers, deadline dates and any other product or price considerations. Therefore it includes both the product and the price elements of the traditional marketing mix.

■ *Tuning/sequencing.* Again, this focuses on issues common to general marketing such as one-shot messages versus campaigns, pulsing versus steady flow of communications, positive and negative seasonal factors and optimum use of repetition. Timing can be crucial in direct marketing – for example, school or public holidays can seriously undermine response to direct marketing campaigns.

■ *Creative/format.* This includes copy, design elements, storyboards, involvement techniques and production considerations such as personalisation and the format restrictions applicable to the chosen medium.

This variable encompasses most of the elements of general marketing's communications mix.

The above four decision variables are listed to their order of importance. To illustrate their relative importance in generating a response, conventional wisdom in the direct marketing industry weights the variables according to the percentages shown below:

Table 8.2 **THE RELATIVE WEIGHTINGS OF THE DIRECT MARKETING DECISION VARIABLES**

Target market: database/list/medium	50%
Offer	20%
Timing/sequencing	20%
Creative/format	10%

Adapted from Roberts and Berger (1999:7).

The above is a generalisation of results gathered by direct marketers over many years. It clearly shows that defining, locating and reaching the target market (that is, the right person) is the key variable in direct marketing.

There is a fifth very important variable that is sometimes forgotten because it comes into prominence only after response has been generated. Nonetheless, it is crucial to long-term direct marketing success and, therefore, carries the same weighting as the target market variable. It is customer service.

■ *Customer service.* It has often been said that direct marketing turns a product into a service. That's because it makes the distribution element of the traditional marketing mix an integral part of the total offer: customers can order and receive the product in the comfort of their own home.

Of course, the efficiency of the fulfilment service (or distribution in general marketing terms) is crucial to the customer's purchase and re-purchase decision. Excellent fulfilment is the key to building customer loyalty.

There are two areas to consider here: the types and levels of customer service. Let's briefly consider these:

◆ Types of customer service are tollfree telephone numbers, free limited-time trials, acceptance of various credit cards, etc. All of these contribute to overcoming customer resistance to purchasing products at a distance (where the actual product is not seen).

◆ Levels of customer service are the speed and accuracy of order fulfilment, handling of customer queries and complaints, guaranteed return policies and fulfilment and many more. All these contribute to encouraging repurchase and to building customer loyalty. They reinforce the convenience of buying through the direct marketing process and inspire the customer's confidence in and loyalty towards the direct marketer.

Therefore, direct marketing incorporates the traditional decision variables of general marketing and takes them further by allowing direct marketers to target with pinpoint accuracy and create loyal one-to-one relationships with the individual customers within their target markets.

8.6   THE ADVANTAGES OF DIRECT MARKETING

Direct marketing offers many advantages. Most textbooks on the subject provide a list of the advantages but one of the best is to frame the advantages in a question which compares direct marketing to general advertising:

Why spend your money on ordinary advertising when you can buy accountable ... added-value ... answer-back ... allegiance ... automated ... appropriate ... action advertising?

Let's review the seven issues listed in the question which are known as the seven A's of direct marketing.

■ *Accountable advertising.* Direct marketing is accountable because it allows the direct marketer to account for each rand spent and each rand earned. Although every aspect of a campaign can be measured, the fundamental measurement is cost per sale because it focuses attention on the conversion rate (replies or enquiries that become actual sales). Once profit margin per product is factored into the calculation the direct marketer has the means to measure bottom-line results.

This means that direct marketing is primarily concerned with quality of response, not simply quantity of response. In this regard the creative appeal of direct response advertising is crucial. It must either sell the product immediately or qualify prospects by attracting serious potential buyers only.

■ *Added-value advertising.* This means that direct response advertising, in addition to making sales, creates product awareness and builds the brand. In fact, if the creative appeal is appropriate, it can do a better job of brand building than general advertising can. Why? For the simple reason that it is 'personalised' – it addresses the prospect by name. Messages that are addressed to us in person are far more powerful than messages that address us as anonymous entities in a large group of other anonymous entities. Therefore brand recognition and recall are enhanced.

■ *Answer-back advertising.* Direct marketing aims at creating a dialogue by inviting consumers to answer back. General advertising is one-way communication, a monologue, because – although it attempts both to impart information and to persuade – it offers the consumer no medium through which to answer back.

Digital marketing creates dialogues and dialogues are potentially the beginnings of relationships, from which sales are a more certain result.

■ *Allegiance advertising.* Direct marketing seeks allegiance from customers. It is a long-term approach for which the lifetime value of each customer becomes a key measurement. Lifetime value is a measurement that many businesses ignore, but it is a crucial one. Applying it gives the marketer a completely new perspective on the use of and return on marketing budgets. It is approximately ten times more expensive to acquire a new customer than it is to sell a product to an existing customer. When standards of quality and service remain constant, the more sales a business makes to an existing customer the more affinity there is for the company and the product.

One of the fundamental objectives of direct marketing is to move the consumer 'up the usage and liking ladder' from the stage of being a suspect (completely unaware of the product) to the stage of being an advocate (loving the product to the extent of 'promoting' it to friends and acquaintances). In other words, the advocate generates positive word-of-mouth advertising.

■ *Automated advertising.* Direct marketing is closely linked with technological innovation. In particular, computers and laser printers have developed in leaps and bounds. And yet as their power, capacity and uses have accelerated exponentially, so their cost has diminished making it possible for large businesses to store vast quantities of customer information and to use that information to create loyal relationships with millions of customers. In other words, automation has allowed direct marketers to reach large markets – one customer at a time. Of course it has also given small business the same power. In this sense, technology is the 'great equaliser' – it allows all businesses to compete equally, no matter what their size or financial resources.

■ *Appropriate advertising.* Appropriate advertising is relevant advertising. It is advertising that pre-selects its target market by matching product or service benefits to the needs of a specific market. This requires careful research prior to a campaign.

If a company has a database that is rich in relevant customer information the research process is relatively simple. The marketer would compile an accurate profile of the target market and then extract from the database the names and addresses of customers who fit the profile. In this case, direct mail, telemarketing or MXit could be used for highly accurate targeting.

If the company does not have an adequate database, the direct marketer will still need to compile a target market profile, but would use it to select appropriate outside lists for purchase or to select appropriate media (media viewed, read or listened to by the target market).

Without careful pre-selection any form of advertising produces 'wastage'. Applied to direct mail, lack of pre-selection results in 'junk' mail, which is simply untargeted mail – mail that makes an offer that is inappropriate or irrelevant to the consumer's needs.

Well-targeted direct mail however, is always appropriate because it is based on knowledge of the consumer's needs. Therefore, it is far more likely to elicit a response.

■ *Action advertising.* Direct response advertising has one fundamental objective – to provoke an action from the prospect. That action can be any one of the following three:

◆ to buy a product or service;

◆ to request further information or follow-up by a salesperson; or

◆ to visit a store to buy the product or service.

In other words, direct response advertising is about making sales. To achieve this it must make a proposition or, as it's called in direct marketing, an offer. This makes direct response advertising different from general advertising which aims at creating brand awareness but leaves the offer vague or implicit. In direct marketing the offer is always explicit. It appeals directly to a need that has been identified by the marketer prior to the communication.

The offer is supported by a compelling sales argument that is based on the reasons why the prospect should buy the product. This entails 'selling the benefits' of the product – what the product will do for the prospect. Direct marketing, therefore, closes the marketing loop by persuading the prospect to act. As mentioned earlier it is often referred to as 'salesmanship in print' because it takes the place of the salesperson. It gives the prospect both the reason and the means to purchase.

8.7   ACHIEVING 'SEAMLESS' MARKETING

Although there are distinct differences between the methods of general and direct marketing, both disciplines aim at the same ultimate objective: creating and keeping customers. In addition, there are areas in which general and direct marketing activities can be integrated to form a powerfully synergistic approach. This requires fundamental integration beginning with the overall marketing plan.

If integration is approached strategically the direct marketer has the opportunity to create what has been termed across-the-line or 'seamless' marketing. This ensures that brand image, product positioning and the total marketing mix (both general and direct) are conveyed to the target market, via the communications mix, as a fully integrated and coordinated whole. Unless marketers achieve this 'seamlessness' they run the risk of confusing the target market and themselves, with the result that both internal and external communications break down and, ultimately, sales suffer.

The strategic approach to integration is essential in modern marketing, especially with regard to the traditional antagonism between general advertising and direct marketing. Perhaps the time has come to abandon the outdated notions of 'above-the-line' and 'below-the-line' advertising and to start practicing 'across-the-line' or 'seamless' marketing. Companies that allow the old antagonism to continue will find that in modern, quickly changing and highly competitive markets internal conflict can cripple effectiveness far more readily than external competition. It is imperative, therefore, that marketers find ways to combine the strengths of general and direct marketing methods.

....

REFERENCES

Koekemoer, L. (ed) 2004. *Marketing communication*. Juta: Cape Town.

Roberts, M. and Berger, P.D. 1999. *Direct Marketing Management*, 2ed Prentice Hall: London, UK.

Stone, B. 1986. *Successful Direct Marketing Methods*. NTC Business Books: Chicago, Illinois.

Toffler, A. 1970. *Future Shock*. Pan Books: London, UK.

WEFA Group. 1995. 'Economic Impact: US Direct Marketing Today?' (Executive Summary and Selected Findings). New York: American Direct Marketing Association.

9   Principles of Public Relations

AIM OF THIS CHAPTER

This chapter's focus is on the nature and functions of public relations, basic concepts of public relations and marketing, the planning of a public relations campaign and establishing integrated marketing communications.

LEARNING OUTCOMES

After studying this chapter you should be competent in:
- defining public relations and discussing the nature and characteristics of public relations
- discussing PR in a marketing context
- identifying some of the key functions of public relations
- identifying key stages in the planning of a public relations programme
- achieving the integration of marketing communications

9.1   NATURE OF PUBLIC RELATIONS

Public Relations (PR) is one of the key tools of marketing communications. On occasion PR is a stand alone tool; most often it is a supportive tool. PR originated as a tool to tell a story, to defend companies against bad publicity, to use propaganda or to achieve reciprocity and to build stakeholder relationships. Today PR is a sophisticated multifaceted discipline able to forge effective two-way communication between an organisation and various internal and external groups.

The International Public Relations Association (IPRA) defines public relations as

> the art and social science of analysing trends, predicting their consequences, counselling organisations' leaders, and implementing planned programmes of action which will serve both the organisation and the public interest.

The one-way concept of public relations leads to propaganda or persuasive communication, the two-way concept emphasises communication exchange and mutual understanding and the organisational adjustment concept puts the function in the role of counselling management on corrective actions. In practice, contemporary public relations reflect a mix of all these concepts. The 'new' strategic management role of public relations, however, emphasises the development of lasting inter-relationships by organisations with all stakeholders.

Thus, the evolution of the concept and the numerous descriptions of the practice lead us to the following conceptual definition (Cutlip et al 1994:6): 'Public relations is the management function that establishes and maintains mutually beneficial relationships between an organisation and the public on whom its success or future depends.'

The definition adopted by the South African Public Relations Institute of Southern Africa (PRISA) states that:

> Public relations is the management, through communication, of perceptions and strategic relationships between an organisation and its internal and external stakeholders (www.prisa.co.za.).

Thus, whatever individuals and organisations may think their image is in the marketplace, the public's perceptions of them are all-important, whether based on fact or fiction. Public relations has a key role to play in developing understanding and support for a particular cause or event. Essentially it helps to define and explain relationships of mutual benefit between organisations and their key stakeholders, both amongst their employees and their customers or clients. These must be managed rather than be allowed to develop haphazardly, as so often happens, so that a fair, balanced and positive image can be created.

9.2 PUBLIC RELATIONS IN A MARKETING CONTEXT

PR and marketing are the two functions that are most often confused, with public relations typically being placed under the larger, more powerful marketing function.

Attempts have been made to clarify the basic concepts behind the two management functions and the following conclusions emerge from discussions of four prominent leaders in the marketing and public relations fields (Kotler, Ehling, Jackson and Jones) in the late 1980s:

- Public relations and marketing both deal with organisational relationships and employ similar processes, techniques and strategies.

- The two functions have to be separated by mission or goal. Public relations has the goal of attaining and maintaining accord with social groups on whom the organisation depends in order to achieve its mission. On the other hand, marketing has the goal of attracting and satisfying customers on a sustained basis in order to achieve an organisation's economic objectives.

- Every organisation needs both a marketing and a PR function. They are equally essential to organisational survival and success.

  Confusion between the two functions exists for a number of reasons. For example, many advertised openings for public relations representatives turn out to be positions as door-to-door sales representatives or telephone solicitors. In many small organisations, as a result of budget constraints, the same person performs both functions. Therefore some have concluded that there is really no difference between the two.

Probably the greatest confusion occurs in non-profit organisations and government when 'non-profit marketing' and 'social marketing' refer to building and maintaining relationships with members, donors and other constituents (Cutlip et al 1994:6).

Those in public relations also add to the confusion with a variety of titles and names used to describe their activities. Many find themselves doing marketing work simply because they and their managers confuse the two functions. Others do marketing support publicity because that is what their firm or agency gets paid to do.

In practice, marketing consists of a coordinated programme of research, product design, packaging, pricing, promotion and distribution. The goal is to attract and satisfy customers (or clients) on a long-term basis in order to achieve an organisation's economic objectives. Its fundamental responsibility is to build and maintain a market for an organisation's products and/or services.

Public relations specialists do help in the marketing effort by writing product publicity stories and by arranging media coverage of new products. They are called upon because of their expertise in 'news' stories and in dealing with the news media, but their efforts are part of the marketing strategy to cause the transaction between the organisation and customers.

Wilcox, (2001:528) lists eight ways in which public relations activities contribute to fulfilling marketing objectives:

- Developing new prospects for new markets, such as people who inquire after seeing or hearing a product release in the news media.

- Providing third-party endorsements – via newspapers, magazines, radio, television and digital media – through news releases about a company's products or services, community involvement, inventions and new plans.

- Generating sales leads, usually through articles in the trade press about new products and services.

- Paving the way for sales calls.

- Stretching the organisation's advertising and promotional Rands through timely and supportive releases about it and its products.

- Providing inexpensive sales literature or articles about the company and its products reprinted as informative pieces for prospective customers.

- Establishing the corporation as an authoritative source of information on a given product.

- Helping to sell minor products that don't have large advertising budgets.

Some organisations treat exchange relationships with customers as only one of many organisational relationships. On their organisation charts, marketing is part of the larger public relations function (Figure 9.1). Other organisations view marketing as the basic function, paying attention only to those non-customer relationship seen as important to the marketing effort. PR is subordinate to marketing in these organisations.

A few put 'customer relations' under PR, making it responsible for non-marketing concerns of customers such as complaints, instructions for product use, safety information and repair service. In many organisations marketing and public relations are separate management functions with different but complementary roles.

These two management functions, therefore, deal with organisational relationships. A major difference is that marketing is typically a line-management function engaged in turning an organisation's inputs into outputs of value to others.

Public relations operates as a staff-management function, providing counsel and other services to support line functions. As a result of the line/staff relationship, PR practitioners often provide publicity and media support for marketing efforts. In too many organisations, however, neither senior line management nor public relations and marketing practitioners clearly distinguish between the two concepts or understand the relationship between the two organisational functions.

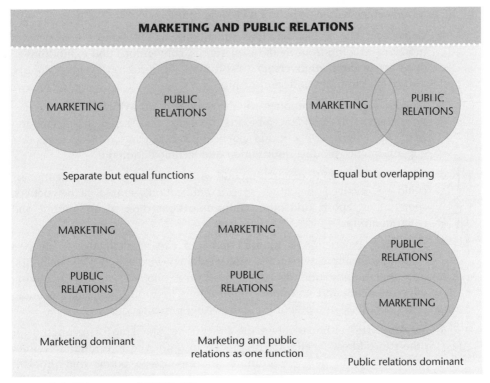

Figure 9.1: Skinner et al (2001:46).

9.3   FUNCTIONS OF PUBLIC RELATIONS

Quite distinct from marketing, PR has a number of key functions. These include the following:

■ *Research.* This involves gathering information about public opinion, trends, emerging issues, political climate, media coverage, concerns of consumer and environmental special-interest groups, etc in order to plan programmes responsive to problem situations. It also includes monitoring programme implementation and assessing its impact to evaluate the effectiveness.

■ *Planning and advising.* This involves determining needs, priorities, goals, target groups, objectives and categories. Essentially it means collaborating with management or clients in a problem-solving process.

■ *Media relations and placement.* This is one of the key functions in which practitioners may be engaged. It involves contacting news media, magazines, Sunday supplements, freelance writers, trade publications and digital with the intention of getting them to publish or broadcast news and features about the organisation. It may also involve responding to media requests for information or spokespersons. Finally, it may mean arranging for the production, booking and placement or broadcasting of corporate advertisements used as part of a PR programme.

■ *Organising.* The public relations practitioner could handle a variety of functions ranging from media conferences, conventions and exhibitions to open-house days, anniversary celebrations, fund-raising events, contests, awards programmes and sponsorship.

■ *Writing.* The PR practitioner should be adept at writing news releases, newsletters, correspondence, reports, booklets, text, radio, television and web copy, film scripts, trade paper and magazine articles, corporate advertisements, product information and technical material.

■ *Editing.* In addition to researching and writing special features, practitioners could be involved in editing special publications, employee newsletters, shareholder reports and other communications directed at internal and external groups.

■ *Production.* Production is multifaceted and very challenging. It involves creating communications using multimedia knowledge and skills (including art, photography and design of brochures, booklets, reports, corporate advertisements and occasional publications; recording and editing audio and videotapes) and preparing audio-visual presentations.

■ *Speaking.* This either involves the practitioner speaking or arranging for others to address meetings. The process of gathering information enables organisations to plan programmes in response to public and problem situations, monitor their effectiveness during implementation and evaluate their overall impact.

■ *Training.* This involves working with executives and other organisational representatives to prepare them for dealing with the media and for presentations and other public appearances. Practitioners could also assist with in service staff development.

■ *Management.* Another very important function is the management of the PR function with regard to personnel, budget and action programmes (Skinner et al 2001:10–12).

Public relations, therefore, incorporates everything that is undertaken to improve mutual understanding between an organisation and all with whom it comes into contact both within and outside the organisation. This includes:

■ advice on the public image of an organisation;

■ action to discover and eliminate sources of misunderstanding; and

■ action to broaden the sphere of influence of an organisation by appropriate publicity, advertising, exhibitions and films – everything, in fact, directed towards improving communication between people and/or organisations.

However, PR is not:

■ a barrier between the truth and the public;

■ propaganda to impose a point of view regardless of truth, ethics and the public good;

■ publicity aimed directly at achieving sales, although public relations can be very beneficial to sales and marketing efforts;

■ composed of stunts and gimmicks – these may be useful at times to put across ideas but fail completely if used often or in isolation;

■ free advertising, or merely press relations, although press work is a very important part of most public relations programmes; and

■ political – its aim in central and local government is to promote democracy through full information and not to advance the policy of any political party.

9.4 PLANNING A PUBLIC RELATIONS CAMPAIGN

Public relations, as one of the organisation's management functions, must involve itself in planning on a strategic as well as a tactical level. The task of PR, as the function concerned with public opinion, is to guide the organisation proactively and reactively to full public acceptance.

Let's consider the planning of a public relations programme. Using the British author Jefkin's model as its base, the model of the Public Relations Institute of Southern Africa (PRISA) identifies seven key stages in the planning of a public relations programme (Figure 9.2).

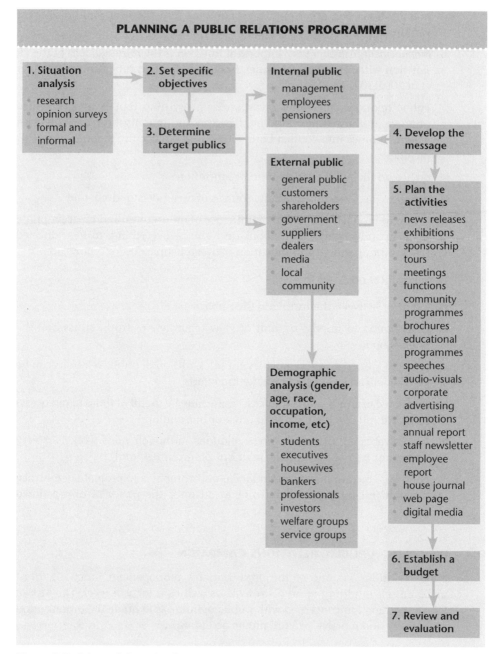

Figure 9.2: Adapted from Koekemoer (2004:405).

9.4.1 Stage 1: Situation analysis

It is important to recognise precisely what the current situation or issue is, what the dynamics are, how it is best defined and the relationship between the underlying problem and the suggested solution.

A useful problem statement summarises what was learned about the problem situation. A problem statement describes the situation in specific and measurable terms and details most of, or all of, the following:

- What is the source of concern?
- Where is this a problem?
- When is it a problem?
- Who is involved or affected?
- How are they involved or affected?
- Why is this a concern to the organisation?

Once the research has been completed (based on the problem statement) enough information should be available to analyse the situation according to a SWOT analysis.

In most instances it has been found that problems can be grouped into the following three general categories:

- Overcoming a negative perception of an organisation, such as resistance by the public to a product on the basis of price and quality or evidence that employees believe their company lacks concern for their interests.
- Conducting a specific one-off project, such as introduction of a new product, conducting a fund-raising project or obtaining shareholder's approval for an acquisition.
- Developing and expanding a continuing programme to sustain a high level of interest, such as maintaining a community's awareness of and confidence in a company's social responsibility programme or convincing the electorate of a political party's interest in their well-being.

9.4.2 Stage 2: Setting the goals and objectives

Objectives are formulated in accordance with the situation analysis. Specific attention should be given to the prioritised internal weaknesses and external opportunities that have been identified.

Objectives need to:

- spell out the key results that must be achieved to reach the programme goal;
- give focus and direction to those developing programme strategy and tactics;
- provide guidance and motivation to those charged with implementing the programme; and

- spell out the outcome criteria to be used for monitoring and evaluating the programme.

Specific objectives must be established to achieve the goal. Objectives are more specific than goals, with each objective contributing to goal achievement. There are basically two kinds of objectives:

- informational objectives; and
- motivational objectives.

One should aim to write the most precise and results-oriented objectives possible that are:

- realistic (achievable);
- credible (the achievement was the result of public relations activity);
- specific (avoidance of vague promises);
- measurable; and
- compatible with the company's overall objectives.

9.4.3 Stage 3: Determining the target groups

Once objectives have been set, the target audience can be determined. In nearly all instances public relations objectives are achieved by influencing someone either to take action or not to take action. The persons to be influenced become the target audience. The temptation often is to describe the target groups in nonspecific terms such as government, media, buying community, population, etc. Such descriptions are insufficient.

The following factors are used alone or in combination to define specific target audiences from among the various stakeholder groups (Cutlip et al 1994:361).

- *Geographics:* natural or political boundaries – indicate where to find people but give little useful insight about important differences within the boundaries. This information is useful for selecting media and allocating programme resources according to population density.
- *Demographics:* gender, income, age, marital status and education – the most frequently used individual characteristics, but they provide little understanding of why or how people are involved or affected.
- *Psychographics:* psychological and lifestyle characteristics (cross-situational) – widely used under the name VALS (Values and Lifestyles System) which segments adults based on 'psychological maturity'.
- *Lifestyle:* Living Standard Measures (LSM) groups
- *Covert power:* behind-the-scenes, political or economic power – describes people at the top of a power pyramid who operate across situations. They exert power over others on a wide range of issues but often not in ways easily observed.

- *Position:* uses the positions held by individuals, not attributes of the individuals themselves, to identify target groups. People are identified as important because of their positions of influence in particular situations.

- *Reputation:* identifies 'knowledgeables' or 'influentials' based on others' perceptions of these individuals. These groups are referred to as 'opinion leaders' or 'influencers'.

- *Membership:* uses appearance on an organisational roster list or affiliation as the attribute relevant to a particular situation; for example, membership of a professional association or special-interest group.

- *Role in the decision-making process:* calls for observing the decision-making process to learn who plays what roles in influencing decisions in a particular situation. This identifies the most active among the active target groups, those who really make decisions, take action and communicate. Or those who block decisions (gatekeepers).

The key to defining target groups is to identify how people are involved and affected in the situation for which the programme intervention is being developed.

9.4.4 Stage 4: Developing the messages

When objectives have been set and target audiences have been identified and prioritised, we can focus on the messages to be communicated. To be understood the message must relate to the interests and concerns of the target groups. They must be able to identify their needs in the message. For any given problem or opportunity there may be several target groups and a different message should be developed to suit each group.

The following aspects have a determining role to play when formulating messages (Cutlip et al 1994:389).

- Firstly, the audience consists of people who are subject to many influences of which the communicator's message is typically only one small source of influence.

- Secondly, people tend to read, watch or listen to communications that present points of view with which they are sympathetic or in which they have a personal stake.

- Thirdly, mass media create their separate communities.

- Fourthly, mass media have a wide variety of affects on individual and collective knowledge, predisposition and behaviour, not all of which are readily measurable.

Careful planning must take into account both the intended and unintended effects of message content. To be effective the message must be explicit (a direct formulated message) or implicit (an indirect message) conveyed by means of different public relations techniques – and it must be ascertained that the messages are related to the objectives.

9.4.5 Stage 5: Planning the activities

PR activities are the tools of communication. They transmit the appropriate message to the target audience. The creativity of the planner is especially crucial. Effective strategy must have action built into it – it must make things happen that relate to the plan's objectives. Planning entails tactical thinking and forms a bridge between strategy and programmes.

The formal action programme will include decisions about:

■ financing;

■ detailed operational steps to be taken in implementation;

■ the time sequence that has to be followed; and

■ the specific tasks that each individual or group associated with the implementation of the communication strategy will have to perform.

The action programme cites a sequence of action plans to be followed and the necessary details (steps) for each separate action plan. Each action plan should be followed by an evaluation and then by a series of decisions concerning the next plan to be undertaken.

The eventual success of a public relations programme depends on behavioural change and there is a step-by-step process to effect change (Figure 9.3 on the following page).

To ease the planning process, however, the following questions should be considered and used with each plan of action to effect the desired change:

■ To whom are you talking?

■ What do you want them to do?

■ Why do you want them to do it?

■ What are you going to say to them?

■ Where will you reach them?

■ When are you going to reach them?

■ Which techniques will you use?

■ How much are you going to spend?

■ What if there is an unforeseen problem?

RELATIONSHIP OF MARKETING COMMUNICATION OBJECTIVES TO OTHER COMPANY OBJECTIVES

Unaware of problem

At this stage the public may not be aware of the problem.

↓

Awareness

Now the public becomes aware of the problem. Normally awareness means a slight or definite uneasiness, but not a concrete definition or knowledge of the problem.

↓

Knowledge

Questions are asked, discussions take place and the problem becomes recognisable – given a 'name', so to speak.

↓

Understanding

During this stage the first signs of a need for change are observed.

↓

Perception

The will to change can only be mobilised once a perception of the need for change is experienced.

↓

Belief

Belief refers to the public's belief in a positive outcome.

↓

Attitude

This can only happen once the attitude changes. In this phase the will to change becomes mobilised.

↓

Behaviour

The process is complete only when behaviour is changed.

Figure 9.3: Adapted from Koekemoer (2004: 410).

9.4.6 Stage 6: Establishing a budget

A marketing jungle truth is that one can spend just enough money to win a battle but lose the war. It's unwise to spend too much, but it's worse to spend too little. When you spend too much, you lose a little money, that is all. When you spend too little you sometimes lose everything because that which you bought was incapable of doing what it was supposed to do.

In established departments, budgets generally relate to one of four factors: total income or funds available, competitive necessity, overall task or goals set for the organisation and profit or surplus over expenses. (Cutlip et al 1994:371):

■ When *total income* or *funds available* is the basis, as in marketing or fundraising activities, public relations is generally allocated a percentage.

■ When *competitive necessity* is the criteria, the amount spent by a similar charity or a competing organisation is matched or exceeded.

■ The *task* or *goals basis* usually provides for public relations to have a share of the funding set aside to achieve the desired end result.

■ The final approach, based on *how much money is 'left over'*, usually sets a fluctuating figure that can go up or down depending on financial circumstances. Not only is it difficult to plan and staff under this option but it also reinforces the impression that public relations is something you do if you have money left after covering the essentials.

The following guidelines may be helpful in drawing up and monitoring the budget:

■ Know the cost of what is proposed. If the plan is to do a special mailing find out the exact cost for photography and artwork, printing and folding, mailing lists, labelling, sorting, delivery, postage and everything else required to complete the job. Do not guess because you will have to live within the approved budget and deliver what was promised.

■ Communicate the budget in terms of what it will cost to achieve specific results. The actual details of variables and fixed costs used to develop the budget may not be of interest to management or to a client. Managers who approve the budget typically want to know how much it will cost to achieve goals and objectives. They look to the PR person to manage the process in a cost-effective manner.

■ Use the power of the computer to manage the programme. Develop a master spreadsheet as well as spreadsheets for individual projects. By tracking each project and linking each to the master spreadsheet one can estimate cash-flow requirements in advance and monitor expenditure against cost estimates.

In the final analysis, practitioners must have realistic budgets, must use them to direct staff efforts, review them frequently with clients and top management and be able to link cost to performance and outcomes.

9.4.7 Stage 7: Review and evaluation

This is a vital step in the public relations programme and it is important to determine the success of each and every activity before follow-up actions are undertaken. The evaluation of objectives is also vital to determine the overall success of the programme. The total process can usually be evaluated according to three criteria.

- *Input*
  - ◆ Was time used economically?
  - ◆ Was the budget management satisfactory?
  - ◆ Were resources fully utilised?
- *Process*
  - ◆ Were there incidents that needed special attention?
  - ◆ Did the process run according to plan?
  - ◆ Did the strategic planning work (objective and action)?
- *Output*
  - ◆ Evaluate the outcome of the project and indicate recommendations for future use where necessary.

A number of measurement tools can be used to determine the effectiveness of a PR programme. These can be divided into formal and informal techniques, and include the following:

- *General feedback.* In a survey undertaken in the USA 'general feedback' was the most popular measurement tool despite the availability of more sophisticated procedures.
- *Press publicity.* This refers to publicity in all types of newspapers and magazines. The traditional accounting method and one that can be effectively measured is counting the number of column centimetres achieved and converting them into rands, using advertising rates as the basis. Sometimes the publication's circulation or number of readers are recorded.
- *Broadcast time.* As with the press, time on the radio or television is another measurement tool – especially if linked to the number of listeners or viewers.
- *Sales results.* Although sales results are difficult to attribute to public relations there is no doubt that a PR programme integrated with the marketing/ sales plan can have an impact on sales results. If the company only used PR, sales can be attributed to it.
- *Opinion polls/surveys.* Studies have shown that companies that use a properly structured audit with clearly defined goals find this method extremely valuable. Unfortunately it is obviously too costly for the 'everyday' PR activity.
- *Subjective internal meetings.* Discussions with sales, marketing and general staff are an effective means of determining how successful a particular

programme or part of a programme has been. Beware of the 'we may not have won but had a lot of fun' feedback.

■ *Complaints and criticism.* Some companies or organisations, such as banks, Telkom, Spoornet, are more prone to complaints or criticism. A programme aimed at negating the issues that tend to cause most of the problems is an obvious and simple yardstick, measurable by the mere reduction in complaints, criticisms or both.

■ *Awards and prizes.* Recognition in the form of awards or prizes in photographic, house journal or advertising competitions is another indication of how successful a particular PR strategy has been. Added to this could be awards for safety, fire protection or personal achievements, all of which contribute to the image of the company.

■ *Fewer government regulations.* PR programmes designed to challenge certain government attitudes or to change or modify policies have proved effective.

Included in this area are lobbying and maintaining close contact with officials. These practices can be of immense help to management in achieving support in such areas as import permits and immigration.

To conclude, there is a growing awareness that PR programmes are vitally needed by companies, organisations and industries. Provided they are formulated by PR professionals with specific knowledge, skills and experience and have top management's full support they can contribute significantly to the success of an organisation in the same way as production, marketing and sales strategies.

9.5 INTEGRATED MARKETING COMMUNICATION

The practice of integrating all the marketing communication efforts is one of the most valuable tools companies can use to gain competitive advantage. Advertising, personal selling, sales promotion, direct marketing, sponsorships, new media and public relations practitioners are busy finding common ground to meet the future challenge of selling to specific customers rather than broad markets.

Don Schultz, Stan Tannenbaum and Bob Lauterborn, authors of *The New Marketing Paradigm* (1994), believe that the critical issue for most marketers is their ability to control the information consumers use to form and adjust their attitudes, especially as most consumers do not differentiate among the sources of information. The antidote, they say, is 'manage the flow through integration'.

They argue, however, that integration can be a limiting concept if it focuses on media choice and execution alone. 'Seamless communications must be built on outstanding marketing strategy and thinking. There is no point in speaking with one voice if the message makes no sense.'

They assert that many companies are held hostage to traditional marketing variables such as product development, price and distribution. 'What most marketers face today is a parity marketplace, in which the only two differentiating features are either logistics or communications.'

Moreover, as the centre of innovation shifts from the laboratory to the customer so, too, will a company's marketing be defined by the customer's agenda. In such an environment the emphasis will be placed more on the relationship and less on the transaction. Because of this and their opinions on the erosion of traditional marketing concepts the authors boldly predict that once logistics are mastered, integrated marketing communications will provide 'the only sustainable competition weapon which most marketing organisations will have in the 21st century'.

IMC is about finding a SMP (single minded proposition). Some ad agencies call it 'The Big Idea'. This SMP is then applied in one or more marketing communications tools. The various practitioners talk to each other to see how each tool can support the other tools. Consumer insights (and sometimes trade insights) are used to pinpoint strategies to approach the target audiences. For example, should the 'tone-of-voice' of our communications be emotional or rational? What kind of language or music should be used?

The key in IMC planning is that all forms of communication are designed to achieve specific objectives. These objectives come from understanding how the marketer can contact the customer or prospect and the message to be communicated. Since the communication goals are driven by the behaviour the marketer wants to change, adapt or reinforce, there is no way any form of communication can stray from that task. The real value of IMC is that it changes the focus from the traditional four Ps (Product, Price, Place and Promotion) to a more customer-focused orientation which emphasises strategic consistency rather than simply independent brand messages.

REFERENCES

Cutlip, S.M., Center, A.H. and Broom, G.M. 1994. *Effective Public Relations*. Prentice Hall: Englewood Cliffs, New Jersey.

Koekemoer, L. (ed) 2004. *Marketing Communications*. Juta: Cape Town.

PRISA. 2010. www.prisa.co.za

Schultz, D.E., Tannenbaum, S.I. and Lauterborn, R.F. 1994. *The New Marketing. Paradigm – Integrated Marketing Communications*. NTC Business Books: Chicago, Illinois.

Skinner, J.C., Von Essen, L.M. and Mersham, G.M. 2001. *The Handbook of Public Relations*. Oxford University Press: Cape Town.

Wilcox, D.L. 2001. *Public Relations Writing and Media Techniques*. Longman: New York.

10 Principles of Sponsorship

AIM OF THIS CHAPTER

To focus on sponsorship as a marketing communications tool, to outline the diverse range of sponsorship objectives and events, to discuss sponsorship selection and how to implement the sponsorship.

LEARNING OUTCOMES

After studying this chapter you should be competent in:
- describing and explaining the nature and scope of sponsorship
- outlining the benefits and potential pitfalls of sponsorship
- planning and managing the sponsorship
- outlining the issues to consider when setting sponsorship objectives and provide typical sponsorship objectives
- discussing sponsorship selection criteria
- discussing the issues involved in deciding between sponsoring an existing event or creating your own event
- discussing broadcast sponsoring
- discussing implementing the sponsorship
- using a sponsorship checklist

This chapter is adapted from *Sponsorship Guidelines*, 1997, of the Association of Marketers and the *Investor's Guide to Sponsorship*, 2002, of the Marketing Federation of Southern Africa, and is published with permission (Koekemoer, 2004).

10.1. INTRODUCTION

The past number of years have seen sponsorships becoming more and more important. It is also a very important part of an Integrated Marketing Communications (IMC) plan. It can extend the impact of other elements of the marketing communications mix, such as advertising, sales promotion, public relations, direct marketing and personal selling, in an environment where consumers are more open and receptive, making key messages more relevant and persuasive.

Sponsorship naturally fits alongside the marketing communications mix and plays a vital role in the marketing communications plan. Isolated from the other elements of the communications mix sponsorship would not be effective, as these elements are required for leverage of the sponsorship programme. Similarly, the other elements of the communications mix should link into the sponsorship and into each other, enabling the communications plan as a whole to flow into achieving the overall marketing communications objectives. Sponsorship is an essential part of an integrated marketing mix and is, therefore, a marketing function.

But what is sponsorship? *Sponsorship is the alignment of a brand with an activity in order to exploit the commercial potential created by the association, thereby positively impacting brand image and/or sales amongst the sponsor's target market, in order to attain marketing and corporate objectives* (Koekemoer 2004:456).

Sponsorship can also be described as the provision of resources (for example, money, people, equipment) by an organisation (the sponsor) directly to a beneficiary or 'sponsoree' (for example, personality, authority, body or code). This enables the beneficiary to pursue some activity (for example, participation by the individual or event management by the authority or body code) in return for rights (which should be detailed in a sponsorship agreement). The choice of sponsorship should be made with regard to the sponsor's marketing communication strategy (cross-impact and leverage between sponsorship and other marketing communication variables employed before, during and after the sponsorship campaign). These should be expressed in terms of corporate, marketing, sales and/or media objectives and measured by linking the objectives to the desired outcome to achieve a return on investment in monetary and non-monetary terms.

A simpler definition is that sponsorship *is a business relationship between a provider of funds, resources or services and an individual, event or organisation that offers association and rights in return, that may be used for commercial advantage.*

Sponsorship offers the opportunity of brand-building and the selling of marketers' goods and services as an alternative to traditional advertising. Sponsorship is an immensely powerful marketing tool. It has the ability to cut through the clutter, providing the unique opportunity to build a relationship with consumers by creating an emotional bond – something rarely spoken of in the business context.

Sponsorship creates the 'feel-good' factor among consumers. For example, a rugby fan will enjoy watching the sport and the appearance of the company's brand name at the event will communicate (in effect) that the company shares the fan's values and interests and is, therefore, his or her type of product. The brand becomes his or her type of brand and if he or she is already a consumer of the brand his or her continued purchase of it is reinforced and the company achieves one of its most sought-after marketing objectives, namely brand loyalty.

Sponsorship is a highly flexible form of marketing communication and can be tailored to meet a wide range of marketing and corporate objectives. It also demonstrates relevance and social responsibility to the consumer, thus showing that the company is caring and concerned about society.

It is for these and many other reasons that globally sponsorship has become an extremely valuable platform for marketing communication and has developed in a relatively short time to become the significant force it is today.

Sponsorship yields some unique benefits but there are some serious pitfalls. Let's review both of these.

10.1.1 Benefits of sponsorship

The long-term benefits and rewards that flow from a committed, well-managed approach to sponsorship are vast and multifaceted, both in business and society. These benefits are unique to sponsorship and include the following:

- *Flexibility.* Sponsorship allows for niche marketing enabling the marketer to manage demographics, psychographics, time and location. Many events and activities can be sponsored in many different ways and events can be selected to fit demographic and psychographic requirements. This provides the opportunity to connect with consumers one-on-one by associating the company (brand or product) with the qualities of the event or activity while simultaneously projecting the company's personality, values and style. This positions the company as 'in sync' with its target market's interests and responsive to their preferences, lifestyles and attitudes.

- *Brand equity.* Sponsorship can provide brand exposure, build association value, even brand exclusivity and can serve as an important branding vehicle that can expand, reinforce and even alter brand personality traits through association with the qualities of an event. This is a unique way of generating brand loyalty and long-term corporate awareness. Sponsorship accrues value over time, increasing its effectiveness and improving the return on investment. When fully integrated and leveraged, events build brand equity.

- *Media exposure.* Sponsorship is the only form of marketing communication in which a marketer can dominate the 'stage' without having to compete with other promotional clutter. It can also extend the value of ad campaigns by creating a dynamic, interactive environment that makes key messages more relevant and persuasive for example, SAB (South African Breweries) with their arrive-alive campaigns and the 'don't drink and drive' campaigns.

- *Cost effectiveness.* Sponsorship enables marketers to obtain coverage and brand awareness at a more favourable rate than traditional advertising, adding greater value to the advertising rand and simultaneously incorporates corporate PR and social responsibility programmes. As the main sponsors of the Soccer World Cup 2010 sponsors such as Coca-Cola and Pick n Pay obtained certain advantages above other sponsors.

- *Industrial labour relations.* A company's reputation and image have bearing on the morale of staff and can encourage the highest quality of future job applications. Discovery Medical Aid/ Legal wise employees receive benefits that attract potential/future job applications, ie free gym memberships, hotel accommodations, kids day-care centres, etc.

■ *Opens doors.* Sponsorship creates long-term relationships. It creates influence. Through corporate hospitality and a good corporate image and reputation, a company's ability to do business with local and national government and other influential people can be enhanced, producing access that would otherwise be extremely difficult and costly to achieve.

■ *Crosses all frontiers.* The involvement of South African companies with South African sporting success is an invaluable tool in the export drive and promotion of the nation. Sponsorship is global. It crosses all barriers of bureaucracy, national prejudice and language, for example, Adidas is an international brand that sponsors football clubs globally and is recognised by the products they offer.

■ *Presents new challenges.* Sponsorship, and the leverage of the sponsorship to maximise the return on investment, presents great challenges for creativity and often reveals ingenuity in marketers.

■ *Unites the nation.* In a nation passionate about sport, sterling performances by national teams help to unify the nation and create feelings of goodwill amongst people who may otherwise be strongly divided. Sport sponsorship, in particular, helps to reduce conflict in the nation. Through association with such activities, sponsors can positively enhance consumer perceptions of their brands in relation to these values.

As a marketing tool, sponsorship can directly influence sales performance, but its real value lies in creating a long-term relationship with the event or activity (sport or arts) and the community at large. The perception that it is adding to the event or activity and to the entertainment available to consumers, enables a company and its brands to achieve a degree of public acceptance and respect that is not necessarily restricted to fans of a particular activity or event. Sometimes the sponsorship is crucial to the future of a sport or art.

Through successful and sensitive involvement in sponsorship, a company can show that it is not merely making a successful brand, but that the brand is part of a wider beneficial involvement in the society of which the consumer is a participating member.

10.1.2 Potential pitfalls

Sponsorship requires specialised skills and expertise and must be very carefully managed. Any aspect that is overlooked could result in devastating consequences for the company. An awareness of the following potential pitfalls will enable sponsors to anticipate them and thereby limit the possibility of their occurrence:

■ *Ignorance of contractual rights.* It is absolutely essential that sponsors are completely familiar with the legal aspects of the sponsorship contract. The rights are the basis of the sponsorship and, therefore, to know what you are buying in terms of your sponsorship investment is a critical aspect and an area where many sponsors make mistakes – purely out of ignorance. It is advisable to work with an attorney when negotiating the contract to ensure that you are fully aware of what your rights include and that they are correctly specified in the contract.

- *Ambush marketing.* This is defined as the attempt of an organisation to create the impression of being an official sponsor of an event or activity by affiliating itself with that event without having paid the sponsorship rights-fee or being a party to the sponsorship contract.

  The ambush marketing tactics that can be and have been used are seemingly limitless. For example, a company may use taglines in its advertising, such as 'We support the South African team', or it may use symbols commonly associated with the event, such as the Olympic flame. This creates confusion in the market about who the sponsor is and dilutes the sponsorship investment.

  Sponsors can protect themselves and the event from ambush marketing, to a certain degree, by ensuring that they are fully aware of their rights to the event. These would include naming, branding, exclusivity, broadcast, licensing and merchandising rights and should be specified in the sponsorship contract. Full knowledge and use of specified rights as well as trademark legislation and licensing will afford some protection against ambush marketing.

- *Broadcast rights.* Many sponsors make the mistake, when negotiating an event sponsorship contract, of assuming that broadcast rights are included in the rights package (often the event rights owner or promoter will lead the marketer to believe this). Broadcast rights are not included in the event sponsorship contract, and in some cases an event sponsor may not even be offered first refusal for the broadcast rights. Therefore, if the company wishes to be the event and broadcast sponsor (the most effective sponsorship programme), it is advisable to negotiate with all the parties concerned at the same time. Tri-party negotiations with the event rights owner (sporting federation in most cases) and the broadcast rights owner (SABC, M-Net, DStv, etc) will eliminate any confusion and ensure a balanced sponsorship programme – even if it is somewhat expensive. This can also prevent the possibility of a competitor purchasing the broadcast rights and thereby ambushing the event sponsorship and drastically diluting the sponsorship investment. If we wish to be the broadcast sponsor it is advisable to consider advertising in and around the broadcast of the event. It should be stipulated in the broadcast contract that no competitive advertising can be accepted.

- *Staff.* As sponsorship is an extremely complex and specialised form of marketing communication it is essential that those managing it have the appropriate skills. Sponsorship is high profile by nature and, therefore, any mistakes or omissions of even the smallest aspect can have potentially devastating consequences for the company. Ensure that personnel are adequately qualified and trained.

- *Expense.* Do not make the mistake of believing that the rights-fee is the total sponsorship investment. It is essential to maximise the investment – ideally, for every rand put into the actual sponsorship, a minimum of a rand for leverage of the investment (advertising and promotional activity) will be required, otherwise the optimum return on the investment will not be achieved.

■ *One-off sponsorships.* Sponsorships that are 'one-night-stands' are seldom successful. The time-period is far too short to successfully build a relationship with a brand. Nike's success in the USA came from the company's commitment to being a major sponsor of basketball, with Michael Jordan as the pivot. This was a long-term project that paid long-term dividends as time passed.

■ *Agents.* It is important to be aware of the following issues when dealing with agents:

   ◆ *Double dealing.* Selling sponsorship rights to more than one sponsor and leading each sponsor to believe that they are buying exclusive rights to the event or activity. Agencies can also mislead marketers into believing that they have the broadcast rights and sell the event on the back of this 'promise'. Their first concern is to get the sponsorship commitment and then they will negotiate rates and rights.

   ◆ *Exorbitant mark-ups and commissions.* The result is that very little money is available for the sport or event sponsored. To prevent this pitfall, which could seriously affect the success of the event, work with an accountant and a lawyer and attempt to get as much information as possible on the event or activity and on the credibility of the agent concerned.

   ◆ *Agency commissions.* Make sure when negotiating directly with the media that your advertising agency does not claim commission without your knowledge. It must be clearly specified, particularly on broadcast sponsorship, whether agency commission is included in the negotiated figure or not. If the sponsor deals with the media there should be no agency commission included in the fee.

■ *The media.* It is important to be aware of the following when dealing with the media:

   ◆ Event sponsors are not given first refusal for the broadcast rights to the event – instead the event sponsor's competitors are approached to purchase these rights. This encourages ambush marketing.

   ◆ Broadcasters sell advertising time to the broadcast sponsor's competitors during the broadcast of the event, which also encourages ambush marketing.

   ◆ The press tends to abbreviate or omit the names of events in their editorials. The sponsor owns the naming rights to the event and, therefore, the name must be used correctly.

   ◆ Ensure that ad breaks do not contain competitive advertising. This needs to be specified up front during broadcast rights negotiations.

   ◆ Make sure that outside broadcasting unit costs are included in the contract.

   ◆ Ensure that clear guidelines and contracts exist for multi-media and multi-sectoral sponsorships.

These guidelines are designed to make sponsorship more effective in achieving marketing objectives by creating awareness of how sponsorship can be used successfully with minimum potential for the pitfalls described above.

10.2 PLANNING AND MANAGING THE SPONSORSHIP

Most integrated marketing plans make provision for sponsorships as part of the total plan. Due to its importance, it can extend the impact of other elements of the marketing mix, such as advertising, sales promotion, communications, public relations and sales, in an environment where consumers are more open and receptive, making key messages more relevant and persuasive.

Sponsorship fits naturally into the marketing mix and plays a vital role in the marketing plan. In planning the sponsorship, as many other marketing mix variables as possible must be used and the desired cross-impact synergy specified. Database marketing is an effective (although by no means the only) way of leveraging a sponsorship effectively. Isolated from the other elements of the marketing mix, sponsorship would not be as effective. Similarly, the other elements of the marketing mix should link into the sponsorship and to one another, thereby enabling the marketing plan as a whole to flow into achieving the overall marketing objective.

The planning of a sponsorship requires a holistic view that relationships exist between the sponsorship management decision-making areas. It is suggested that the following should be linked:

- The sponsor sets a range of sponsorship objectives given the selected target audience. The objectives can fit into categories decided on by the sponsor. They can range from corporate to marketing to sales objectives.
- Select the appropriate sponsorship.
- Implement and leverage the sponsorship.
- Evaluate the effectiveness of the sponsorship.

Let's look at these issues in more detail (see also Figure 10.1).

10.2.1 Sponsorship objectives

The diverse range of objectives for which sponsorship can be used effectively illustrates its highly flexible nature. Sponsorship can be applied directly to the bottom line, for example, in the generation of sales and is often used to augment other marketing communication with objectives such as creating brand awareness, enhancing corporate and brand image, building relationships and developing goodwill in the community. The following should be considered when setting objectives:

- Sponsorship objectives must be clearly defined.
- Sponsorship objectives must match overall marketing objectives to ensure that they contribute to the achievement of the marketing objectives.

- Well-defined, quantifiable sponsorship objectives enable the marketer to develop clear selection criteria for events or activities to be sponsored.

- Strategies for leverage of the sponsorship should be developed directly from sponsorship objectives.

- Clear and measurable sponsorship objectives facilitate the integration of objectives during implementation as well as effective evaluation of the 'success' of the sponsorship.

- Always ensure that sponsorship objectives are clearly expressed and understood by all involved, internally and externally.

- Ensure that the objectives are realistic and achievable considering aspects such as budget allocation and types of events or activities available for sponsorship. It is also advisable to consider external factors such as competitors' activities, their involvement in sponsorship and their sponsorship objectives.

The following are common sponsorship objectives:

- *Corporate objectives*
    - increase (or maintain) awareness;
    - enhance or change corporate image;
    - change target market perceptions or attitudes; and
    - develop an involvement with the community.

- *Marketing objectives*
    - enhance or change a brand image;
    - create positive associations with a brand amongst the target audience;
    - establish brand relevancy with target audiences;
    - facilitate dialogue and consumer interaction;
    - build business or trade relations; and
    - build 'goodwill' amongst customers, business contacts and key influencers, forge links with opinion leaders.

- *Sales or service expansion objectives*
    - increase sales or market share (sales and trade promotions);
    - increase target market awareness of brand;
    - identify or build product image;
    - strengthen brand preference;
    - media coverage and wireless or Web distribution;
    - increase sales and market share via licensing arrangements (for example, Castle Lager and Springbok rugby jerseys); and
    - increase sales and market share through product endorsement (for example, Nike and Tiger Woods for many years. In spite of Tiger Woods' personal life drama Nike decided to continue sponsoring him).

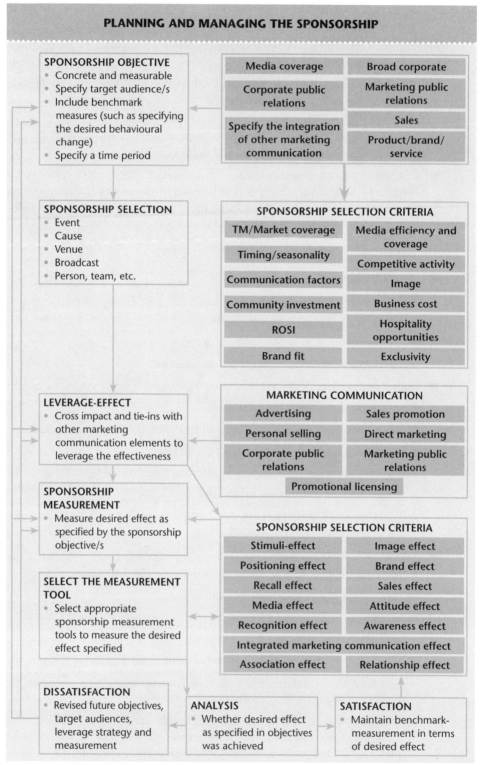

Figure 10.1: Adapted from Coggin (2002).

10.2.2 Sponsorship selection

The event or activity selected must stand out from the crowd and not be perceived as a 'me too' sponsorship. Selection is a critical phase of sponsorship requiring thorough consideration and investigation of many different factors before the particular event or activity is chosen and the sponsorship contract is signed.

The sponsorship selection criteria consist of the factors that have a direct bearing on the choice of event or activity to sponsor. Basic research into each of the areas described can make the difference between a successful sponsorship and a significant marketing failure. Sponsorship selection is usually based on the following criteria:

- *Target market coverage.* A fundamental requirement is that the sponsored event must reach the consumers with whom the marketer wishes to communicate. In order to achieve this, detailed information must be obtained relative to the sporting or arts interests of the target market as well as the degree to which media coverage of the proposed event will reach these people.

- *Timing/seasonality.* Consider the corporate marketing needs, product seasonality, other marketing communication strategies, etc. Establish that the event does not take place on the same day as a major sporting event, as the media coverage may then only consist of a few minutes or column centimeters.

- *Competitor activity.* This involves general market investigation to obtain information on competitors' sponsorship involvement. If a decision is taken to sponsor an activity or event similar to one being sponsored by a competitor, ensure that the event is high profile enough to dominate the attention of the target market.

- *Communication factors.* Consider the 'type' of sponsorship on offer (such as title sponsorship, presenting sponsorship, co-sponsorship, etc; or federation, league, event, team, individual, facility, etc; or broadcast, etc) as these convey different messages and will determine communication strategies and leverage as well as media interest.

- *Event profile (history, previous sponsors).* Consider the degree to which the previous sponsor created a lasting bond with the event/activity and whether you can displace the equity built up by the previous sponsor in the target market.

- *Potential media exposure.* Consider the likely level of media exposure to be achieved through on-site branding at the event. Generally, TV exposure is one of the most important features of a sports sponsorship. Potential on-screen branding can be established through timing analysis of previous editions of the event or of similar events.

- *Product or brand relevance.* The perceived synergy between sponsor and event can be an advantage. For example:
  - direct brand link (Coca-Cola sponsoring a soccer event: FIFA);
  - indirect brand link (MTN sponsoring the soccer zone promotion on TV);

- image link (Sony sponsoring a rock concert); or

- corporate image link (Nedbank sponsoring an arts festival).

■ *Image.* Consider the image to be projected. The event or activity must fit the corporate and brand image and conform to the sponsorship policy of the company. As a rule, 'brand fit' is essential for effective sponsorship.

■ *Budget/costs.* Is the sponsorship affordable and if so, does it represent value for money? Consider the relative value of media delivery, focusing on TV. This will entail analysing a range of events (previous sponsorship or packages on offer) to establish a cost versus media valuation relationship. This calculation involves sponsor exposure time per hour, hours of broadcast, audience delivery and the normal costs of reaching that audience through 30 second spot advertising, ie either spot costs or cost per thousand (CPM) or cost per gross rating point (CRP). Results can be plotted to establish whether the sponsorship offer appears to be good, average or poor value in comparison with other events.

It is also advisable to ensure that sufficient funds are available and that the budget is flexible enough to allow for unforeseen expenses.

■ *Hospitality opportunities.* Consider the hospitality potential that the event sponsored may offer. Examine factors such as the suitability of the event, the venue and the facilities for entertaining VIP guests.

■ *ROSI.* Return on Sponsorship Investment. ROSI may not only be financial, it may also relate to factors such as changing brand perceptions, cross selling opportunities, hospitality opportunities, relationship building, etc.

■ *Exclusivity.* Exclusivity is ideal as other sponsors involved could dilute the impact of the main sponsor or other sponsors.

In selecting the type of sponsorship to get involved in, prospective sponsors should be aware of the following considerations:

■ *Levels of sponsorship in sport.* There are various levels of sponsorship in sport and the level selected will depend on the requirements determined in the selection criteria and on the sponsorship and marketing objectives. The sponsorship rights-fee and the rights afforded to the sponsor may differ at each level. One or a combination of the following levels may be chosen:

- *National team sponsorship* (for example: Vodacom sponsors a number of national teams; Nike, Castle and Wellington Brandy sponsor the Springbok rugby team).

- *Provincial team sponsorship* (Mr. Price sponsors the Natal Sharks rugby team; Vodacom sponsors the Bulls and the Stormers).

- *League sponsorship* (Castle Lager sponsors the Premier Soccer League).

- *Individual club sponsorship* (Sasol sponsors Sasol Super Squad U23 soccer).

- *Individual athlete sponsorship* (Nike sponsors Roger Federer and Tiger Woods).

- *Development sponsorship* (PPC Cement sponsors cricket development).

◆ *Multi sponsorships* (Energade sponsors cycling events, triathlons and is the official sports drink of Super 14 rugby).

In considering a combination of levels in sport sponsorship a company could, for example, select a national team for its primary sponsorship programme and then get extra value by sponsoring development in the same sport.

It is advisable for companies to have a development component as part of their transformation or reconstruction and development programme. Creative leverage of a development sponsorship can yield many benefits for sponsors, even though it would not normally receive the same coverage as any of the other levels in sports sponsorship.

■ *Technical sponsors in sport.* Apart from the primary sponsorship (such as national team sponsorship with naming rights) there are technical sponsors who are entitled to secondary sponsorship rights. In the case of FIFA, Technical sponsors supply the team's kit. For example, Adidas may be the official shoes and clothing supplier, and Coca-Cola the official drink supplier. In addition, there may be different suppliers for balls, bats, racquets, caps, sunglasses, sunscreen, etc all entitled to various rights and, depending on the sport, to branding rights on kit items. Individual stars' equipment can also be sponsored, for example, golf clubs, cricket bats, tennis rackets, etc.

■ *Licensing and merchandising.* This is an important factor in sponsorship selection. It can be immensely profitable and provide added value to the leverage of the sponsorship. It is critical that the naming-right holder (primary sponsor) makes use of the licensing option to prevent ambush marketing.

As a means of generating funds many sporting bodies will award a licensing contract or develop a licensing programme. The sponsor should take up this licensing option and specify in the rights agreement that because of the trademark or theme mark, it may be resold to licensees.

The sponsor may sell merchandising rights to an official supplier or merchandiser for event-related articles that would feature the logo and/or theme piece (T-shirts, caps, etc). The merchandiser then pays royalties for the use of the logo and theme piece.

It is essential to approve all items that will feature the logo and this requirement should be specified in the contract. If there is no control the merchandise may be of inferior quality or the logo may be incorrectly printed, which would have a negative impact on the company and the sponsorship programme.

■ *International factors.* If a national team is invited to an overseas fixture the sponsor must be aware of their rights on an international level. The following five issues are usually relevant:

◆ *Exclusivity.* This aspect can be illustrated by the following example. There are two levels of sponsorship rights for the Olympic Games, world and national. World rights are sold by the IOC (International Olympic Committee) and give the sponsor rights to use their association with the Olympics throughout the world. National sponsorship rights for South Africa are sold by NOCSA (National Olympic Committee of South

Africa). A conflict arose in relation to the 1996 Olympics sponsorship. VISA held world rights, giving any banking institution that held a VISA franchise in any country in the world the right to use their association with the Olympic Games. The problem arose when Nedbank became a National Olympics sponsor. Fortunately for Nedbank, their exclusivity clause prevented VISA or any VISA franchise from using their Olympics association in South Africa. Without this clause, Nedbank's investment would have been wasted as any bank with a VISA franchise could have ambushed their sponsorship.

◆ *Know exactly what you are buying.* Obtain this information by asking the body you are dealing with (for example, BMW South Africa would not want to be involved in an international event called the Nissan Shield).

◆ *Check branding signage opportunities.* Determine whether signage will give value to the sponsorship or will have no significance in the international market.

◆ *South African copyrights* may be of no consequence internationally as they are only registered within South Africa.

◆ *Maximise team sponsorship* by ensuring that the international event is covered by the local press and manage publicity campaigns accordingly.

10.2.3 Sponsoring an existing event versus creating your own event

Sponsors may be faced with a choice between sponsoring an existing event or creating their own event.

A marketer may be approached by an agent wishing to sell the rights to an event on behalf of the rights owners (usually sporting bodies). Agents and intermediaries tend to approach regional and national companies first as these companies have bigger brands and budgets and can spend more on an event. Agents generate their revenue through:

■ sponsor fees;

■ tickets to the event;

■ programmes and advertising in them;

■ concessions;

■ merchandise royalties; and

■ TV revenue.

The success of an existing event depends on the organiser's experience and skill, as well as the answers to the following questions:

■ Who is responsible for promoting the event?

■ Will spectators come to the event?

■ How can attendance be maximised?

■ Do you understand rights-fees and admin costs?

■ Once the rights-fees are paid, what budget is set for leverage of the sponsorship? Consider the 1:1 ratio for leverage: as stated earlier, for every rand invested in the sponsorship, the sponsor must be able to match it with a rand for promoting the sponsorship. This is essential for optimum return on the sponsorship investment.

■ Strategic considerations in selecting on existing event. The following must be considered when evaluating an event:

◆ Who are the other sponsors? For example, for a multiple sponsorship event are any of the other sponsors competitors?

◆ How many sponsors are there at each sponsorship level?

◆ What are the other sponsors' rights and how do they differ from your rights?

◆ Did the other sponsors gain rights commensurate with their payment? Did you?

◆ How did the agent or federation or broadcaster arrive at their asking price?

◆ What is included in the rights-fee?

◆ Other sponsors. Is their business compatible with yours or is it in conflict? For example, the core businesses of McDonald's and Weigh-Less are incompatible and they should not sponsor the same event. If this situation arises determine whether contact (signage, location, etc) between the conflicting businesses can be kept to a minimum. If you have negotiated an exclusivity clause in the contract the agent would have to replace the conflicting sponsor.

◆ Cluttered events. If the event is cluttered (that is, there are a lot of different sponsors) be creative and find ways to ensure that your branding is visible. This requires considerable additional spending. Leading brands (such as Coca-Cola and South African Breweries) can negotiate limitations on the type and number of other sponsors. They can also negotiate 'clean stadia', that is, limits to signage in and around the stadium.

◆ What opportunities are there for hospitality and are these suitable for VIP guests?

◆ If the event was previously sponsored by another company, are you confident that enough brand association can be built to dilute and eventually overpower the brand association built up by the previous sponsor? This will require significant expenditure for leverage and promotion of the event.

■ *Creating your own event.* The objective of creating an event is to control and dominate it. Creating your own event gives a degree of control over:

◆ where the event will take place;

◆ how your company is positioned (branding, image, etc);

◆ the timing of the event;

◆ how your customers and VIPs are treated (hospitality);

◆ how much you spend;

◆ number and types of other sponsors;

◆ quality of the event; and

◆ selection of various media partners.

However, creating your own event involves increased risk and, therefore, it is advisable to seek the advice of lawyers and insurance professionals, contract with a professional event or sports marketing company and work very closely with everyone involved.

10.2.4 Broadcast sponsorship

In selecting the appropriate sponsorship, the decision on whether or not to get involved in broadcast sponsorship is important. Broadcast sponsorship provides the best coverage of the widest possible audience. The most successful sponsorship programmes are those where the sponsor is involved in sponsoring the event as well as the broadcast of the event – this is the most balanced approach.

In recent years, a clear distinction between event sponsorship and broadcast sponsorship has developed. The most likely reason for this is that broadcast sponsorship is extremely costly – it is the most expensive component of the total sponsorship cost. Therefore, many sponsorships consist of the event sponsor who owns the rights to the actual event and the broadcast sponsor, who owns the rights to the broadcast of the event.

Broadcast sponsorship is appealing to marketers because communicating to consumers through an independent third party (the media) results in a more subtle selling message than the direct approach of traditional advertising. Broadcast sponsorship is the only form of marketing communication that provides the marketer with an opportunity to dominate the stage entirely without having to share it with competitors and, therefore, has the ability to break through the promotional clutter which traditional advertising is often unable to do.

The media, especially television, is well aware of this power and its ability to attract audiences. It must be remembered, however, that without the event sponsor there would be no event to broadcast.

The following issues must be taken into account when deciding on broadcast sponsorship:

■ *Coverage and exposure*

◆ *Market coverage.* Know the market coverage of the event broadcast and ensure that key markets are included in the coverage.

◆ *Estimated audience.* Get a clear picture of the estimated audience and know how those numbers were developed, including audience guarantees. Check this by examining the previous year's ratings for similar programming. Factor these audience estimates into any competing programming.

◆ *Logo visibility.* Carefully assess the placement and value of the logo's exposure during the broadcast. Logo visibility during a broadcast can create a cost-effective impression.

◆ *Advertising space.* When advertising space is included in the broadcast sponsorship, review the sponsorship objectives and evaluate how the event advertising would:

- coincide with the advertising flighting pattern;

- expand the brand reach against its core target;

- enable the brand to reach a new target audience; and

- support the brand and/or corporate image.

◆ *Competitor merchandising.* Will they allow competitors T-shirts, caps, etc. in the stadium? This can detract from the sponsor's exposure. The media is best able to decide on the level of commercial exposure acceptable to its audience and the sponsor will decide whether the exposure opportunities on offer represent good value for money.

■ *Assessing the cost effectiveness of the broadcast sponsorship package.*

To assess if the amount to be paid for the broadcast of the event is good value, calculate the CPM or the CRP. Weigh these factors against a typical advertising buy, see how much of a premium is being asked and then determine if the higher cost is worth it. It is advisable to rely on experienced media buyers from the ad agency or a specialised media buying service.

Actual audience delivery is a critical component in the evaluation process and in determining success of the broadcast sponsorship. To determine the total impression, do a post-event broadcast evaluation of publicity and broadcast ratings.

■ *Problems and complexities surrounding broadcast sponsorship.*

It is advisable to consider the following problems and complexities surrounding broadcast sponsorship before entering into a broadcast sponsorship contract:

◆ *Ambush marketing.* If it is decided not to purchase the broadcast rights to the event, the televised coverage could be sponsored by a competitor (which in effect amounts to ambush marketing). This is extremely detrimental to event sponsorship investment and to the sport or arts sponsored. Ambush marketing also occurs when the broadcaster allows competitive advertising to be placed during the broadcast of the event.

◆ *Broadcast sponsorship only (usually short term).* Marketers who only sponsor broadcast of events often use it as a short-term tactical tool to create awareness. This result in less funds, if any, going back into the event or activity which may well be in danger of losing the event sponsor if they are not offered television exposure. Consideration should, therefore, be given to ensuring that a proportion of the revenue generated by broadcast sponsorship is ploughed back into the event or activity (sport or art).

◆ *Provision of event-related services.* Some complexities arise in the sponsor/ media relationship with the provider of services such as timing, results and result analyses (watch and computer companies). These can supplement media coverage and provide enhanced information for spectators that would not otherwise be affordable.

◆ *Broadcast sponsorship is expensive.* Broadcast sponsorship is high profile and important to many sponsors, but it can lack the flexibility and targeted communication available through other media at a lower cost.

◆ *Some sponsors feel that sponsoring television coverage of a major event on a small budget* means that they can only be small fish in very big ponds and therefore prefer to sponsor minority sports enabling a closer, more recognisable link.

10.2.5 Implementing the sponsorship

■ *Prerequisites.* Before implementing the selected sponsorship four issues need to be addressed:

◆ Does the sponsorship fit into the strategy for the brand? A number of criteria could be used to evaluate the fit or to select the ideal sponsorship. The following matrix (Figure 10.2) can be used where the best fit is where the brand's exposure/association is high and the customer experience/ bond is high:

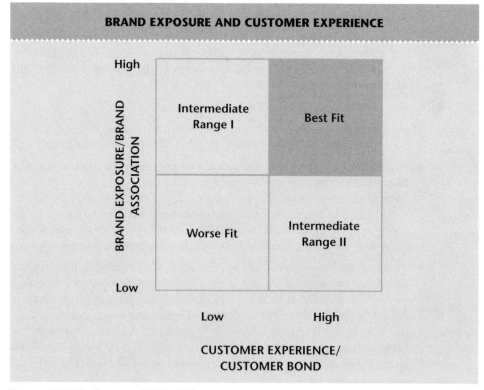

Figure 10.2: Koekemoer (2004:474).

◆ A second prerequisite is to be satisfied that the parties involved are professional, that they have the necessary credentials to organise or promote the event and that there is full disclosure of pertinent information.

◆ A third is to eliminate the risk of ambush marketing by either association or by intrusion.

◆ Finally, dot every i and cross every t. Ensure that all the legal aspects are taken care of, that the interests of all parties are secured and that all rights and obligations are understood.

■ *Implementation requirements.* A sponsorship must emanate from the marketing objectives and plan and must contain its own marketing plan or strategy that flows directly from the sponsorship objectives. This can involve building internal support and agreement across the entire marketing department that is the advertising manager, sales manager and public relations manager, to ensure better management of the sponsorship and to maximise the return on the investment.

Throughout the sponsorship the support of senior management and stakeholders must be obtained and maintained by providing them with periodic reviews and updates of progress towards sponsorship objectives and ultimately marketing and corporate objectives. The support of senior management and stakeholders is crucial to gain approval for expenditure.

Maximising the return on investment requires imaginative, creative and skilful exploitation of the sponsorship. To do this effectively will require investing money in promoting the association with the event by transferring 'brand footprint' across all media in terms of tone and manner, message, brand positioning, image, etc. This is expensive and will require dedicated and flexible planning and management. Sponsorship management, as with advertising, is not a 'nine-to-five' profession.

Accountability is essential. The sponsor must ensure that all funds can be adequately accounted for and it is advisable to work with an accountant who can keep accurate records of expenditure so that if any questions do arise, proof of where the money has gone is available. In implementing the sponsorship, the event marketing strategy must:

◆ support corporate objectives and marketing objectives;

◆ work with the brand strategy directed to the same targeted audience;

◆ support sales and marketing plans;

◆ consist of a strategy to secure internal support and encourage key stakeholders to endorse the sponsorship;

◆ ensure a leverage ratio of at least 1:1; and

◆ include qualitative measurements of 'success'.

■ *Leverage of sponsorship.* Herein lies the difference between a mediocre sponsorship and a successful sponsorship. The key is imaginative and creative exploitation involving maximising the brand's or company's visibility in order to maximise coverage and awareness, and ultimately to maximise the return on the sponsorship investment – from launching the sponsorship (which can achieve immense media exposure), to hospitality and to the publicity during and after the event.

Effective leverage requires a budget that at least matches – and ideally doubles – the sponsorship investment. This ongoing promotional activity creates exposure that adds considerable value to the event and to the sponsorship investment.

Developed directly from the sponsorship objectives, specific leverage objectives include:

◆ to reinforce, enhance or alter brand image;

◆ to strengthen corporate image;

◆ to create the opportunity for product sampling and trial;

◆ to increase and maintain market share;

◆ to open new channels of distribution;

◆ to forge new links with opinion leaders;

◆ to improve employees' morale;

◆ to gain a competitive advantage; and

◆ to launch a new product or service.

It is important to ensure that the objectives set are communicated and understood by all involved in implementing leverage strategies and tactics.

To leverage the sponsorship to the maximum one must understand leveraging, prepare a leveraging plan, execute the plan and evaluate the plan.

■ *Understanding leveraging.* Leveraging goes beyond branding and/or signage and just 'being there'. It is all about making the sponsorship work for you by interacting with your target market in a relevant way. Look for opportunities that bring your brand to life in an environment where your audience has chosen to be. It is also about bringing your target market closer to what your brand stands for – your mission and values – and to market your company's core business, products or services. Your leveraging rand should be spent driving your brand and product message via the sponsorship theme.

■ *Executing your plan.* Ensure that you have followed the necessary protocol in executing your plan. Make certain that you have followed your rights, that the necessary approvals have been passed, that your activities will not clash with other co-sponsors and that your measurement criteria and tools are in place for evaluation after the event. Take control of your message and bring your brand to life within every element of the sponsorship leverages. Exploit your sponsorship rights ... and more!

■ *Measurement and evaluation.* This is a critical element of sponsorship. There are many measurement tools available to evaluate the success of your sponsorship against your objectives. They should be utilised and budgeted into the sponsorship investment.

■ *Hospitality.* An important objective of sponsorship is to provide access to influential people and VIPs who would otherwise be extremely difficult and costly to reach. Hospitality at the event provides the perfect opportunity to build a relationship with influential VIPs in a relaxed atmosphere. This should, however, be carefully planned. Every detail must be meticulously attended to during planning and implementation, from the arrival of the guests to their departure. The following aspects should receive attention:

◆ *Venue.* It is critical to ensure that the event's venue has facilities conducive to hospitality and entertaining VIP guests – it is essential to check this beforehand.

◆ *Budget.* Ensure that the budget is adequate to meet the scope of the intended hospitality. This will require a budget separate from the sponsorship budget – add 10 to 15 per cent to cover contingencies.

◆ *Guest list.* Carefully devise a list of the appropriate VIPs to invite. It is advisable to have a backup list in case many are unable to attend. Send out formal invitations well before the event. Follow up on those who did not respond. Stipulate that VIPs cannot pass their tickets on to family or friends.

◆ *Ticket distribution.* Develop a reliable method of distributing tickets, parking passes and, if necessary, directions to VIPs. It is critical to ensure that all receive their tickets.

◆ *Programme of events.* This would include speeches, presentations, celebrity appearances, etc. It is advisable to print a programme containing this information.

◆ *Staff.* Ensure that those serving the VIPs are appropriately trained to provide excellent service.

■ *Hospitality contingency planning.* This is a vital aspect in hospitality. Prepare for all eventualities that can and will happen, covering aspects such as:

◆ catering:

◆ extra seating;

◆ extra staff and backup staff; and

◆ backup celebrities, speakers, etc.

■ *Finishing touches.* Try not to overlook anything. Remember that even the smallest detail can create a lasting impression. Be creative. Aspects such as gifts (event-related goods), sending out letters to thank guests for attending, spelling names correctly – these are all important in the overall impression.

The more detailed the hospitality or public relations plan, the better. A plan carefully rehearsed and implemented by informed, well-mannered, trained and enthusiastic staff is the key to hospitality success and results in extremely beneficial spin-offs.

■ *Contingency planning.* Unforeseen things can and do happen. It is essential to avoid potentially harmful and damaging situations. An effective contingency plan is detailed, up to date and correctly funded. The following issues should receive attention:

◆ Review the following carefully, step-by-step, and consider everything that could go wrong:

- leverage (promotion, advertising and public relations plans);
- on-site activities; and
- hospitality.

◆ Ask the staff and promoters to help. Decide how to deal with each eventuality. Review this with the sponsorship team and ensure that they know what to do and who to contact. Hire a specialised event marketing agency to help with contingency planning. They can ensure that all the elements of the event are executed smoothly with minimal alterations to the original plan.

■ Potential situations to anticipate are:

◆ athlete/player strikes or lockouts;

◆ extreme weather conditions;

◆ celebrity no-shows;

◆ talent strikes;

◆ sudden negative publicity;

◆ ambush marketing; or

◆ others such as power failures, sabotage, violence, collapse of the event facility, etc.

The sponsor should try to provide for all of the above factors in the sponsorship contract and question what guarantee the organiser can provide against some of these eventualities. Successful events are conscientiously planned and skillfully coordinated and executed at each and every step along the way.

SPONSORSHIP CHECKLIST

The following questions will provide a guide to ensure that all aspects of the sponsorship are carefully considered:

1. Why are you entering into sponsorship?
2. Do your sponsorship objectives match the marketing objectives and contribute to their achievement?
3. Does everyone involved in the sponsorship (internally and externally) clearly understand the sponsorship objectives?
4. Are your objectives realistic and achievable relative to factors such as:
   - your budget allocation?
   - the types of events and activities available to sponsor?
   - your competitors' activities?
5. Is your company fully committed to making the most of the sponsorship in the short term and in the long term?
6. Do your sponsorship objectives provide clear benchmarks by which you can effectively measure sponsorship 'success'? →

7. Do you have clear sponsorship selection criteria?

8. Does the proposed sponsorship reach the target consumers with whom you wish to communicate?

9. Will your sponsorship branding have a reasonable chance of being seen and noted during the broadcast?

10. How does the proposed sponsorship fit in with your corporate marketing needs, product seasonality and existing or planned marketing communication strategies?

11. Are your competitors involved in sponsorship? To what extent?

12. Is your event high profile enough to result in a dominant association?

13. What is the event profile of the proposed sponsorship (history, previous sponsors)? Can you displace the equity built up by the previous sponsor?

14. How relevant is the proposed sponsorship to your product or service? Is there synergy between the sponsor and the event or activity?

15. Does the proposed sponsorship convey the image you wish to project? Is there 'brand fit'?

16. Is the company prepared to fully market the proposed sponsorship?

17. Is the sponsorship affordable? If so, does it represent value for money?

18. Have you introduced leverage costs into your budgetary calculations? Does your budget for leverage or least match your sponsorship investment?

19. Have you added at least ten per cent to allow for contingencies and unforeseen expenses?

20. What hospitality opportunities does the proposed sponsorship offer? Are these conducive to entertaining your VIP guests?

21. If the proposed sponsorship involves sport, what level of sports sponsorship does it involve – national team, provincial team, league, club, individual athlete or development sponsorship?

22. Who are the technical sponsors involved in the proposed sponsorship? What are their branding rights? Will you be able to approve all technical sponsors involved?

23. What licensing and merchandising options are being offered as part of the proposed sponsorship? Do you have a control mechanism in place allowing you to approve all items that will feature your logo or theme piece?

24. What rights to exclusivity will be afforded to you nationally and internationally?

25. If you intend to sponsor a broadcast, what coverage and exposure opportunities are on offer?

    *   Are your key markets included in the coverage?
    *   Do you have a clear picture of estimated audience?
    *   Are audience guarantees included?
    *   How visible will your logo be during the broadcast? Have you assessed the placement and value of your logo's exposure during the broadcast?
    *   Is advertising space included in the broadcast sponsorship?
    *   Are there guarantees regarding the placement of your ads?
    *   Does the broadcaster allow the placement of your competitors' ads in and around your broadcast? →

- What allowances does the broadcast sponsorship contract make for product category exclusivity?
- What rights are you entitled to under the broadcast sponsorship contract?

26. Who owns the rights to the event?

27. Have you thoroughly investigated the event/sports marketing agent's credentials? Are you fully satisfied with the credentials?

28. Has a working committee been formed between you and the event organiser? Is there clear identification and agreement on each party's roles and responsibilities in operating the sponsorship?

29. What are the fees involved in the sponsorship and what rights are you entitled to under the contract?

30. What is the duration of the sponsorship and what are your rights to extension and renewal of the contract?

31. Does the contract offer protection from ambush marketing?

32. What is the payment schedule as specified in the contract?

33. Does your contract stipulate the means by which you will measure performance?

34. What cancellation terms for performance clauses are specified in your contract?

35. What geographical and territorial considerations are specified in the contract?

36. What contractual stipulations are there regarding dispute resolution?

37. What efforts have you made to build internal support and agreement across the marketing department, that is, with the advertising manager, the sales manager, the public relations manager, etc?

38. How do you intend to gain and maintain the support of senior management and stakeholders in the company?

39. How do you intend to account for and record all expenditure?

40. How do you intend to leverage your sponsorship involvement – what are your leverage objectives and tactics?

41. Have you considered all aspects in planning hospitality at the event – budget, venue, guest list, ticket distribution, programme of events, staff, contingency planning and finishing touches?

42. Do you have a detailed contingency plan?

43. Is your contingency plan funded?

44. Can you plan for any of the possible contingencies in your sponsorship contract?

45. What guarantees do the organisers provide against contingencies?

46. What measurement procedures will you use to evaluate the sponsorship?

47. What key areas will you evaluate?

48. What decisions will you need to make based on the results?

49. Who needs information about the results?

If you can provide informed answers to these questions you will be taking the skilful, well-managed approach to sponsorship enabling you to answer the ultimate question: *Has the desired return on investment been achieved?*

....

REFERENCES

Association of Marketers. 1997. *Sponsorship Guidelines*. Johannesburg.

Cant, M.C. 2006. *Marketing Management*, 5ed JUTA,Cape Town.

Coggin, T. (ed) 2002. *Investor's Guide to Sponsorship*, 2ed Marketing Federation of Southern Africa, Systems Publishers: Johannesburg.

Koekemoer, L. (ed) 2004, *Marketing Communications*, 3ed JUTA Academic, Cape Town.

Marketing Federation of Southern Africa. 2002. *Investor's Guide to Sponsorship*. Johannesburg. See www.mfsa.co.za.

Yeshin, T. 2004. *Integrated Marketing Communications*, 2ed Jordan Hill, Oxford.

11 Principles of Digital Marketing

AIM OF THIS CHAPTER

This chapter highlights the nature and scope of digital marketing and discusses the following digital marketing opportunities: website, search engine marketing and optimisation, online advertising, email, blogging and podcasting, viral, affiliate, mobile and social media marketing. Finally this chapter poses the question: is digital marketing an asset or a threat to the brand?

LEARNING OUTCOMES

After studying this chapter you should be competent in:
- outlining the nature and scope of digital marketing
- discussing the website as a digital marketing tool
- discussing search engine marketing and search engine optimisation
- discussing online advertising
- discussing email marketing
- discussing blogging and podcasting
- discussing viral marketing
- discussing affiliate marketing
- discussing mobile marketing
- discussing social media marketing

11.1 THE NATURE AND SCOPE OF DIGITAL MARKETING

It has been said that there will be more technological changes in the next 10 years than in the past 100 years. The fast pace of technological change, especially in the information and computer arena, is fuelled by hardware and software innovation, interlinked telecommunications, the Internet and the emergence of the sovereign individual with increased power due to an almost unlimited freedom of choice and access to information.

The advertising scene has changed dramatically and will keep on changing in the years to come. Brands are no longer just advertised in above-the-line media. They are to be found on the Internet, in Web sites, they are discussed in Facebook and Twitter and promoted via cell phones, on MXit, etc. Brand communications aiming to tell and sell are being replaced with attention grabbing messages in the digital space. In this space information is not scarce.

There is no doubt that the Internet is playing an increasingly important role in business. Digital marketing is an inevitable technological trend that sweeps today's industries and includes such applications as e-commerce, Internet marketing and networking, even demographic and product research.

The commercial use of the Internet represents one of the most fundamental business developments of the previous century. The Internet and its technologies now impact on almost every business in some form. Marketers face new challenges as they attempt to leverage the opportunities offered by the Internet. The Web encompasses a new marketspace (the electronic version of a marketplace) and a new sales channel, as well as new methods of advertising and it allows new ways of communications, customer relationship building and sponsorship. The Internet has enabled marketers in the new marketing environment to consider consumers individually and to customise their products and services even better, mainly due to the unique and powerful characteristics of the World Wide Web (www).

It is essential for a company not to underestimate the impact that the Internet will have on its strategies, organisation, job policies, marketing and advertising strategy and operations. Although some businesses are applying the tools of technology to excel in the information age, too many are still charting a path to the future guided by the images in their rear-view mirrors. Marketers and their ad agencies will have to prepare for the world of the new 'customer of power' of the digital era and learn how to use the marketing and communications tools of this era effectively.

So how does digital marketing differ from traditional marketing communications? Digital marketing endeavours not only to provide information but to build and maintain customer relationships through online (digital) activities. Its main differences are interactivity and individuality. Above-the-line advertising (TV, print, radio etc) is one message to many whereas digital marketing is a high-tech strategic and tactical extension of information gathering, direct marketing, social interaction and customer feedback. All of these are important aspects of an integrated marketing communications strategy.

In this chapter we will briefly consider the following digital marketing opportunities: website, online advertising, email, blogging, affiliate marketing, viral marketing, mobile and social media. Reference will be made to search engine optimisation, PPC (pay per click) etc in these discussions.

11.2 WEBSITE

One of the most important aspects of a website is the information it provides to those interested in learning more about the company or brands. Whether it be a prospective client, a potential investor, a student doing research or a future employee, whoever arrives at the website should find it usable for the purpose they came there.

A detailed description of the offering and its unique selling proposition (USP) is a must on any website. Here one should be informing the prospective client, as mentioned above, about the unique service and why they should choose this product or service rather than the others they have come across. More and more customers will gauge the service or product offering by what they see and read on the website and by what other websites say about the organisation.

The Internet provides a great opportunity to a prospective client to find out everything about a company and its services from the comfort of their own home or office. For this reason the website should be the ultimate marketing tool.

Online brochures, downloadable documents, games, screensavers and sound or video clips can all add to the marketing of the organisation online. The Internet, being an interconnected web of related websites, can add great additional value to the business from a pure linking (from various other websites) and ranking (on search engines) point of view.

It is this linking from other websites which will get more users to the website and market the company's business in a much greater way than one can ever accomplish with a similar type of budget spent on print, radio or TV. This linking will also help the site achieve higher rankings on search engines and thus gain the company greater exposure when a prospective client searches for this type of service or product using search engines such as Google, Yahoo!, Bing, Asl and AOL Search.

Although the website can be a company's greatest marketing tool, one still has to market the website. Because of the multitude of websites on the Internet, it is foolish to assume that users will just stumble across the website in numbers significant to make a difference to the company's business. In order to ensure that the website can fulfil its role as a major marketing tool for the organisation, one needs to drive as much traffic to the site as possible.

11.1.1 Using the website as a marketing tool

When using the website as a marketing tool special attention should be given to the following:

- *Marketing copy.* A company's product or service description is often required for advertising, articles and inclusion in various types of documents. Placing approved short, medium and long versions of the product or service offering ensures that the message that goes out is always consistent, of high quality and controlled by the organisation rather than left to outsiders to decide. This can also be applied to the CVs of members of the company that are regularly required for introductions at presentations, speeches and seminars.

- *Contracts.* Agent and distributor agreements, commission structures and other relevant documents can be made available for download from a 'trade zone'. These documents can be made available in PDF format, making it impossible to alter any important details such as rates and dates.

- *Logo and image downloads.* Companies often have to supply their logos for print and various types of online advertising. Instead of mailing such logos or even emailing them, the corporate section of the company website can be utilised for this purpose. This will ensure that the colours, style and quality of the logos are always used in the correct manner. Different sizes, as well as different colour combinations (full colour, two-tone or black and white), can be made available for download. The company can decide whether to request full details, after which a password will be supplied prior to allowing someone to download the logo or whether it simply requires basic contact information and a reason for the use of the company logo. The same principle applies to photos of directors or special events (prize giving and award ceremonies), celebrity endorsements, etc.

- *Media/news section.* Most of the large firms have dedicated media sections on their websites. Here media specific information can be found. Press releases with photos can be made 'live' on a site's media section to coincide with traditional media releases.

Countries with restrictions on access via the Internet limit the effectiveness of marketing online marketing activities, especially when a company is involved in global marketing. An annual report compiled by the Paris-based non-governmental organisation Reporters without borders listing the 'enemies of the Internet' and 'countries under surveillance' for Internet censorship. Marketers involved in global e-commerce need to be aware of the restrictions and limitations placed on the Internet in the countries where their intended target audience may not be able to access the information and which would result in ineffective marketing.

11.2.2 Using the website to sell

If a company is in the business of selling a product or service, the website should be an extension of their sales team. Many businesses rely very much, if not solely, on their website for sales. Whether it is a Bed & Breakfast, a framing company or one that sells specialised books, the website can easily be their most valuable sales 'person'!

The marketing aspect of a website centers on the provision of information about products and services. Although this is very important in assisting future clients in their decision-making process, it is useless if it cannot lead to new business. This can be compared to a beautiful glossy brochure that does not lead to sales. A website, like any good brochure, should entice the user to buy the product. If the website does not allow for this to happen, the company is not capitalising on the true value of its site as a sales tool.

But one needs to:

- make someone responsible for online enquiries;
- ensure that all the organisation's contact details are on the site;
- design the website with different target audiences in mind;
- provide information that can add value to the Internet user; and
- keep the information up to date if sales people use the website as part of their sales pitch.

11.2.3 The website as a communications tool

The website can be used for the following forms of communication:

- *Online news.* An online news section on a site has several advantages. Besides being an excellent way to communicate with the customers and cultivate long-term relationships with them, such a news section is cheap to manage and easy to update. Various content management programmes are available, allowing for in-house management of news. Company news can be posted any time of the day or night, making it a true source of current news.

- *Community building.* The Internet is a perfect platform from which to create an interest group. 'Community building' refers to a virtual community sharing a joint interest through an online forum. Community members can post their comments on the current topic and participate by means of an Internet chat room. Online communities can be set up by any business with a website.

- *Online polls.* Online surveys are a great tool for determining the needs of corporate or trade clients. Another way of using the website for communication is to post online polls with a special focus on the individual user, customer or client.

Surveys provide a platform for such users to communicate with the company. A poll could ask the customer to give comments on products, services, facilities, rates and prices, etc. This feedback is invaluable in providing customers with services they want and need. The cost saving through online polls and surveys is enormous, as there is no printed material, handling, mailing or processing costs.

11.3 SEARCH ENGINE MARKETING

Search engine marketing has become one of the most important tools in the overall digital marketing sphere. Ensuring that the website can easily be found by means of search engines will greatly increase the traffic to a website.

Why is search engine marketing so important? When a user is searching for a product or service, or even just information, that person is in search mode. This means that he or she is actually looking to find information on a certain company, topic, product or service.

Once in search mode, a Web user is much more receptive to the right type of information than when it is merely 'thrown' at him or her. It is therefore of paramount importance for the product or service to be 'findable' when it is sought for. The principle is very much the same as that of having your name in the telephone directory. If your name is there, it does not mean that you will be phoned all the time. If, however, your name is not in the telephone book, you simply cannot be found by someone looking to make contact with you.

Although one often hears about the multitude of search engines on the Internet, the bulk of all worldwide searches are performed on, or supported by the following global search engines:

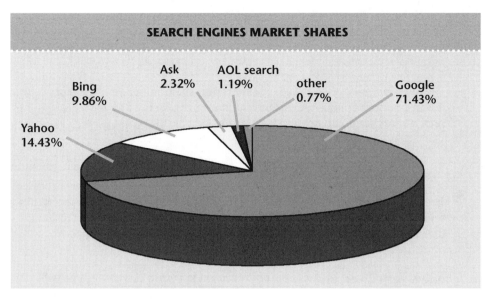

SEARCH ENGINES MARKET SHARES

Ask
2.32%

AOL search
1.19%

Bing
9.86%

other
0.77%

Google
71.43%

Yahoo
14.43%

Figure 11.1: www.seoconsultants.com

Figure 11.1 clearly shows the dominance of Google. There are, of course, various niche search engines that focus on a particular market segment or even geographical area. Some new search engines that have been receiving a lot of press and gaining market share internationally include:

- Kayak.com
- Wolfram Alpha
- Sidestep.com
- Ananzi.co.za
- Aardvark.co.za

11.3.1 Search engine optimisation (SEO)

If the site information is up to date, the site is user-friendly and it has a definite call to action, then search engine marketing will increase business.

Take the example of a new resident in Polokwane. Once moved into his new house, he realises that he needs a garden service to mow the lawn and maintain the garden. Although there is always the trusty Yellow Pages or other guides and directories, search engines make it easy to find the service one is looking for.

The new Polokwane resident can now go to a search engine such as Google (www.google.co.za) or 24.com and type in 'garden services polokwane'. This should yield a number of results. The total number of results depends on the number of websites vying for that phrase or parts of that phrase.

Internet users commonly only pay attention to websites listed on the first page of the results. This could be anything from 10 to 50 results, depending on the search engine and depending on your preference settings for the number of results per page.

The question most often asked is 'Why is that site number one?' The fact is that it does not happen by chance! One can optimize a website for search engines in such a way that it can achieve higher rankings on the various search engines.

11.3.2 Linking strategy

The www in an Internet URL stands for World Wide Web. This is because everything is linked in some way or another, the same way as in a spider web. This adds to the overall value of the Internet as a resource for research, entertainment, online purchases and more.

A link is an image or a line of text on a page within a website that will take the user to another page within the same site or to a completely different site when clicking on it. Linked text is usually underlined (but needn't be) within the text of a paragraph or as a freestanding word or phrase. When hovering over a linked image or text, your cursor will indicate that you are on a link.

It is very important that a site is linked to other websites with content and information that can enhance the website, without giving up valuable traffic in the process. Links within the site can also enhance the site's searchability and usability.

The search engines consider a link to a company's website from another website as a vote of confidence in that site. Google, for instance, places a very high value on incoming links to a website.

11.3.3 PORTAL LISTINGS

A portal is a website that serves as a directory for other websites. From here, one can get more information about various services and products that relate to a certain theme or business segment. Tourism, news and sport portals are very popular. Such sites offer links to other websites for more information on a specific topic or product.

A website for a town can therefore be considered a Web portal. If the site for Mossel Bay (www.visitmosselbay.co.za) lists all the various retail shops, restaurants, hotels, builders, electricians, estate agencies, hairdressers, etc for that town with a link through to the website of each of those listed, it serves as a portal.

Some portals charge a fee for a full listing with a Web link and a certain amount of information on their site. Others offer a free listing and then sell advertising space. Some are association sites where members of that association get a free listing as part of their membership. The most important aspect is to note that a link from a quality portal with a good ranking will improve the ranking of your own website on the various search engines.

Portal sites exist for household services, property, restaurants, accommodation, health matters, women's interests, sports etc. Some examples of portal sites are:

- www.sportal.com
- www.health24.com

11.3.4 Pay per click (PCC)

Organic search engines offer free listings but there's little guarantee that a site will be listed where you want it to be.

Paid listing is the only guaranteed way of getting onto the first page of a search engine. One either pays for it or you bid for it.

As an advertiser, you bid for a spot relating to the search phrase you wish to advertise. Once the search engine accepts the bid, the ad can appear within the next 24 hours on the search engine's site. The turn-around time is therefore very short.

A Web searcher who then clicks on that advertisement will be directed to that website. The beauty of the system is that the company only pays once a person clicks on their ad – no click, no pay! For this reason, these ads are also referred to as a pay per click or PPC.

11.4. ONLINE ADVERTISING

There are two primary uses for online advertising which, if utilised correctly, can be a very effective marketing tool. The first is a brand-building medium and the second is to drive sales.

If the objective is response or immediate sales, then measurable online advertising becomes a powerful marketing weapon. By calculating precise figures (cost per customer) for acquiring customers through different forms of online advertising, one can ensure that an advertising budget is spent in the most efficient and productive manner possible.

Using online advertising as a brand-building tool is an entirely different story. The brand building can add a great deal of value to an overall campaign by creating awareness for a product or a brand.

A great deal of good and bad has been said about online advertising. In the hey-day of the dotcom explosion, online ads were a much-used marketing tool by traditional as well as new media organisations. With the 'bursting' of the dotcom bubble, online advertising lost a lot of its appeal. This type of advertising has, however, made a comeback and can form an integral part of any overall business strategy for online marketing.

But how does it work? When arriving on a website that displays banner advertising, one can see either a horizontal banner across the top, a skyscraper along the right-hand side or a combination of different banners. A banner is a form of an image with or without accompanying copy.

In most cases, the banner gets 'served' from a remote ad server. This is a computer that is normally operated by a third party that delivers and tracks advertisements and is independent of the website where the ad is being displayed. Use of an ad server helps establish trust between an advertiser and publisher since the statistics are maintained by an objective third party.

This software allows users to see the advertisement when they arrive on a particular website. Once they click on the advert, users arrive on the advertiser's website, the landing page or a page within the advertising website, specially created for the advertiser.

11.4.1 Online advertising forms

Let us briefly review 11 forms of online advertising:

- *Horizontal banners.* These are graphics that appear on a Web page that is usually hyperlinked to an advertiser's website. They may be in a variety of formats including GIF, JPEG, MPEG, Flash, HTML, Java, JavaScript and more. This type of advertisement is the most common online advertisement. Horizontal banners can be placed at the top of the page, at the bottom or anywhere else within a page. This type of banner is also quite commonly used in email newsletters. These banners can either be static or animated. A static banner displays one image which can be seen by the Internet user when arriving at the page displaying the banner. An animated banner displays a number of images alternating in the same space. This is very similar to a rotational billboard where one image is replaced by another every few seconds. Such an animated banner is still just advertising one product or service.

- *Buttons.* A button is a type of advertising unit that is smaller than a banner and usually placed in parts of a Web page where space is limited, such as in narrow columns on the left or right side of a page.

- *Skyscrapers.* These are vertical banners – a type of ad unit that is much taller than it is wide. They are often used in columns of Web pages where there is a lot of unused vertical space but limited horizontal space.

- *Fixed tiles.* A tile is a background graphic element. A fixed tile is one that stays locked in place and doesn't scroll with the content when the user scrolls the browser window.

- *Pop ups.* This type of advertisement is automatically displayed in a second smaller browser window when you load or unload a normal Web page. Pop-up advertisements tend to cost advertisers more since their visibility is higher, but they are often considered annoying by website visitors since they are considered intrusive. This can, however, be circumvented by users by blocking pop-ups which will decrease their effectiveness. Also called interstitials, these ads are a form of interruption marketing. This type of advertisement appeals to advertisers who feel Web advertising needs to be more like a broadcast medium to be effective.

- *Pop-unders.* This type of advertisement is automatically displayed in a second smaller browser window behind the current window when you load or unload a normal Web page. Pop-under advertisements tend to cost advertisers more since their visibility is higher, but they are considered less annoying than pop-ups by website visitors, although they can be blocked in a similar fashion.

- *Contextual links/text ads.* Text-based ads, although common in email, have been dominated on the Web by their graphic-based counterparts. Although affiliate marketing is one area where text ads have flourished, many mainstream advertisers are only beginning to discover the power of text.

- *Sponsorships.* In this type of advertising an advertiser pays to sponsor a section of a website. It may take the form of the typical banner and/or text that mentions 'This section sponsored by'. This works best when the content of the sponsored Web page is directly related to but not in competition with the advertiser's products or services. An example will be where a foreign currency provider sponsors an exchange rate calculator on a travel website.

- *Rich media.* This is technology that often includes richer graphics, audio or video within the advertisement. Unlike static or animated GIF banner advertisements, rich media advertisements often enable users to interact with the banner without leaving the page on which it appears. A rich media ad may take the form of an interactive image with sound and items or images that can be manipulated or moved around by the user.

- *Micro sites.* A micro site is, in effect, a customer's own section within another website. This should be promoted throughout the main site for the micro site's duration. Within such a micro site, one can create a number of pages, place articles about the advertiser and any areas of business that the client is involved in or wants to be involved in.

- *Ad features.* An ad feature is a cost-effective way to gain presence on a news website or a specific section within such a website. Most of the above-mentioned types of online advertising can be used here in combination with one another.

11.5 EMAIL MARKETING

Email has become so much part of our day-to-day lives that it is difficult to imagine a world without it. Whether it is an anecdotal video clip from a family member, an invitation to a party from a friend or a confirmation of a business meeting, life just won't be the same, or that fast, without email.

Email marketing can be a very effective communications tool to market a business or service, to announce special offers and to maintain relationships with existing clients and others interested parties.

Great success can be achieved by having a well-structured email marketing plan in place. Before looking at email newsletters as a marketing tool, however, it is important to get the basics of the day-to-day emails right:

■ *Email signature.* Every email sent from a business or organisation's email address should be considered as an image building business communication activity and as such should have the organisation's branding and information details. The very least one has to do is to set up a proper email signature. This should contain the following:

◆ Your name and surname, title or position, telephone and fax numbers, cellphone number (if so desired), email address, website address, company name

◆ In addition, one can also include: company logo, company slogan and a link to an email newsletter subscription form.

This can be set up on most email clients/programmes following the prompts for 'Tools', 'Options' and then 'Mail format' on the toolbar.

■ *'From' set-up.* Consider what the recipient will see. Pay special attention to how you set up your email address as many emails are deleted before they are opened.

■ *Subject line.* When sending an email, the subject line is probably the most important aspect to consider. Think for a moment about all the unwanted emails you receive daily. Even if you see an email from a known source (friend, colleague or family member), it is still the subject line that will determine how soon after receipt you will read it, if at all.

■ *Attachments.* Most computer viruses get spread through email attachments. Some simple rules to keep in mind:

◆ Don't open any attachments from unknown email addresses, no matter how interesting or appealing they may appear.

◆ Only open attachments from known senders when you are expecting such attachments.

◆ Update the virus protection programme daily.

■ *Spelling.* Enabling the spell checker on your email client is a very easy task. This can usually be set up under 'Options' within the email programme. An email might be the first contact one is making with a prospective client, investor or partner and it is therefore imperative that a professional image is portrayed.

■ *Inserts.* It has become quite common to include some type of branded insert into every email message. Doing this allows each email to also serve the purpose of an electronic business or promotion material in addition to other communication with the recipient. The principle is that every email is an opportunity to tell someone more about the organisation.

11.5.1. Email Newsletters

The uses of email newsletters have become very popular. These are effective digital communications opportunities. What is involved?

- *Set up a newsletter template.* The template (HTML designed) should reflect the look and feel of the organisation's website in order to relate to the company or its brands/services.

- *Obtain consent.* One cannot send email newsletters (or bulk mail) to anyone without permission. Email newsletters can only be sent to users who have consented to receive such newsletters.

- *Create the message.* The newsletter should contain newsworthy, new, interesting, relevant information.

- *Decide on the frequency.* Should the email newsletter be sent out daily, weekly, monthly, quarterly etc?

- *Personalise the message.* Emails allow for personalisation of messages. Every newsletter should be personalised as much as possible (eg preferred language, male/female specific news, a preference relating to the company or brand etc).

- *Write a clear message.* Focus on what the recipient(s) want to hear.

- *Track open and click-through rates.* Monitor the open and click-through rates. Test alternative messages and appeals for success.

- *Improve the response.* Improve the response by trying and testing different fonts, designs, articles, styles etc.

11.6 BLOGGING AND PODCASTING

11.6.1. Blogging

The Internet and the software developed to run on it have made it extremely easy for anyone to publish content that is made accessible to millions of people. In effect, consumers have been given a voice to air their views to a massive audience, something that could never have happened before the advent of the Internet.

In recent years, one of the leading examples of this has been the massive growth of weblogs or blogs, wikis, podcasts, vlogs (video blogs) and moblogs (mobile blogs). Together they form what is loosely known as citizen media – the ability for anyone to publish almost any content without the typical costs and hindrances associated with traditional media.

But what is a blog? Wikipedia.com describes a blog as follows:

A blog or weblog (derived from Web + log) is a Web-based publication consisting primarily of periodic articles (normally, but not always, in reverse chronological order). Although most early blogs were manually updated, tools to automate the maintenance of such sites made them accessible to a much larger population, and the use of some sort of browser-based software is now a typical aspect of 'blogging'.

The best way to understand what blogging is about is to visit and read a few blogs. Blogs come in a huge variety of shapes and sizes, from individual diaries shared mainly with friends and family members to political campaigns and media programmes. Blogs also range in scale from the writings of one occasional author (known as a blogger), to the collaboration of a large community of writers. Many weblogs enable visitors to leave public comments, which can lead to a community of readers centred on the blog. Others are non-interactive.

The totality of weblogs or blog-related websites is often called the blogosphere. When a large amount of activity, information and opinion erupts around a particular subject or controversy in the blogosphere, it is sometimes called a blogstorm or blogswarm.

The format of weblogs varies from simple bulleted lists of hyperlinks to article summaries or complete articles with user-provided comments and ratings. Individual weblog entries are almost always date-and-time-stamped (but this is not a pre-requisite for being a blog) with the most recent post at the top (or bottom) of the page and reader comments often appearing below it. Because incoming links to specific entries are important to many weblogs, most have a way of archiving older entries and generating a static address for them; this static link is referred to as a permalink.

Blogging is a useful tool for creating publicity (PR tool) although it must be remembered that:

■ in blogging one engages in trying to spark conversations, not just provide information;

■ blogging is not time bound;

■ blogs are mostly personal and informal;

■ blogging is best used where sharp questions are asked or strong opinions exist;

■ blogging works best where information is kept short and to the point; and

■ blogging lends itself to good news but can also create bad publicity.

11.6.2. Podcasting

Following closely on the heels of blogging, podcasting is emerging as an explosive form of citizen media. According to Wikipedia, podcasting is a method of publishing audio programmes via the Internet, allowing users to subscribe to a feed of new files (usually MP3s). This became popular in late 2004, largely due to automatic downloading of audio onto portable players or personal computers.

The name podcast can be somewhat misleading because it does not require an iPod, nor is it a broadcast. Instead podcasting is all about the receipt. This makes it distinct from other types of online media delivery, because of its subscription model.

Podcasting enables independent producers to create self-published, syndicated 'radio shows' and gives broadcast radio programmes a new distribution method. Listeners may subscribe to feeds using 'podcatching' software (a type of aggregator), which periodically checks for and downloads new content automatically.

The most popular platform for podcasting distribution is Apple's iTunes software.

11.6.3. Blogs and search engine optimization

Because search engines love fresh, relevant content, blogs are a great way to give them exactly this. Essentially, a blog allows you to add a fresh page of content to your website every day by writing one daily post.

It is important, however, that the blog is set up to be as search engine friendly as possible. This means considering two important points:

- All blog posts should be assigned a unique page, which is easily indexable by the search engines. This can be achieved by ensuring that each page has a link to it, which the search engines can find and follow.

- Pages must be tagged with keywords relevant to the SEO strategy. This means putting important keywords in the post headings, page URL and meta tags, particularly the title tag.

The nature of blogs also makes them an excellent source of links to a website. Provided the content is engaging, other bloggers will link to it and search engines view these links as popularity votes for the website, thereby assisting in improving the rankings.

11.7 VIRAL MARKETING

11.7.1. The essence and scope of viral marketing

Viral marketing is a marketing technique that makes use of social networks to increase brand awareness. It is delivered by word of mouth, and is used very effectively online. It makes good use of the network effect of the Internet and can be very useful in reaching a large number of people rapidly. The term 'viral' is used because the information is spread in a socially organic way, not unlike the physiologically organic spreading of pathological viruses.

It focuses on building brand image whilst creating a list of qualified prospects with whom the organisation can communicate. Often the ultimate goal of viral marketing campaigns is to generate media coverage via 'offbeat' stories worth many times more than the campaigning company's advertising budget. It can therefore be used to describe the use of blogs in Web-based marketing to create word-of-mouth advertising for a new product or service. Some people even refer to it as 'word-of-mouse' advertising. Blogging provides the perfect environment for the passing on and building up of brand awareness.

Viral marketing also include strategies that encourages individuals to pass on a marketing message to others, creating the potential for exponential growth in the message's exposure and influence. Driven by a good and exciting concept, viral marketing can provide great awareness for a product, service or brand.

Clients, investors and others with an interest in the company's products or services know others like themselves, with similar interests, needs and lifestyles. Loyal clients are usually the best advocates and will pass on a message that they believe can add value to others they know. The message can be in the form of a video or sound clip, an HTML email, a tweet, bloglink, or the like.

The result is a new pool of qualified prospects and sales leads that were hand-picked by existing, loyal customers from among their own colleagues, friends and family.

An effective viral marketing strategy does the following:

- ■ *It gives away products or services.* 'Free' is the most powerful word in a marketer's vocabulary. Free attracts eyeballs. Eyeballs bring valuable email addresses, advertising revenue, and ecommerce sales opportunities. Give away something – sell something.

- ■ *It provides for effortless transfer to others.* The medium that carries the marketing message must be easy to transfer and replicate: email, website, graphic or software download. Viral marketing works famously on the Internet because instant communication has become so easy and inexpensive. The digital format makes copying simple.

- ■ *It scales easily from small to very large.* To spread like wildfire, the transmission method must be rapidly scalable from small to very large.

- ■ *It exploits common motivations and behaviours.* Clever viral marketing plans take advantage of common human motivations. Design a marketing strategy that builds on common motivations and behaviours for its transmission and you have a winner.

- ■ *It uses existing communication networks.* Most people are social. Social scientists tell us that each person has a network of eight to twelve people in his or her close network of friends, family and associates. A person's broader network may consist of many more depending upon his or her position in society.

- ■ *It takes advantage of other people's resources.* The most creative viral marketing plans use other's resources to get the word out. Authors who give away free articles seek to position their articles on other's web pages. A news release can be picked up by hundreds of periodicals and form the basis of articles seen by hundreds of thousands of readers.

11.7.2 Viral marketing activities

Viral marketing does not start and end with email campaigns, whether controlled or left to spread naturally.

Any type of online activity that is exciting or worthwhile enough will get users talking, and in the process pass it on to others with similar interests. This can apply to various other online activities. The two essential principles when putting any such campaigns in place remain brand building and data gathering.

The following activities can also fulfil the role of viral campaigns when set up correctly:

- *Competitions:* It is a good idea to have a competition running on a website. Many people will fill in a competition form when arriving at the site on purpose or by chance. As long as the prizes are worthwhile and one can gather relevant information on current and potential clients, it may be worthwhile to run such competitions. Entrants will tell others, making the viral concept work for the company.

- *Quizzes:* A quiz on the website with either general news, questions or questions related to the site and then answers somewhere else on the site is not only a source of additional fun and entertainment but can drive extra visitors to the site. This will be especially true if the top scores are kept online, ranked with the name of the top 'quiz king'.

- *Games:* Online games serve as a great source for traffic to a website. Users have to register to stand a chance of winning a prize. For example, a pharmaceutical company that handed out lip balm with the web address: www.painrelief.co.za printed on it. On arriving at the site, users were offered the opportunity to play a game after registering their details.

- *Ecards:* Electronic postcards are a great way for users to send images from an organisation's website to others they know. The image can be one that relates in some way to the company's product or service offering or of a group or individual dealing with the company. This can be well applied to guests at a game lodge, hotel or restaurant. The owner takes photos and then places them on the company's website. Users visit the site's gallery where they have the opportunity to send the images as electronic postcards to friends and family. The recipient then receives the image or a link that takes him or her back to the website.

- *Articles:* many professional services companies (legal firms, marketers, consulting firms) spend a great deal of time writing articles that can be downloaded for free from their website. One can either have an entire article posted on the website for users to read or have an abbreviated article on a site with the full article available upon registration only.

11.8 AFFILIATE MARKETING

11.8.1. The nature of Affiliate Marketing

The concept of referral or network marketing is well known and its success documented. This type of marketing has been used for many years and has helped manufacturers of certain products and brands gain a place in the market without having to utilise the traditional retail channels. Referral or network marketers often use those networks that only sell their products and services through their partners. This is mostly used in the various multi-level marketing organisations across the world.

Affiliate marketing is the online version of rewarding referrers for business and leads generated as a result of their efforts. It puts the Internet's connectedness to work by creating links into your website from other sites.

If affiliates are incentivised with either a commission or fixed fees for certain deliverables, their sites should send far greater volumes of potential customers to your site. What distinguishes affiliate marketing from online or any other type of advertising is that, unlike advertising, one only pays the affiliates when they perform. No referral, no fee!

Running various affiliate programmes from one website has become a popular way of generating income from the Internet. People now have websites built with the sole purpose of acting as affiliates for one or more merchants. These sites don't sell any other product or service but derive all their income from being affiliates to a number of different merchants.

11.8.2 Using affiliate marketing

Affiliate marketing can create awareness for a brand, especially when similar campaigns are run at the same time on TV, radio, in print and outdoor etc.

It can create leads or enquiries. Easy to complete enquiry forms can be used containing all the relevant information one might seek of the prospective client. Client feedback can be given and further interaction encouraged.

The affiliate campaign could be primarily aimed at generating sales. The primary purpose of any banner, button or text link will therefore be to get the user to click on it, to learn about the product in a very easy and user-friendly way and then to buy.

11.9 MOBILE MARKETING

(Retrieved from http://en.wikipedia.org/wiki/Mobile_marketing)

Mobile marketing is not to be confused with moving media marketing (eg road shows, bus advertising, moving billboards etc). Mobile marketing refers to marketing on or with a mobile device (ie a cellphone). In South Africa 9 million people use cellphones daily.

In November 2009, the Mobile Marketing Association updated its definition of Mobile Marketing:

> *Mobile Marketing is a set of practices that enables organizations to communicate and engage with their audience in an interactive and relevant manner through any mobile device or network.*

By using the cellphones of target audiences marketers can distribute promotional or advertising messages, even personalised information to promote goods, services and ideas via SMS, MMS, Games, Web, mobile marketing via Bluetooth, etc.

Let's briefly consider these options:

- *Via SMS.* Over the past few years SMS has become a popular and legitimate advertising option. Initially people were complaining about receiving SMS 'spam'. However, one can opt-in or opt-out and thereby grant permission to the sender to send the SMS message. The public can also request info or a brand message (eg special offer) by sending a SMS to a shortcode.

- *Via MMS.* MMS messages can contain a timed slideshow of text, images, video and audio. This message is delivered by MMS (Multimedia Message Service). All colour screen cellphones are capable of receiving and sending a standard MMS message. In some countries and in some networks brands are able to send and receive MMS's and to sponsor messages that are sent person-to-person (P2P). Consumers can, for example, send their mobile photos (eg entry for a competition) to a marketer or blog their images online.

- *Via In-Game.* In-Game mobile gaming includes casual (simple) games, interactive real-time 3D games, massive multi-player games and social networking games. Brands are promoted via promotional messages within mobile games or they can sponsor a game to acquire consumer engagement. This is called Mobile Advergaming.

- *Via Web.* Mobile devices (cellphones, BlackBerries, IPhones) can be used to access emails and advertising on web pages. Google, Yahoo, etc have been selling advertising on their properties for many years.

- *Mobile marketing, via Bluetooth.* Since its initiation in Europe in 2003 the Bluetooth 'hotspot' systems have been used for marketing purposes. It is permission based, offer high transfer speeds, is a radio – based technology and is free.

- *Via Location-based Services (LBS).* Some cell phone networks offer marketers an opportunity to send custom advertising and other information to cellphone subscribers based on their current location. The network obtains the location from a GPS chip built into the phone or they use radio location and trilateration (based on the signal strength of the nearest cell phone tower).

A final comment on mobile marketing: mobile marketing differs from most other forms of marketing communication as it often originates with the consumer and it requires the express consent of the consumer to receive further communications. Although Mobile Marketing has become more and more popular, consumers are concerned about their privacy and mobile spam.

11.10 SOCIAL MEDIA MARKETING

The online social media and network environment is an ever-evolving platform for various issues and topics affecting people's daily lives. Due to the nature and ease with which users can connect to each other and share their opinions about issues, it has become a platform that businesses and organisations of any size companies cannot ignore.

Social media is the Web 2.0 preferred mode of media and communication. Users respect what their peers say and many online influencers have followers who read and comment on the written opinions of those they follow. Although social media started out as a platform for individuals to share messages, news, photos, video clips and music with each other, commercial and other organisations have now embraced this communication channel.

Once an organisation has decided to embrace the online social media space in a planned and controlled manner, it should plan to

- listen to;
- engage with; and
- initiate

online conversations about topics that affect people's lives and behaviour and are of importance to their long term goals of sustainability, marketing and communications with regards to its brand and products.

Though there are literally hundreds of thousands of social media sites, services and applications, the most popular ones are:

- *Blogs:* discussed in section 11.6
- *Twitter:* a micro-blogging platform allowing for only 140 characters of content per "posting" or tweet
- *Facebook:* the world's biggest social media network with over 500 million users. In South Africa 3.3 million people spend an average of 55 minutes per day on Facebook.
- *Flickr:* this is purely an online photo sharing platform and one that can be utilised to store large amounts of photos.
- *YouTube:* there are approximately 120 million videos on YouTube with about 200 000 new uploads per day.

Social media has changed the traditional media landscape. Newspapers now publish their content online, commentaries are invited, print stories can be supplemented online with video etc. TV commercials can be placed online for free via channels like YouTube.

The benefits of Social Media to marketers are (Stokes, 2008: 140, 141):

- It is easier to switch off or ignore traditional advertising, particularly TV or radio. Social media give brands te opportunities to interact with customers through targeted communications which customers can choose to engage with on their terms. For example a consumer may visit a branded YouTube channel as opposed to deliberately ignoring advert breaks on television.

- Social media's potential to go viral is one of its greatest benefits – if users like the content they will share it with their own communities.

- Social media allows one to create an online community for the brand and its supporters.

- Social media can tie in nicely with other online marketing tactics – a holistic eMarketing strategy is always the best strategy.

- Social media allows engaging with an online community and allows one to connect the brand to the appropriate audience.

- Social media has created a forum for brand evangelists. Companies should embrace as well as monitor this as users with negative opinions of the brand have access to the same forum.

- The various platforms allow access to a community with similar interests – networking without borders.

- The numerous interactions allow feedback from communities.

- Feedback from social media sites helps drive both future business as well as marketing strategies.

- The range of media enables one to learn more about the audience's likes, dislikes, behaviour etc. Never before has this much information been available to marketers – market research just got a whole lot cheaper.

- Niche targeting just got a whole lot easier.

There are huge risks as well as opportunities. Social media facilitates a two-way conversation between customer and company. This necessitates that the company shifts approach from "deploy and watch" to one of constant involvement with the audience.

The most important elements to consider when using social media as a marketing or communications tools are:

- Ensure that you have a social media policy in place.

- Decide what you wish to accomplish by using social media; have a strategy in place.

- Always be open, honest and respectful to your users, followers and fans.

11.11 DIGITAL MARKETING : ASSET OR THREAT?

Kickstarted by the Internet, digital marketing has grown at a spectacular speed. Clients' heads are spinning from the accelerated flow of digital marketing tactics, web statistics, growth in South African cellphone use, regulatory issues and digital marketing experts speaking a language few others understand. Some marketers believe digital marketing merely offers different media options. Others believe mass marketing, branding and marketing communication will soon change forever.

People are now talking to each other online; they find brands and ideas in the digital space. Young people don't read any more and they hardly watch TV. But almost all of them have cellphones! And many have access to the Internet or cellphone browser capacity.

Despite the fact that the Regulation of Interception of Communications and Provision of Communication-related Information Act 70 of 2002 is already eight years old, it has only been since mid-2009 that the compulsory registration of cellular SIM cards has come into effect. Despite the fact that this has been viewed with distrust by many in the general public, many marketers have realised its potential regarding effective marketing strategies.

Many marketers have already realised that mobile technology is the most measurable marketing channel. While sending and receiving emails and mobile browsing, sites are capable of logging the mobile numbers which allows marketers not only to identify the potential target market, but also to determine the effectiveness of their mobile marketing strategies.

However, until now, the proliferation of unregistered cheap pre-paid SIM cards has meant that people frequently changed mobile numbers. With the compulsory registration of SIM cards demanded by RICA, mobile numbers will become more valuable as a marketing tool, since the registered numbers will lead to long-term use of mobile numbers which, in turn, will allow for more accurate profiling of users and their preferences. This, in turn, will allow the marketer to develop strategic and highly personalised marketing strategies for different target audiences.

The continued advances in cellphone technology and the steady penetration of smartphones in the South African (and world-wide) cellphone user market have created vast new areas of mobile marketing potential. Users now literally carry the Internet in around in their pockets and can access information at anytime, anywhere...as long as they have sufficient GPS connectivity. Mobile websites (mobi-sites) have carried limited advertising until recently, but has potential to be developed by marketers world-wide. The restrictions of mobile devices require compatible web-content and optimisation of content in order to fulfil the user's expectations. In many cases companies will find that their current websites are not compatible with the requirements of mobi-webs and will either have to change the format of their websites or host dual, device dependant, websites for a company.

Marketers are scared to miss out on 'brands not tweeting', the company not having a blog, a poll, a forum, an avatar, favicon or YouTube profile. Even non-marketers want to be paid to play with marketers' brands in the digital space.

Now more than ever a marketer needs to understand and preserve its brand's DNA. A combination of traditional and digital media may be necessary based on the target market, the brand positioning and the key communication objectives. Digital marketing is uniquely positioned for its measurability, interacting, sharing, commenting, communication and transacting ability. But marketing principles and brand DNA should inform the choices you make or digital marketing could just be the biggest threat to your brand's health (Moffat, Advantage; June 2010: 27).

REFERENCES

Swanepoel, J. 2006. *The e of Marketing*. Juta: Cape Town.

Mobile Marketing, Available at: http://en.wikipedia.org/wiki/Mobile_Marketing [Accessed on 2010/08/10].

Moffat, D. June 2010. 'Could digital be the greatest brand threat?' *Advantage*. Johannesburg.

Stokes, R, 2008. eMarketing. *The essential guide to online marketing*. Quirk eMarketing (Pty) Ltd.